Four Approaches to Counselling and Psychotherapy

D0216986

Four Approaches to Counselling and Psychotherapy provides an essential introduction to and overview of the main therapeutic approaches used in psychotherapy and counselling today. Written clearly and concisely, it will have international appeal as an ideal introductory text for all those embarking on psychotherapy and counselling courses.

The authors trace the development of counselling and psychotherapy, and examine the relationship between the two. They then consider the four main models of psychotherapy – psychodynamic, humanistic, integrative/eclectic and cognitive-behavioural – before focusing on the most popular approach from each, including: person-centred, rational emotive behavioural, and multimodal. Each approach is clearly examined in terms of its historical context and development, its main theoretical concepts, and its aims.

In the final chapter these approaches are compared, with the examination of a case vignette from the point of view of each approach by four well-known therapists.

Four Approaches to Counselling and Psychotherapy will prove invaluable to students requiring a clear introduction to the subject.

Windy Dryden is Professor of Counselling at Goldsmiths College. He is the author or editor of over one hundred books in the field of counselling and psychotherapy.
Jill Mytton is a Chartered Counselling Psychologist and a Senior Lecturer at the University of East London.

Four Approaches to Counselling and Psychotherapy

Windy Dryden and Jill Mytton

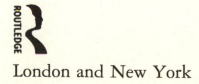

London and New York

First published 1999 by Routledge
11 New Fetter Lane, London EC4P 4EE

Simultaneously published in the USA and Canada
by Routledge
29 West 35th Street, New York, NY 10001

© 1999 Windy Dryden and Jill Mytton

Typeset in Garamond by
BC Typesetting, Bristol
Printed and bound in Great Britain by
TJ International Ltd, Padstow, Cornwall

All rights reserved. No part of this book may be reprinted or reproduced or
utilised in any form or by any electronic, mechanical, or other means,
now known or hereafter invented, including photocopying and recording,
or in any information storage or retrieval system, without permission
in writing from the publishers.

British Library Cataloguing in Publication Data
A catalogue record for this book is available from the British Library

Library of Congress Cataloging in Publication Data
Dryden, Windy.
        Four approaches to psychotherapy/Windy Dryden and Jill Mytton.
                p.   cm.
        Includes bibliographical references and index.
        1. Psychotherapy.   I. Mytton, Jill, 1944–   . II. Title.
RC480.D79   1999
616.89′14–dc21   98-37422
                                                                         CIP

ISBN 0–415–13992-9 (hbk)
ISBN 0–415–13993-7 (pbk)

Contents

Figures and tables

Figures

Tables

Acknowledgements

We wish to thank the following people for their very useful feedback and comments on this book: Jane Aebi, Nicole Aebi, Paul Bebbington, Judy Cooper, Albert Ellis, Arnold Lazarus, Stephen Palmer, Lawrence Spurling, Roger Stott, Brian Thorne, Rachel Tribe, and the client 'Mary' who consented to allow us to use her story. However, we wish to stress we take full responsibility for the content of this book.

1 Counselling and psychotherapy

'When *I* use a word,' Humpty Dumpty said in a rather scornful tone, 'it means just what I choose it to mean – neither more nor less.'

'The question is,' said Alice, 'whether you *can* make words mean so many different things.'

'The question is,' said Humpty Dumpty, 'which is to be master – that's all.'

From *Through the Looking Glass*, Lewis Carroll (1871)

If we told you that exorcism, shamanism, hypnotism, even witchcraft all have something in common with counselling and psychotherapy, you would probably be very surprised. Yet they all represent humanity's response to the healing of emotional problems down through the ages. Long ago in Paleolithic times emotional distress was thought to occur when the soul left the body, either accidentally or when it was stolen by ghosts or sorcerers. The healer, or shaman, cured the individual by searching for this lost soul and restoring it to its owner. A later idea was that frustrated wishes led to disease; lovesickness and homesickness were considered prime causes. Therapy among the Iroquois Indians of North East America in the seventeenth century used dreams to access unfulfilled wishes. In a grand Festival of Dreams, the person would be given whatever it was they desired in the belief that this would effect a cure.

Like counselling and psychotherapy, all these methods involve a professional relationship between the person with a problem seeking help and a trained specialist offering to provide help. They all have theories about how emotional problems come about and these theories determine what kind of help is given. The seminal book *The Discovery of the Unconscious* by Ellenberger (1970) describes the wide variety of methods used in ancient times right up to the present day; today's diversity is nothing new.

The growth of counselling and psychotherapy

Counselling and psychotherapy are relatively recent phenomena and are currently enjoying enormous popularity. A glance in the national papers shows that there has been a tremendous increase in training courses and a similar increase in advertised jobs in a very wide range of settings from large organisations to small doctors' surgeries.

Many reasons have been put forward for this growth in counselling and psychotherapy. Some say it is because fewer people are religious now and this, combined with the scattering of the extended family, has removed many of the traditional social and familial supports. Troubled individuals no longer turn to priests, or Great Aunt Mary for help, and even the family doctor's time is more severely restricted than it used to be. It may also be a reaction against orthodox medicine which tends to view individuals in bits. Many approaches to counselling and psychotherapy take a more holistic approach – the well-being of the total person is taken into account.

What are counselling and psychotherapy and are they really different?

If we were to ask you, 'What are counselling and psychotherapy?' you would probably have some sense of what they are, but your answer might be rather vague or uncertain and may be very different from another person's answer. But you would probably be able to say which of the two following conversations could possibly be between Beth and a counsellor (or psychotherapist) and which could be between Beth and an acquaintance.

First conversation

BETH: Oh I'm feeling so yucky today.
JOHN: Yucky?
BETH: Yeah you know, kind of down and fed up, can't seem to get anything right. I know I ought to be feeling happy, I've got a good job, loving husband, two adorable kids blah blah blah – but I don't feel happy, I actually feel miserable.
JOHN: (tentatively) You say you ought to be happy and yet you're not, you're feeling really down and . . . perhaps guilty too?
BETH: Yeah definitely, I mean other people have it real bad, no home or they're sick or whatever. I've got it good, I've no right to feel down.
JOHN: And yet that is how you feel.
BETH: (thoughtfully) Yeah – it's like something is still missing but I'm not sure what.

Second conversation

BETH: Oh I'm feeling so yucky today.
CARL: Yucky! What have you got to feel yucky about?
BETH: I dunno, oh don't listen to me, I'm just being silly I guess, I mean I've got a good job –

CARL: (interrupting) and a good husband and a nice home. Come on, cheer up, you should be feeling really great, things are going so well for you.

BETH: But I don't feel great, I can't help it.

CARL: Stop thinking about it, pull yourself together – you're not going to feel better if you keep dwelling on it. Focus on what you've got.

BETH: (sighing) Yeah, I suppose you're right.

The first conversation could easily be between a counsellor or psychotherapist and a client. John is encouraging Beth to explore why she is feeling low. He is not being judgmental nor is he 'rubbishing' how she feels. Of course, a conversation like this could also be between Beth and a good friend or a relative. Most of us at various times will listen to another person in distress and, like John, try to understand without being critical in any way. There are a number of differences between such conversations with friends and what happens in a counselling or psychotherapy session. The former are usually spontaneous events whereas counselling and psychotherapy are deliberately planned and involve an explicit agreement between two or more people. Usually clients contact counsellors and psychotherapists who are offering their services and the two parties agree to work together for the benefit of the client. Another major difference is that the conversation between client and counsellor is always focused on the client. If the conversation between John and Beth continued as follows then we would know that this was not a counselling session.

JOHN: Oh I used to think that. Remember the time when I was unhappy at work and I couldn't work out why? I had the same empty feeling then, like there was, yeah as you say, something missing.

BETH: Yes I do remember and I also remember it took you some time to figure out what it was.

John is now talking about himself and his past problems. Such a conversation would not occur in a psychotherapy or counselling session.

The conversation between Carl and Beth is extremely unlikely to be between a therapist and client. Carl cannot understand why Beth should feel so miserable. Instead of accepting her feelings Carl is discounting them and makes no attempt to understand things from her point of view. His responses stop the conversation dead.

There are probably as many definitions as there are misunderstandings about the nature of counselling and psychotherapy. There is, and probably always will be, considerable debate about the differences between counselling and psychotherapy. Historically the term psychotherapy came first and is a combination of the words 'psyche' meaning mind and 'therapeia' meaning treatment. It was probably first used in the late 1880s (Efran and Clarfield, 1992) at a time when it was believed that if there were ways of treating the body then there should also be ways of treating the mind.

The use of the word counselling applied to psychological problems appeared during the 1930s when Carl Rogers was developing his person-centred approach in the United States. At that time, in the United States only medical people were legally permitted to practise psychotherapy. Calling his therapy 'counselling' enabled him and other psychologists to practise, thus side-stepping the legal restrictions.

Rogers' decision to use the term 'counselling' is perhaps an unfortunate one, since it is a word with a wide variety of meanings. For example, in common speech it is frequently used as a synonym for advice-giving, as in debt counselling, financial counselling, or even energy conservation counselling. This is hardly surprising since the word counsel has been in the English language at least since the thirteenth century, when the word meant consultation or advice. Later it also came to be used for legal advisers or advocates. Today's dictionaries usually still define a counsellor as someone who advises students or others on personal problems or academic and occupational choice and often make no mention of the therapeutic kind of counselling. Perhaps Alice should have asked Humpty Dumpty not whether we *can* make words mean so many different things but whether it is wise to do so.

Therapeutic counselling and psychotherapy have, in the main, little to do with the giving of advice. This is one of the hardest lessons a trainee has to learn. When listening to other people's problems for the first time they often display a strong need to 'fix-it' for that person and can be heard to say 'If I were you I would . . .'.

So, what is the nature of counselling and psychotherapy if these activities do not involve giving advice? The British Association for Counselling has this to say about the nature of counselling:

> The overall aim of counselling is to provide an opportunity for the client to work towards living in a more satisfying and resourceful way. The term 'counselling' includes work with individuals, pairs or groups of people often, but not always referred to as 'clients'. The objectives of particular counselling relationships will vary according to the client's needs. Counselling may be concerned with developmental issues, addressing and resolving specific problems, making decisions, coping with crisis, developing personal insight and knowledge, working through feelings of inner conflict or improving relationships with others. The counsellor's role is to facilitate the client's work in ways which respect the client's values, personal resources and capacity for self-determination.
>
> (From the BAC Leaflet, *Invitation to Membership*, 1994)

The definitions of psychotherapy sound remarkably similar to those of counselling. For example, Brown and Pedder (1979: ix) say that psychotherapy is:

Essentially a conversation which involves listening to and talking with those in trouble with the aim of helping them understand and resolve their predicament.

Another definition given by Aveline (1992: 11) states that:

> The unique feature of psychotherapy is the structured professional relationship between the therapist and one or more patients . . . who meet in a relationship which is genuine, equal in feeling but asymmetrical in disclosure, and which is directed towards assisting the patient in making changes in personal functioning.

These definitions make psychotherapy sound synonymous with counselling. Both are about the provision of an environment of respect in which a therapeutic relationship can develop and an atmosphere in which clients can themselves discover their own solutions to their problems. Nevertheless, clients coming for the first time often do have the expectation that they are going to be given advice and will actually ask for it. One of the first tasks for a counsellor or psychotherapist is therefore to educate the client about the therapeutic process – a somewhat difficult task given that it is so hard to define unambiguously what counselling and psychotherapy are. Perhaps what is most important here is that the consumer, that is the client, is not misled especially in the area of what can be achieved – no false promises explicitly or implicitly.

Looking at what counsellors and psychotherapists actually do, it is seen that often both are doing the same things. They use identical approaches so that one talks, for example, of psychodynamic psychotherapy or psychodynamic counselling. Counsellors and psychotherapists use identical techniques, for example both will use behavioural techniques to treat phobias. Both see the same kinds of clients. So perhaps the use of two different terms is purely historical. Or maybe Humpty Dumpty is right and the question really is which is to be master.

Often different labels are used according to the agency employing the therapist. For example, HIV agencies tend to use the title of counsellor whereas agencies dealing with children might use the term child psychotherapist. Sometimes the term psychotherapist is used as a way of selling the service – it is often considered an up-market or elite term. It seems that whichever term is deemed more acceptable to the proposed clientele is used regardless of what the service is actually offering.

In this book we are using the two terms interchangeably as we do not perceive any real differences between them. This is in line with the British Association for Counselling which has acknowledged that no final distinction can be made between the two labels. We do recognise, however, that others see counselling and psychotherapy as different activities.

Where do counsellors and psychotherapists work?

It is thought that about one third of people going to see their general practitioner are actually suffering from some kind of psychological problem – often of a very temporary nature. People are reluctant to turn to mental health professionals for a number of reasons. Partly this is due to the stigma attached to the label of mental illness, and partly to the fact that people prefer to maintain the image they have of themselves as being strong and able to cope. Those who do ask for help from the state health system often find that what is on offer is usually a long waiting list for a limited number of sessions only. Much of the expansion of counselling and psychotherapy has been in the private sector although in the last few years even the National Health Service in the United Kingdom has increasingly employed counsellors, especially in primary care. This has opened the door to those who cannot afford private counselling.

- *Voluntary agencies*
  Many counsellors and psychotherapists work in voluntary agencies such as Relate (formerly the Marriage Guidance Council) and CRUSE (for bereavement problems). Some of these organisations use highly trained staff, others such as the Samaritans operate with staff trained in the use of counselling skills, such as active listening, but who do not call themselves counsellors. Usually clients refer themselves to voluntary organisations.
- *The public sector*
  In the public sector, clients may be referred for therapy to counsellors, psychotherapists, clinical psychologists, counselling psychologists, psychiatrists, community psychiatric nurses, or family therapists. Unlike the previous group, not all of these clients have asked specifically for counselling or psychotherapy, but have been referred by their general practitioners. Some may in fact be reluctant to attend. Counsellors or psychotherapists work in community mental health centres, general practitioners' surgeries, psychiatric hospitals or psychiatric units in general hospitals, and in specialist clinics like the drug rehabilitation centres and alcoholic advisory services.
- *Education*
  In education, the term counselling rather than psychotherapy is normally used. Counselling is rare in secondary schools in Britain but has become quite common in tertiary education. University and college counsellors can sometimes find themselves having a dual role: that of counsellor helping the students with the usual wide variety of emotional problems, and that of adviser helping students with study difficulties, or financial and immigration problems. In this setting clients usually refer themselves though sometimes they are referred by their tutors.

- *Private sector*

   Many counsellors and psychotherapists set up in private practice, often operating sliding scales for their fees. There is also a growing number of private organisations offering counselling services such as the Institute of Family Therapy in London or the Centre for Stress Management in Blackheath. Some private training institutions offer therapy which may be free or at low rates to those who cannot afford to pay – for example the Westminster Pastoral Foundation.

- *Service and commercial organisations*

   Large service and commercial organisations such as banks, insurance companies, the police forces, the fire brigade and so on, increasingly are making counselling and psychotherapy available to their employees. Some are investing large sums of money in providing help. For example, in 1996, due to the increasing numbers of employees experiencing traumatic events at work, London Transport set up a specialist unit for the treatment of post traumatic stress disorder. Linked to this is a large treatment outcome study, investigating three different approaches to the treatment of this disorder. They have recognised that making this provision is a valuable, efficient way of looking after one of their main resources – people.

The historical context

Limited space in this book prevents us from doing more than a rapid gallop through the decades of history that predate the professions of counselling and psychotherapy as we know them today.

Prehistory and BC

The search for causes of and treatment for emotional problems and abnormal behaviour is something that has probably always absorbed human beings. We have already mentioned some of the cures around during prehistoric times. Most early theories focused on supernatural causes including possession by evil spirits or the devil. Evidence of belief in demonological thinking can be found in the records of early Chinese, Greeks, Babylonians and Egyptians. Cures ranged from drugs, ointments, massage, and diet through to confession, exorcism, and mechanical extraction of the foreign spirit believed to be living in the person.

Hippocrates in the fifth century BC rejected the supernatural idea that the gods sent physical and mental disturbances as punishment. Instead he believed that mental problems were symptoms caused by some kind of brain pathology. Hippocrates classified mental disorders into three categories: mania, melancholia, and phrenitis or brain fever. He believed that mental health depended on the balance between the body's four fluids or humours:

blood, black bile, yellow bile, and phlegm. Too much phlegm resulted in a person becoming sluggish and dull hence the use of the word phlegmatic today. Too much black bile led to melancholia, too much yellow bile to irritability and anxiety and too much blood to a changeable temperament.

Anno Domini up to Freud

During the first two centuries AD Greek and Roman philosophers such as Epictetus and Marcus Aurelius put forward the idea that the way we think is what causes our problems – a theme we take up in the chapter on rational emotive behaviour therapy (chapter 4). These philosophers advocated learning how to live and encouraged the use of mentors and tutors. After this the Greek and Roman civilisations went into decline and the so-called Dark Ages began. The churches and monasteries cared for the mentally disordered during this period. Treatment included prayer, being touched with relics and drinking strange potions. Demonic possession, witchcraft and other supernatural causes were again considered responsible for insanity as people sought an explanation for the famines and plagues that frequently occurred. Witchhunts were common, often instigated by the Pope. In 1486 a manual *Malleus Maleficarum* (The Witches' Hammer) was issued which stated that an individual's loss of sanity was the result of demonic possession and that burning was the only way to drive the demons out.

History also records that from the thirteenth century onwards, the state began to take over some of the activities of the church including the care of the insane. Lunatics were put on trial to determine their mental state and if judged insane the Crown became guardian of their estate (Neugebauer, 1979). Until the fifteenth century there were very few mental hospitals. With the ending of the Crusades, leprosy gradually disappeared as contact with the eastern sources of the infection ceased. The leprosy hospitals were turned into mental asylums where both beggars and disturbed people were taken in and put to work.

In 1247 the Priory of St Mary of Bethlehem in London was founded. By 1403 it had admitted its first patient with psychological problems. The idea was to keep those who had lost their wits incarcerated until their reason was restored. In 1547 Henry VIII handed it over to the City of London as a hospital for the insane. There was only one treatment available for mentally ill patients who were seen as vagrants and dangerous – they were chained, tortured and put on show to an admission-paying public. The word 'bedlam' is a mispronunciation of Bethlehem and came to mean chaos because of the scenes of uproar and confusion existing in the hospital resulting from this inhumane treatment which continued for three hundred years.

Benjamin Rush (1745–1813), usually regarded as the father of American psychiatry, believed that the insane could be cured by blood-letting or through inducing extreme fear. This was done by convincing them that they were about to die. One particular story reports how a New England doctor put his patients into a box and then immersed them in water until the bubbles stopped rising. They were then brought out and revived – if possible (Deutsch, 1949).

Towards the end of the eighteenth century, scientific approaches to the understanding and treatment of the mentally ill took over from religion, superstition and witchcraft. Phillipe Pinel (1745–1826) is seen as an influential figure in the movement towards more humanitarian treatment of the insane. He was put in charge of the large asylum in Paris called La Bicêtre. He outraged his fellow physicians by cutting the chains of the people being held at the hospital.

> The mentally ill, far from being guilty people deserving of punishment, are sick people whose miserable state deserves all the consideration that is due to suffering humanity. One should try with the most simple methods to restore their reason.
>
> (French physician Philippe Pinel, 1801,
> quoted in Zilboorg and Henry, 1941)

Treating the mentally ill as sick rather than as beasts led to many being released as they regained their sanity. However Pinel reserved his humane treatment to those in the upper classes; the lower classes continued to be treated with punishment and containment.

Around the same time, William Tuke, an English Quaker, founded the York Retreat which also provided more humane treatment – an approach that came to be called 'moral treatement'. Patients were encouraged to discuss their difficulties with the staff in an atmosphere of calm and quiet, and they were encouraged to work. Many North American hospitals were influenced by the work of Pinel and Tuke.

This more compassionate approach was not found everywhere. To quote the editorial of the British Journal of Psychiatry in 1858: 'Insanity is purely a disease of the brain and the physician is in charge of the lunatic and will ever remain so'. Moral treatment gradually declined and the cure of the emotionally disturbed became the responsibility of the asylum doctors who believed that all mental illness was the result of some brain damage or disease. Drugs, herbs and some rather bizarre treatments were used, including spinning people round with water wheels and various forms of electrical treatment. In 1883 a textbook by Emil Kraepelin (1856–1926) was published describing a classification of mental disorder (Kraepelin, 1981). He believed that the symptoms he observed occurred frequently enough to be grouped together as syndromes, which had an underlying physical cause. He suggested two major groups of severe mental disorder; dementia praecox (an early description of schizophrenia) and manic-depressive psychosis. In 1905 the idea that mental illness had a physical cause gained popularity when it was discovered that the syphilis germ caused mental and physical deterioration.

Freud and the beginning of the 'talking cures'

Despite the attempts to find physical causes for all mental disorders, in western Europe many doctors focused on finding psychological causes. There was considerable interest in the nineteenth century in psychic phenomena such as hypnotism, spiritism, and states of multiple personality. All these phenomena suggested the existence of an unconscious mind.

Psychological theories of the cause of mental illness centred on the ideas of conflict and the duality of human personality – the conscious self and the unconscious. The philosopher Friedrich Nietzsche (1844–1900) challenged the ideology of science and of the possibility of man ever reaching any truth. He saw the unconscious as an area of confused thoughts and feelings. He described humans as self-deceiving beings; our feelings, attitudes, opinions, and acts are founded on unconscious lies. Many nineteenth century writers also recognised the existence of the unconscious, including William Wordsworth (1770–1850), Samuel Coleridge (1772–1834) and Charles Dickens (1812–1870).

Sigmund Freud (1856–1939) was born at a time when the philosophical climate was ready for his ideas. Concepts such as sexual instincts, drives, repression, reaction formation, the pleasure principle and mental energy were already in vogue. Freud was not the first to talk of the unconscious mind and its powerful effect on the personality, nor was he the first to interpret dreams or encourage catharsis. His main achievement was that he took all these ideas and put them into a coherent model of the human mind. Out of this he developed psychoanalysis and out of psychoanalysis came psychodynamic counselling and psychotherapy. World War I provided a boost for the development and popularity of psychoanalysis. Many soldiers were returning from the war with shell shock (now labelled post traumatic stress disorder). The psychiatrists with their medical model were unable to help these men so the government in their need to get men back into the trenches as soon as possible, turned to psychoanalysis. Psychodynamic approaches to counselling and psychotherapy developed from Freud's theories of psychoanalysis which we describe in chapter 2 in this book.

Until the late 1940s the treatment of mental illness was largely in the hands of psychiatrists and psychoanalysts. The psychiatrists used drugs, electro-convulsive therapy, and in some cases psychosurgery which involved drilling holes in the skull and severing some of the brain tissue (known as lobotomy or leucotomy).

The development of behaviour therapy

It is not an easy task to describe the development of behaviour therapy in a chapter of this length, there is only space to mention the main players. One of these was John Watson who published a provocative paper in 1913 just as psychoanalysis was developing in both the United Kingdom and the United States of America (Watson, 1913). He put forward a view that was a complete reaction against what he saw as the 'mentalism' of psychoanalysis. He believed psychology should not be the study of the mind but should only be the study of behaviour. Since psychology was a science it must be objective: the only thing about human beings that can be seen and measured is what people do. He believed we can only speculate about what people think and feel and so we cannot scientifically study these internal aspects of a person.

Watson's famous experiment with 'Little Albert' is often cited as the beginning of behaviour therapy (Watson and Rayner, 1920). He had noticed that this one year old healthy infant showed no fear at all if he was presented with a white rat, however he did show fear if someone banged loudly on a piece of metal behind his head. Watson experimented by showing Albert the white rat at the same time as making the loud noise. Watson repeated this pairing a few times and each time Albert showed fear. He then presented Albert with the white rat alone and discovered that Albert was now afraid of the animal too. He had learned to become afraid of the rat as a result of the association with a loud noise. This experiment was cited as evidence that neurotic behaviour is learned behaviour. Albert's fear of the white rat generalised to anything that resembled it like a white rabbit or even Father Christmas's beard. Watson and his co-workers concluded that human phobias were also learned emotional responses.

During the 1950s a South African psychologist Joseph Wolpe began trying to apply the behavioural approach to the treatment of neurotic disorders (Wolpe, 1958). His method involved training people suffering from fears and phobias to relax. While in a relaxed state they were then introduced step-by-step to the situation they feared. Gradually the association between anxiety and the feared object would be weakened. This technique became known as systematic desensitisation. Wolpe's contribution had a major influence on the development of behaviour therapy.

In the United Kingdom, British psychologists at the Maudsley Hospital, London, such as Hans Eysenck, Jack Rachman (Eysenck and Rachman, 1965) and psychiatrists such as Isaac Marks (Marks,1987) all became interested in behaviour therapy and played significant roles in its development. Meanwhile Arnold A. Lazarus (whose work is the focus of chapter 5) was influential in spreading behaviour therapy in the United States (Lazarus, 1971). The actual term 'behaviour therapy' is frequently attributed to Lazarus.

We have not devoted a chapter specifically to behaviour therapy as it is rarely found in its pure form today. Rather, elements of behaviour therapy are incorporated in other approaches such as rational emotive behaviour therapy (chapter 4) and multimodal therapy (chapter 5).

The humanistic model

By the mid 1950s there were two schools of thought dominating psychology: psychoanalysis and behaviourism. Both these approaches are deterministic; our behaviour is determined either by the drives of our unconscious or by events in our environment. The late 1950s and 1960s was a period of rapid social change with a movement away from traditional ideas and towards the exploration of new ideas and attitudes. Traditional psychiatry with its emphasis on a medical model came under considerable criticism. In the field of psychology dissatisfaction with psychoanalysis and behaviourism was also growing. These schools of thought were criticised for leaving out core aspects of human existence such as the conscious self, the capacity for personal growth, and our ability and power to choose.

Out of this dissatisfaction emerged the humanistic movement, which Abraham Maslow called the 'third force' (Maslow, 1968). Unlike psychoanalysis and behaviourism (the first and second forces) humanism has a more positive opinion of human nature and potential. Maslow believed we have an innate drive for growth and we are by nature active and resourceful. We could take charge of our lives; we are not pawns under the control of either our unconscious or of the environment. The best known humanistic approach in use today is the person-centred approach of Carl Rogers, the subject of chapter 3.

The cognitive-behavioural approach

By the 1970s behaviour therapy had become the treatment of choice for many psychological problems such as phobias, obsessions, and anxiety. Despite considerable success there were certain problems it did not seem to help. In particular, behaviour therapy did not seem to work with people suffering from depression. Change came about not from within behaviourism but from two psychoanalysts, Albert Ellis and Aaron Beck, who became aware of the importance of their clients' thoughts and beliefs about themselves. The term cognitive-behaviour therapy is a generic term embracing a number of approaches which all have in common the assumption that our thoughts or cognitions have a great influence on our emotions.

In the 1950s, Ellis realised that emotional disturbance was the result of the unhelpful way individuals think about themselves, others and the world. As Shakespeare's Hamlet says, '. . . there is nothing either good or bad but thinking makes it so' (Hamlet, Act II, Scene ii). Ellis developed an approach to counselling and psychotherapy now called rational emotive behaviour therapy which we describe in chapter 4.

Cognitive-behaviour therapy did not become a popular approach until the 1970s. Arnold Beck, also a psychoanalyst, carried out research on depression to test the psychodynamic idea that depression resulted from unexpressed anger being turned inwards (Beck, 1967). He found little support for this idea. Instead he discovered that depressed people saw the world, themselves and their future in unrealistic, negative ways – he called this the 'negative triad'. He developed what is now probably the most widely used form of cognitive-behaviour therapy, known as cognitive therapy, aimed at identifying and changing maladaptive thinking.

By the time Ellis and Beck had developed their cognitive approaches to counselling and psychotherapy, dissatisfied behaviour therapists were also recognising that their clients' thoughts seemed to be affecting behaviour and emotion. Reducing the complexity of human beings to units of behaviour seemed too simplistic. Donald Meichenbaum developed a type of cognitive-behaviour therapy called self-instructional training (Meichenbaum, 1977). He noticed that people with examination anxiety, for example, seem to have recurring thoughts, which affected their behaviour. For example in examination situations their thoughts would focus on how poorly they were doing rather than on the task at hand. He developed ways to help his clients control their task-irrelevant, stressful thoughts.

Cognitive approaches are often collectively referred to as 'cognitive behaviour therapy' (CBT) since most now include behavioural components. Proponents believe that for therapy to be successful not only must a client's cognitions change but also their behaviour. Some problems seem more amenable to behavioural techniques while others respond better to cognitive techniques.

Variety is the spice of life – or is it?

Over the last 40 years there has been an explosion of approaches to counselling and psychotherapy – more than 400 have now been listed. Many of these are rather obscure and are not widely used. This variety of approaches can be very confusing both to the uninitiated and also to those of us actually working in the profession. Perhaps this medley of different approaches to counselling simply reflects the uniqueness of each human being and our seemingly innate search for truth and meaning in our lives.

A more cynical person might say that each new approach is simply aimed at trying to corner the market and make a name for its protagonist. Under scrutiny many of these so called different approaches are in fact very similar although the language used to describe them may be very different. New words are invented for old ideas – a 'new lamps for old' policy. It has often been pointed out that there are more similarities between the approaches than differences. Jerome Frank (1974), an influential writer in this area, argued that therapy is effective not through the specific techniques identified by the different models as essential, but through common or non-specific factors. He identified the following features common to any influential counselling or psychotherapeutic approach:

- the therapeutic relationship;
- a rationale which includes an explanation of the patient's distress;
- the provision of new information;
- a strengthening of the patient's expectations of help;
- the provision of success experience;
- the facilitation of emotional arousal.

The idea that it is these non-specific factors that help a person to change and not the much advertised specific techniques such as dream analysis, interpretation, or the challenging and changing of beliefs, is controversial and has stimulated a lot of debate. Proponents of each approach try to convince us that it is their specific techniques which are most effective in helping people get better. Research does not fully support this idea – it would seem that all the main approaches are equally effective, although for certain specific problems, specific techniques or strategies are called for.

It may be that we need 'bespoke' therapy. Human beings are unique; each of us has our own personality and idiosyncrasies. Perhaps it really is a question of tailoring the approach used to suit the person, the problem, the time in life and the social and family context. For example, a person who normally solves problems quickly and efficiently is likely to become impatient with the slower methods of psychoanalysis or the growth model of person-centred counselling. They might find cognitive-behaviour therapy more helpful with its focus on specific problems and its structured directive approach. On the other hand a person who finds thinking about their thinking difficult might do better with the person-centred approach.

The move to integration and eclecticism – the fourth force?

Partly in response to the recognition that in reality the so-called different approaches have many similarities, attempts have been made to move towards integrating different models. Partly this has been an attempt to restore order to the chaos caused by what John Norcross has called sibling rivalry among the different orientations (Norcross, 1986). Rather than regard rival approaches as contradictory, integration and eclecticism regard them as complementary.

Eclecticism is defined in Webster's Collegiate Dictionary as the 'method or practice of selecting what seems best from various systems'. Eclectic approaches do not subscribe to any one theory and in fact do not believe that present theories are adequate to explain the diversity of human behaviour. Eclectic therapists are more concerned with using what research has shown is effective; the theoretical ideas from which the techniques are drawn are regarded as unimportant. Integration is the combining of elements from different theories to make a new theory. In a sense Freud did this by integrating concepts from philosophy, biology, medicine and even literature to create a new model. Cognitive-behaviour therapists likewise have integrated cognitive and behavioural approaches to counselling and psychotherapy. Integrationism is more theoretical and eclecticism more technical. Integrationists create something new by combining parts to make a whole whereas eclectics take from what already exists. In practice the terms are often used interchangeably.

Eclecticism and integrationism were developing around the same time as cognitive-behaviour therapies, that is in the early 1970s. About one third of practitioners today describe themselves as eclectic or integrative (O'Sullivan and Dryden, 1990). In chapter 5 we describe one of the best known of these: the multimodal approach developed by Arnold Lazarus.

Closing comments

In this chapter we have given a brief overview of the historical context of counselling and psychotherapy and have attempted to define what these activities are. The bookshops where once a few shelves were enough to contain the books on counselling and psychotherapy now allocate large sections to them, such is the proliferation of literature. At the end of each chapter on the four approaches described in this book we give suggestions for further reading.

One of the current debates is around the issue of whether counselling and psychotherapy help or harm. Part of this is due to the many charlatans who practice under the guise of 'counselling' and give it a bad name. Unfortunately in the United Kingdom there are at present no regulatory mechanisms that control the professions of either counselling or psychotherapy. This means that people can and do set themselves up as counsellors with no qualifications and little or no training. The British Association for Counselling (BAC) and the British Psychological Society (BPS) both have accreditation schemes but there is no state regulation. In 1993 the United Kingdom Council for Psychotherapy (UKCP) was set up and now has over 70 member organisations and, like the BAC and BPS, is trying to find ways to regulate the professions of counselling and psychotherapy. Soon after, the British Confederation of Psychotherapists (BCP) was established, which is composed of psychoanalysts and psychodynamic psychotherapists. As can be expected there is some tension between the BCP and the UKCP. The BAC has set up a United Kingdom Register of Counsellors (UKRC) which took effect in 1996. Only qualified counsellors and psychotherapists can register with these organisations. Steps are being taken in the right direction but none of these professional bodies have statutory powers and they cannot impose legal sanctions on 'mal-practitioners'. Meanwhile the lack of regulation means that we cannot be certain how many people in the United Kingdom claim to be working as counsellors or psychotherapists. In 1993 the *Sunday Times* newspaper estimated that there were about 30,000 paid and 270,000 volunteer counsellors and psychotherapists.

As a final note we would urge anyone wanting to see a private counsellor or psychotherapist to check their training, qualifications, the professional body to which they belong, their experience, whether they are currently in clinical supervision and whether they are continuing with their professional development.

REFERENCES

Aveline, M. (1992) *From Medicine to Psychotherapy*. London: Whurr.

Beck, A. T. (1967) *Depression*. New York: Harper & Row.

Brown, D. and Pedder, J. (1979) *Introduction to Psychotherapy*. London: Tavistock/ Routledge.

Deutsch, A. (1949) *The Mentally Ill in America*. New York: Columbia University Press.

Efran, J. S. and Clarfield, L. E. (1992) 'Constructionist therapy: sense and nonsense', in S. McNamee and K. J. Gergen, *Therapy as Social Construction*. London: Sage.

Ellenberger, H. F. (1970) *The Discovery of the Unconscious. The History and Evolution of Dynamic Psychiatry*. New York: Basic Books.

Eysenck, H. J. and Rachman, S. (1965) *Causes and Cures of Neurosis*. London: Routledge.

Frank, J. D. (1974) 'Psychotherapy: The restoration of morale'. *American Journal of Psychiatry*, 131, 271–4.

Kraepelin, E. (1981) *Clinical Psychiatry*. (A. R. Diefendorf, trans.) Delmar, NY: Scholar's Facsimiles and Reprints. (Original work published 1883.)

Lazarus, A. A. (1971) *Behavior Therapy and Beyond*. New York: McGraw Hill.

Marks, I. (1987) *Fears, Phobias and Rituals*. Oxford: Oxford University Press.

Maslow, A. (1968) *Toward a Psychology of Being*. 2nd edn. New York: Van Nostrand.

Meichenbaum, D. H. (1977) *Cognitive-behavior Modification*. New York: Plenum.

Neugebauer, R. (1979) 'Mediaeval and early modern theories of mental illness'. *Archives of General Psychiatry*, 36, 477–84.

Norcross, J. C. (1986) *Handbook of Eclectic Psychotherapy*. New York: Brunner/Mazel.

O'Sullivan, K. R. and Dryden, W. (1990) 'A survey of clinical psychologists in the South East Thames Region: activities, role and theoretical orientation'. *Counselling Psychology Forum*, 29, 21–6.

Watson, J. B. (1913) 'Psychology as the behaviorist views it'. *Psychological Review*, 20, 158–77.

Watson, J. B. and Rayner, R. (1920) 'Conditioned emotional reaction'. *Journal of Experimental Psychology*, 3, 1–14.

Wolpe, J. (1958) *Psychotherapy by Reciprocal Inhibition*. Stanford, CA: Stanford University Press.

Zilboorg, G. and Henry, G. W. (1941) *A History of Medical Psychology*. New York: Norton.

2 The psychodynamic approach

INTRODUCTION

> . . . he merely told
> The unhappy Present to recite the past
>   Like a poetry lesson till sooner
>   Or later it faltered at the line where
>
> Long ago the accusations had begun,
> And suddenly knew by whom it had been judged,
>   How rich life had been and how silly,
>   And was life-forgiven and more humble.

From *In memory of Sigmund Freud*, W. H. Auden (1939)

The psychodynamic approaches to counselling and psychotherapy are based on the psychoanalytic theories and practice of Sigmund Freud. They focus on the belief that a large part of our mental functioning is unconscious. The unconscious part of our mind contains memories, thoughts and feelings which we have repressed in order to avoid the pain and conflict they might cause. This material is in a sense 'out of mind', but this does not mean that it no longer affects us. The psychodynamic approaches assume that it continues to have a profound influence on our behaviour, thoughts and feelings.

The quotation at the head of this chapter is from a poem written in memory of Freud soon after his death. It expresses the central belief of the psychodynamic approach – that our emotional problems have their origins in childhood experiences. As long as the troubling thoughts, feelings and memories of these experiences are repressed by the unconscious processes they are inaccessible and therefore cannot be understood or resolved. Psychodynamic therapy aims to bring the unconscious into conscious awareness so that the individual may gain insight and understanding. Freud once said 'One cannot fight an enemy one cannot see'.

The word psychodynamic is a combination of two words, both of Greek origin. 'Psyche' originally meant soul, but is now often translated as mind, spirit or self and also includes the emotions. 'Dynamic' conveys the idea of forces, often moving in different and opposing directions. Freud put forward a model of the human mind based on the idea that our experiences are dynamic, the outcome of conflicting forces, wishes, impulses and ideas.

Sigmund Freud has been called the grandfather of all psychodynamic schools. The family is not a united one; it contains the usual family feuds, separations, divorces and reconciliations. Freud, while he was alive, was at the centre of an ever-changing circle of friends and disciples. Those who left his circle and those who came after him evolved their own theories about personality development. The term psychodynamic is a generic or umbrella term that covers a number of theoretical schools which, although they all have their origins in Freud's ideas, have evolved their own psychodynamic models. The differences between these various schools of thought are mainly questions of theoretical emphasis; they have each played down some aspects of Freud's ideas and emphasised and elaborated others. When it comes to therapeutic practice, they are all very similar. This heterogeneity can seem confusing to the beginner, but if we look closely there are many similarities between the different schools. What unites them all is the underlying work of Freud.

It is beyond the scope of this chapter to examine all these different schools. We can, however, introduce you to Freud's basic ideas, an essential prerequisite to understanding all other psychodynamic theories. Some of the concepts presented in this chapter may be already familiar since they have infiltrated everyday language – the Freudian slip, phallic symbols, the meaning of dreams and the ego, to name but a few. Freud's theories have had a profound effect on Western society; many of his ideas have so permeated our culture that we are often no longer aware of their origins.

SIGMUND FREUD

Family background and early life

Sigmund Freud once said that he wanted to be remembered for his ideas rather than for his personal life and therefore repeatedly destroyed private documents such as letters and diaries. Even his lecture *An Autobiographical Study* (1925) contains little personal material. However, since the development of many of his ideas came from his attempts to understand himself, his life story has some relevance.

Sigismund Schlomo Freud was born on 6 May 1856 in Freiberg, Moravia (now Pribor, Czech Republic) the eldest of eight children. When he reached adolescence he decided to call himself 'Sigmund' in preference to his given names. His father, Jakob, was a wool merchant and a rather remote and authoritarian figure. Sigmund's parents were Jews and had high expectations of their oldest son. When he was four years old, the family moved to Vienna for economic reasons and because there was increasing anti-Semitism in Moravia.

Sigmund was his mother's favourite child and he was later to trace the origins of his strong self-confidence to her love and pride in him. Her favouritism seems to have made him a bit of a tyrant at times. He objected so vehemently to his sisters practising the piano while he was studying, that the piano was sold and they were deprived of the musical education that was usual for young ladies in Vienna. Freud attended secondary school from 1866 to 1873, where he was an excellent student, coming top of his class for seven years.

University life

At that time, strong anti-Semitism made it difficult for Jews to enter any professional careers except medicine and law. Freud chose to enter the Faculty of Medicine at the University of Vienna in 1873; but even here he was to encounter prejudice. He later wrote:

> I found I was expected to feel myself inferior and an alien because I was a Jew. I refused absolutely to do the first of these things. I have never been able to see why I should feel ashamed of my descent. . . . I put up, without much regret, with my non-acceptance into the community.
>
> Freud, 1925: 9

Freud did not have any particular desire to become a doctor but he was moved 'by a sort of curiosity, which was more directed towards human concerns than towards natural objects' (Freud, 1925: 8). He changed the focus of his studies several times before eventually finding his niche in the physiological laboratory run by Ernst Brücke. His interest was in neurological research and he neglected his medical studies. He did not take his degree as a Doctor of Medicine until 1881.

Early career and professional development

After graduation Freud continued to work for Brücke but promotion seemed unlikely. Since Freud wanted to get married, he had to do something about his poor financial position. Reluctantly he turned his back on a theoretical career, left Brücke's laboratory and began work at the General Hospital in Vienna as a clinical assistant.

During the next three years, Freud worked in various departments of the hospital including psychiatry. He also studied nervous diseases and published papers on the anatomy of the brain and on the organic diseases of the nervous system. In 1885, he was appointed lecturer in neuropathology at the University in Vienna. His career began to look very promising.

In 1886, Freud married his fiancée, Martha Bernays, after a long engagement. They had six children, one of whom, Anna, became a distinguished psychoanalyst in her own right. To supplement his income he set up in private practice as a specialist in nervous diseases.

By the beginning of the First World War Freud was seeing eight patients a day and had published numerous papers and books not only on his theory of psychoanalysis but also on law, religion, education, art, mythology, war and other subjects. Despite his busy schedule he found time to meet with friends, visit his mother, address conferences and give lectures in the University of Vienna.

A few years after the end of the war Freud was faced with his own mortality. He was diagnosed with cancer of the jaw and in the years that followed he had over thirty operations to cut out pre-cancerous growths. His hearing and speech became affected and he was in considerable pain. For many years he had to wear a prosthesis to replace his jaw and palate which had been partly removed. Despite the pain, Freud kept on working and continued to publish books and papers.

Freud's enthusiasm extended into many other areas including the nature of civilisation and the existence of God. In 1927 he published *The Future of an Illusion* which is 'an essentially negative valuation of religion' (Freud, 1925: 257). In 1930 he published *Civilisation and its Discontents* in which he suggested that civilisation required the suppression of instinctual needs of sexuality and aggression; these disadvantages being offset by the advantages of protection and provision of comforts.

In 1933 Hitler came to power and the rise of Nazi Germany posed an enormous threat to all Jews including Freud and his family. In 1934 his books were burned publicly in Berlin. His friends tried to persuade him to emigrate, but it was not until 1938 that he left the town where he had lived since the age of four, and moved to England. In London he was received with great honour and was made a Fellow of the Royal Medical Society. He died at the age of eighty-three on 23 September 1939.

Sigmund Freud the person

Freud was a hard working and ambitious person, a man of strong likes and dislikes. One of his sons described Freud as a kind father but one who found it difficult to accept modern innovations, such as the bicycle and the telephone.

Some of his contemporaries described him as a bitter man who bore grudges and resentment towards those who offended him; a man so convinced of the correctness of his theories that he did not allow any contradiction. This was seen either as intolerance or as a passion for the truth. Other contemporaries depicted him as a kind and civil man, full of wit and charm.

Freud possessed the attributes of all great writers, including an extensive vocabulary and a wonderful feeling for language. He was possessed with deep curiosity and enjoyed observing people, trying to understand their lives and attitudes. He loved writing; this was demonstrated by the 900 letters he sent to his fiancée, his numerous publications and the long involved correspondence with Willhelm Fliess, an ear and throat specialist he had met in 1887 who became his confidante and mentor.

DEVELOPMENT OF THE PSYCHODYNAMIC APPROACH

Freud took over 40 years to develop his theory of psychoanalysis. In this introductory chapter we can only refer to the main points; the interested reader will find suggestions for further reading at the end of this chapter.

Initial approach to therapy

Freud's fascination with psychopathology (the study of mental disorder) began in 1885 when he went to Paris to study under Charcot, a professor of neuropathology. Charcot was interested in hysteria – a condition in which patients, mainly women, suffered with a variety of physical symptoms such as paralysis, anaesthesia, blindness and deafness without any real (or at that time detectable) nerve or muscle damage. It was regarded as either a peculiar disorder of the womb (hence the term 'hysteria') or as a faking or imagining of the symptoms. Charcot demonstrated that the symptoms were genuine and could be produced in otherwise normal people by suggestion under hypnosis and that they could be removed in a similar way.

Freud, inspired by the possibility that some nervous disorders could be caused by psychological factors, returned to Vienna anticipating fame and success. His colleagues, however, rejected the new theories. Undeterred, he withdrew from academic circles and continued with his own observations and ideas. Since many of Freud's private patients suffered from hysteria, he needed to find an effective method of treatment if he was to stay in business. He began using hypnosis with suggestion as Charcot had done and achieved some success.

In the late 1870s Freud met Josef Breuer, a Viennese physician. Breuer told him about a patient of his, referred to as Anna O. She had suffered from paralysis and episodes of mental confusion since the death of her father. Sometimes she seemed to be in a trance-like state during which she would tell Breuer about some of her past experiences. Noting that symptoms related to these experiences then disappeared, Breuer began artificially inducing the hypnotic state and encouraged Anna O to keep talking about her past life. She began to refer to her treatment as the 'talking cure'. It was as if the mental distress, which had been building up inside her like steam inside a pressure cooker, was released through talking about it while in the hypnotic state.

Freud and Breuer began to work together on what they now called the 'cathartic' (purging of the emotions) approach using hypnosis to encourage emotional release rather than using it with suggestion. In a joint publication *Studies on Hysteria* in 1895 they suggested that hysterical symptoms are related to some psychic trauma which was so painful to the patient that they had excluded it from consciousness. These dammed up emotions resided in the unconscious where they continued to have energy. If the expression of this energy was prevented, it was converted into physical symptoms. This was Freud's first book about his developing ideas on psychoanalysis.

Many of Freud's patients recalled sexual abuse in childhood while under hypnosis; with the female patients this was almost always by the father. Freud believed that he had discovered the roots of neurosis; the essential cause of hysteria was 'repression' of the memories of childhood sexual seduction. This was later called the 'seduction theory'.

During this period Freud began to develop his ideas about the importance of the relationship between patient and doctor (later to be called 'transference'). This was triggered by an incident with one of his patients who flung her arms around Freud's neck at the end of a session of therapy. When something similar had happened to Breuer with his patient, Anna O, his reaction was to terminate therapy. Freud reacted differently and regarded the problem as one of scientific interest needing analysis.

Dissatisfaction

Hypnosis was not the success story Freud had hoped it would be. Sometimes he was unable to hypnotise the patient, or he could not put them into as deep a state of hypnosis as he would have wished and he often found that relief from symptoms was only temporary.

Searching for an alternative, he tried to insist that his patients reveal their past traumas without hypnosis. He found this hard work and too coercive. One of his patients, Elizabeth von R, got cross with him one day for interrupting her flow of recollections with questions. Freud took the hint and silently allowed her to speak freely without any interruption from him; this proved to be helpful. He realised that his patients' apparently meandering words were associated in some way and that there was a force working within the person directing and determining their thoughts. He called this new method 'free association'.

The key case

In 1896 Freud's father died after a long illness. This seems to have sparked off a neurosis in Freud himself. He said 'inside me the occasion of his death has reawakened all my early feeling. Now I feel quite uprooted' (Jones, 1961: 280). Freud began to analyse his own unconscious; he believed that in order to understand human nature he needed first to understand himself. He became his own key case and also the first psychoanalyst.

Freud spent much of his self-analysis observing and investigating his own dreams. What he discovered from this and from the dream work with his patients he published in a book *The Interpretation of Dreams* (1900), considered by many his major work. One of his dreams about his niece, Hella, he interpreted as really being about his own sexual wishes towards his eldest daughter; evidence he used in support of his seduction theory.

Then doubts began to creep into his mind. He had noticed that his brother and some of his sisters were exhibiting hysterical symptoms, which meant that, if his seduction theory was correct, his father was incriminated. This thought was untenable. He began to think that, regardless of whether parents had incest wishes towards their children or not, the root of the problem was incest wishes of children towards their parents. These fantasies could be re-awakened in later years. He wrote to Fliess of his surprise and bewilderment brought by this realisation; it challenged the notion of childhood innocence. Yet he said, 'I have the feeling of victory rather than of defeat' because out of this realisation he developed his theories on infantile sexuality. Through his dreams and recollections of his childhood, he had discovered his deep child-hood passion for his mother and his jealousy of his father and he believed that such feelings were common to all people. He recalled travelling with his mother, when he was about four years old, in a sleeping compartment of a night train and being sexually aroused when seeing her naked.

Another recollection that emerged during this period of self-analysis, was the birth of his younger brother, Julius. Before this event Sigmund had had the exclusive love of his mother. When Julius subsequently died at the age of eight months, Freud viewed his death as a fulfilment of his own jealous wishes. These and other memories which Freud analysed were to play an important role in the development of his ideas.

Freud's period of self-analysis was a creative time when ideas emerged and were developed with great rapidity. The end was marked by two important developments: the interpretation of dreams and his growing appreciation of infantile sexuality. He emerged from this stage a 'serene and benign Freud, henceforth free to pursue his work in imperturbable composure' (Jones, 1961: 277).

Transition

Freud has referred to his years of self-analysis as 'a glorious heroic age' and a 'splendid isolation' (Freud, 1914 in 1957: 22). This feeling of isolation ended in 1902, when a number of young doctors gathered around him including Alfred Adler, Sandor Ferenczi, Carl Gustav Jung, and Ernest Jones. They were some of the founder members of what came to be known later as the Vienna Psychoanalytic Society.

In 1901 Freud published *The Psychopathology of Everyday Life* in which he explored slips of the tongue, misreading of words and forgetting of names (known collectively as parapraxes). In the same year he gave an account of the psychoanalytic method which no longer involved hypnosis. Instead free association in which patients should say anything that came into their minds was combined with the analysis of resistance and the interpretation of dreams and parapraxes (see later in this chapter for a description of these).

In 1905 *Jokes and their Relation to the Unconscious* was published followed by *Three Essays on the Theory of Sexuality* in which he spelled out his ideas on the development of the sexual instinct. Up to this point, Freud had been regarded as the explorer of the unconscious and the interpreter of dreams; from this time on he was regarded more as the proponent of a sexual theory.

In 1908 the first International Psychoanalytical Congress was held in Salzburg. The first psychoanalytic journal was founded in 1909 and in the same year Freud was invited to lecture in America on 'The Origin and Development of Psychoanalysis'; a journey he made with Jung and Ferenczi. This was the first time Freud spoke publicly about psychoanalysis. He was awarded a doctorate by Clarke University, Massachusetts, a moving moment for Freud; at last he was being treated with honour in academic circles after years of contempt.

In 1910 at the second International Psychoanalytical Congress, the International Psychoanalytic Association was founded. Psychoanalysis had become a movement despite the opposition that continued in psychiatric circles.

Final developments

In the final 35 years of his life Freud continued to develop his ideas. He was enjoying his increasing fame and success. At the same time many of his closest followers defected from his close circle and developed separate schools of thought. Despite this the psychoanalytical movement continued to grow. The First World War had a major impact on its growth; conventional psychiatry had little to offer the soldiers returning from battle with shell shock, whereas psychoanalysis provided an explanation and a method of treatment.

During the war, Freud's three sons and many of his followers were called up and his private practice diminished. His thoughts turned to the subject of death and aggression, publishing his ideas in *Beyond the Pleasure Principle* (1920). In 1923 Freud published *The Ego and the Id*: a revision of his earlier model of the mind. He also revised his theories about anxiety and defence mechanisms and published *Inhibition, Symptoms and Anxiety* (1926).

Freud's contemporaries

In this section we introduce you very briefly to a few of those who knew and worked with Freud. They are among the many who have modified Freud's ideas, in some cases forming separate schools of thought.

Alfred Adler (1870–1937)

Like Freud, Adler graduated as a doctor in Vienna and became interested in the neuroses. His association with Freud began in 1902 when he became a founder member of the Vienna Psychoanalytical Society. In 1911 a number of disagreements, particularly over Freud's belief that the sexual drive was of primary importance, led to a split.

Adler founded the school of Individual Psychology, which emphasises the uniqueness of the human personality and pays attention to the way individuals perceive their reality. He focused on social factors and what might be called egoistic elements of the personality, such as self-esteem and assertiveness.

Sandor Ferenczi (1873–1933)

Although born in Hungary, Sandor Ferenczi was another of Freud's followers who graduated in medicine in Vienna. Freud met him in 1908 and Ferenczi became one of his 'inner circle', the Vienna Psychoanalytical Society. His friendship with Freud lasted many years despite his divergence from classic psychoanalysis. He became frustrated at Freud's lack of interest in therapeutic technique and wanted to find ways to make psychoanalysis more effective.

Carl Jung (1875–1961)

Jung was born in Switzerland and unlike other early psychoanalysts was not Jewish. He graduated in medicine and psychiatry in Zürich. He met Freud in 1907 and became interested in psychoanalysis. He was often referred to as 'the favourite son' and was expected to be Freud's successor as leader of the psychoanalytic movement. However the friendship ended in 1912 partly because of Freud's insistence on the sexual bases of neurosis.

Jung became known for his concepts of extroverted (outward-looking) and introverted (inward-looking) personality types. He believed that we are born with a psychological heritage as well as a biological one and that just as the human body is the result of a long evolution, so too is the mind. He spoke of a collective unconscious which includes materials that do not come from personal experience. Within the collective unconscious are psychic structures or archetypes. After his split from Freud, Jung developed new psychotherapeutic techniques and promoted what he called analytical psychology.

Melanie Klein (1882–1960)

Melanie Klein like many other early psychoanalysts was a Viennese Jew. Just before the First World War she read some of Freud's work and was particularly intrigued by his theories of child development. Later she became a patient of Ferenczi who encouraged her to begin exploring the possibility of using psychoanalysis with children.

In 1926 she was invited by Ernest Jones, one of Freud's loyal supporters in England, to work in London where her approach gained wide acceptance. Klein was a strong influence on the development of the 'British' school of psychoanalysis and her ideas continue to have far-reaching effects particularly on the 'object relations' school of thought (see later in chapter).

Anna Freud (1895 – 1982)

Anna was Freud's youngest daughter. She was fond of her father and took an active interest in his work. Freud analysed her himself; a practice that would be severely frowned on today as being unethical. She was an elementary school teacher and through her observation of children she became interested in child psychology. She is one of the founders of child psychoanalysis.

Anna emigrated to London with her father in 1938 and was his constant companion and carer during his terminal illness. She worked at the Hampstead Child-Therapy Clinic until 1945. During the Second World War she wrote three books about the effect of war on children. In 1947 she founded the Child Therapy Clinic in London.

The psychodynamic approach today

While Freud was alive, he expected and even demanded a high level of agreement from his followers. He did not tolerate dissent and, as we have described above, many broke away from his circle to form associations and training centres of their own.

In London, Ernest Jones worked hard to introduce psychoanalysis to Britain and under his leadership the British Psychoanalytic Society was formed in 1919. It was largely due to his efforts that the British Medical Association recognised psychoanalysis in 1929. When Freud and the other Jewish psychoanalysts came to London, considerable tensions arose between them and the followers of Klein, who had already been there a few years. Freud in particular was suspicious of Klein since her ideas conflicted with those of his daughter Anna. After Freud's death these controversies escalated and the British Psychoanalytic Society seemed to be heading for a split. However, following a series of talks a compromise was reached. Two separate groups were established within the society: the Kleinians and the Anna Freud group. Later a 'middle' group emerged to be known as the Independents.

The object relations school originated in Britain and is strongly influenced by Klein's emphasis on the importance of relationships in early life. Human beings are essentially social and their primary need is for relationships with others. Klein was not a scientist and therefore did not follow the biological approach of Freud with its system of drives and instincts. The use of the word 'object' is nevertheless a carry over from Freud's idea of the goal of an instinct. The 'object' the individual is relating to can be a complete person or it can be part of a person such as the mother's breast when the infant is feeding. The 'self' develops under the influence of these relationships with people or objects in the external world. At the same time there is a developing pattern of 'internal' relationships; the way in which different aspects of the personality react to and relate with each other. Our experience of the external world is determined by these inner relationships.

The object relations school has had a powerful effect on Western society as well as on the world of psychotherapy. For example, the belief in the importance of close continuous relationships in early life has led to greater efforts to prevent separation of young children from their parents in hospital and children are now placed as far as possible in foster homes rather than in large institutions.

In America psychoanalysis had became a major force by the 1950s and 1960s. Large numbers of psychoanalysts had fled Hitler and Nazism to emigrate to the United States of America. Gradually the Freudian family began to split up and various schools of thought developed under the influence of Freud's ideas. For example, Hartmann (1939) developed 'ego psychology' which emphasises the importance of an adaptive ego. Kohut (1977) developed an approach similar to the British object relations school referred to as the 'self theory'. This places the development of the self at the centre of the psychodynamic theory and emphasises the crucial role of relationships with others.

More recently time-limited or brief psychotherapy has developed. Psychoanalysis is usually associated in people's minds with years of therapy of three or more sessions per week, although Freud in fact carried out successful therapy over short periods of time. For example, it is said that he analysed Gustav Mahler, the composer, and cured him of his sexual problems in only four sessions. As psychoanalysis became a more complex theory, treatment began to be a lengthy business. Ferenczi was one of the first who argued that the therapist should take a more active role and set definite time limits on therapy. Later other psychoanalysts promoted these ideas; one reason for this was the need after the Second World War to help the thousands of soldiers returning from the war with emotional problems. With huge numbers needing help, long-term therapy was not feasible. It was also around this time that group therapy was developed in army psychiatric units at the Northfield Military Hospital in Birmingham. Today both group and individual psychodynamic counselling and psychotherapy are common both in private practice and in hospital settings.

THE THEORY

Overview

Despite their differences, psychodynamic approaches hold certain key concepts in common and use Freud's psychoanalytic theory to inform their work. Freud's theories were not as revolutionary in his time as people today often think. Most of the concepts had already been put forward by other prominent people such as Nietzsche (see chapter 1) and clearly his model is influenced by the zeitgeist of the nineteenth century. What Freud achieved, however, was to put all the ideas and concepts together into one model that sought to explain the complexity of human personality and behaviour.

In this chapter we have already met Breuer and Charcot who both inspired and influenced Freud. Other important influences include Moritz Benedikt (1835–1920) who believed in the importance of the sexual element in hysteria. Like Freud he achieved success with his patients through psychotherapy aimed at revealing the pathogenic secrets he believed were causing their difficulties. Freud was also influenced by Charles Darwin (1809–1882) in basing his theory on the biological concept of instincts or drives.

Freud's theory is deterministic; that is he assumes that all behaviour has a specific cause and that cause can be found in the psyche. Nothing we do is accidental but is governed by the innate drives of our unconscious. Even events like forgetting someone's name have psychological determinants (causes) which can be identified if we examine them closely. The reason for forgetting might be that we do not like that person, or that the name is the same as that of an old enemy. The unconscious plays a fundamental role in determining a person's behaviour. This idea that we have limited conscious control over what we do is seen by many as essentially pessimistic.

Many psychodynamic approaches today take a more optimistic view than Freud. Erik Erikson, one of the German psychoanalysts who emigrated to the United States, believes we do have control over our future and that by developing our 'ego identity' we can learn to master life crises. Jung saw humans as more positive, forward-moving people and in his interpretations of dreams saw beauty and growth whereas Freud only saw, often sinister, symbols of repressed wishes, sometimes sexual in nature.

Personality theory

In this section we describe Freud's ideas about human personality. Where space allows we have indicated where other psychodynamic approaches differ. Many psychodynamic terms are difficult to understand and often the same words are used in different ways by the various schools of thought. The terms chosen by Freud's interpreters are themselves often incomprehensible without explanation; terms like id, super-ego, libido and transference. The aim of the rest of this chapter is to present an introductory account of

Freudian concepts which will provide a foundation on which to build with further reading.

The unconscious

The concept of the unconscious is an underlying theme that runs throughout Freud's model of the mind; he often defined psychoanalysis as the 'psychology of the unconscious'. Before his time, the unconscious was seen as a passive dustbin where everything that we no longer had any need to remember could be thrown. However, for both Freud and Nietzsche the unconscious was a place of 'wild, brutish instincts that cannot find permissible outlet . . . and find expression in passion, dreams and mental illness' (Ellenberger, 1994: 277). Freud often used the metaphor of a 'seething cauldron'. This expresses the idea of active forceful mental processes which would be dangerous if permitted to enter into our conscious minds. Unlike a dustbin, which can be emptied, the memories in our unconscious do not vanish but are stored away and they act as hidden but powerful motivating factors for our conscious behaviour.

The levels of consciousness are often likened to an iceberg. The tip of the iceberg represents the conscious part of our awareness, those thoughts and feelings of which we are currently aware. The much larger part of the iceberg lies beneath the sea and cannot readily be reached and represents the unconscious. Between these two, parts of the iceberg are revealed and then lost again as the sea laps against the ice. This part of the mind Freud called the preconscious. All the thoughts, memories and emotions of which we are not currently aware reside here; they can be recalled into consciousness relatively easily. The boundaries between what is preconscious and what is unconscious alter as forces within the mind vary: in our metaphor, as the sea ebbs and flows. Thoughts and feelings of which we are unaware may manifest themselves in our behaviour. The contents of the unconscious can leak out, like the radiation leaking out of Chernobyl, without our awareness, and be just as noxious.

Evidence of the unconscious

Slips of the tongue

Slips of the tongue or the pen are examples of this leaking out. Sometimes when we make a slip there may be two contradictory thoughts: the one we intended to convey and the one we did not intend to convey but held as an underlying thought. For example, a psychology student preparing for a statistics tutorial rang her tutor and asked 'When is the next tuchorial?'. The intended thought is clear, but the unintended thought of these tutorials being a chore was not in the student's conscious awareness.

Dreams

Freud often described dreams as the 'royal road to the unconscious' and said that the essence of them is the fulfilment of some hidden wish. As he analysed his own and his patients' dreams during his 'creative illness' he came to the conclusion that dreams operated on two levels. The manifest content was the often absurd actual content of the dream as we remember it. However, the unconscious does not leak out in dreams in an obvious way. The true meaning of the dream is usually hidden by converting it into symbols. This true meaning of a dream Freud called the latent content. By 'censoring' the latent content and converting it into symbolic form sleep is less disturbed. Dreams also often contain material from the previous day, usually events that show some relationship to the disturbing memory. They can also include events that are currently happening such as driving rain against the bedroom window.

Drive theory

Drives or impulses are pressures coming from within ourselves but without conscious thought. A need arises in our body, we then strive to reduce this need and to find satisfaction. The amount of energy used to satisfy the impulse depends on the strength of the need. Freud's views on the motivating forces that accounted for behaviour, changed a number of times as a result of his experiences. His final views were strongly influenced by the First World War which led him to become somewhat pessimistic about the future of human beings. In *Civilisation and its Discontents* (1930) Freud described two basic drives: Eros and Thanatos (love and death in Greek). Eros, a positive creating force, is the life instinct and includes self-preservation and therefore the need for food, water, and shelter. It also includes the preservation of the species, making sexuality a powerful force. Freud focused on the sex drive, believing it to be central to human nature. By sexuality he meant more than adult sexual behaviour and included all forms of physical pleasure. The energy force of Eros he called the libido. Thanatos refers to the drive that provokes us to aggressive behaviour including self-destructive acts. Freud believed that, since animate beings evolved out of inanimate things, there was a tendency for them to return to this inanimate state, often referred to as the death wish.

The conflict between the opposing forces of Eros and Thanatos are present throughout our lives. The existence of this intrapsychic (within ourselves) conflict is something we all experience and any differences between us are only a question of degree: high or low conflict; more or less intense; more or less manageable. Throughout our life we experience variations in this intrapsychic conflict.

When our innate drives are not satisfied, we experience frustration and tension. Freud assumed that normal healthy behaviours are directed at reducing tension to acceptable levels. For example, a hungry baby energised by its libido has the goal of obtaining nourishment. The object of that goal is the mother's nipple. If the goal is not achieved tension is felt by the baby and it will continue to behave with the goal of reducing this tension by sucking anything in reach.

Other schools of thought agree that the conflict connected to drives is of central importance though they disagree over how to categorise them. Adler believed that Freud's insistence on biological drives was very restrictive. He believed that we all suffered from inferiority complexes and that the main goal of human beings was therefore to achieve superiority. Jung saw the sex drive as a small cog in a very much larger wheel containing a number of other important drives, such as spiritual and cultural drives. Klein, as we have seen, suggested that the primary motivation of human beings is to seek relationships with other people or objects.

The structure of the mind

Freud's model of the mind has three elements, which his translators have called by the Latin words, the id, the ego and the super-ego. Freud used the German words das Es, das Ich and das Uber-ich which, literally translated, are the it, the I and the over-I. He believed that human behaviour is determined through their interaction. The three structures do not correspond to any anatomical areas within the brain but should be seen as metaphors which we can use to understand the workings of the mind. They are linked to his ideas about the unconscious.

The id is the most primitive part of our personality and the part we are born with. Perhaps Freud called it 'the it' because this part of the mind does not differentiate us much from other people. The id contains the basic biological drives such as hunger and thirst as well as the sex drive. It does not know 'right' from 'wrong' and knows nothing about what is possible or impossible in the real world; it simply knows what it wants and drives us to go and get satisfaction. To avoid psychic pain the id operates according to the 'pleasure principle'; it seeks immediate satisfaction. The id is totally unconscious; it drives us without our awareness.

We are not born with a super-ego (the over-I) but acquire it during childhood. Unlike the id, which is made up of demands from within individuals, the super-ego is made up of demands from outside, from our parents, society and culture. It is as if a critical and ever-watchful parent is inside our heads, waiting to challenge any behaviour driven by the id which does not conform to its dictates. The super-ego is partly unconscious and partly conscious; we are unaware of some of our internalised moral judgements, but we are aware of others. We develop an idea of what kind of person we should be; Freud sometimes used the term the ego-ideal to refer to this idealistic standard.

Mediating between the primitive id and the vigilant super-ego is the ego (the I). We can think of this structure as the adult part of our personality. The ego is concerned with rational thinking and brings the various parts of the personality together. It contains the sense of self and also includes functions such as memory, perception, and learning.

> The poor ego . . . serves three masters and does what it can to bring their claims and demands into harmony with one another. . . . Its three tyrannical masters are the external world, the super-ego and the id.
>
> Freud, 1933: 77

The super-ego maintains the moral code of an individual through feelings of guilt and depression if the ego does not listen to its demands. When the ego acts in harmony with the super-ego, for example, by resisting temptation, the super-ego can reward it by increasing self-esteem.

> Megan was tempted by her school friends to skip class and go to the park. Her super-ego 'told her' that this would be severely disapproved of by her very strict parents, while her pleasure-seeking id urged her to join her friends. She resolved this conflict by deciding not to go to avoid feeling guilty in her parents' presence afterwards. When her friends were caught and punished, her super-ego rewarded her with feelings of superiority.

Both the id and the super-ego are unrealistic and either can dominate the personality. A healthy personality is seen as one with a strong ego capable of working out compromises between the three forces, enabling the individual to adjust to the real world while at the same time satisfying at least partially the demands of the id.

Defence mechanisms

Freud believed that the ego was largely conscious but one role that it plays is probably completely unconscious. To enable us to lead comfortable lives free from feelings of anxiety resulting from the conflict between its three masters, the ego employs a variety of defence mechanisms to ward off the forbidden impulses of the id. Defence mechanisms play an important role in normal development and we all use them. As we shall see later in this chapter they also play a role in the development of psychological problems and in maintaining these problems.

Repression

Repression is central to psychodynamic theory. Unwanted or unacceptable thoughts, wishes, experiences, fantasies and so on are pushed out of awareness into the unconscious usually because they are causing too much guilt, anxiety or fear. Freud believed that almost all traumatic events of early life are repressed.

Repression is not the same as suppression which is a conscious way of trying to forget something distressing – often people say 'I just want to forget it, put it out of my mind and get on with life'. Repression is an unconscious process and requires a great deal of psychic energy which is then not available to the ego for other functions.

> Marisa was sexually abused by her older brother when she was seven years old. The experience was so traumatic that she completely repressed it. She always felt uncomfortable and scared in the presence of her brother without knowing why. Later in life she had considerable difficulty in her relationships with the opposite sex, usually ending them as soon as they became intimate.

Denial

As the name suggests this defence mechanism involves denying reality by distorting thoughts, feelings and perceptions in order to avoid overwhelming feelings of anxiety and distress.

> Aled was a train driver on the London Underground. One day a woman jumped in front of his train as it approached the platform and she was killed. Two days later when Aled was asked to attend the mandatory debriefing he refused, saying that he had no need to talk about what had happened since he was fine and in no way distressed. At the time he believed that this was true. He returned to driving the trains normally, but became very taciturn. A few months later, a drunk man lurched towards the edge of the platform. Aled screamed and applied the emergency brakes. Following this all his distress about the original incident flooded into his conscious mind.

Projection

Often called 'the pot calling the kettle black', projection involves attributing our own unacceptable feelings to others. In this way we 'get rid' of our own unacceptable feelings by assigning them to others. For example, James accused his wife of hating him and speaking ill of him to her friends. In fact it was he who hated her, but these feelings were unacceptable since he was a Christian and was 'supposed to love her'.

Rationalisation

In one of Aesop's fables we read of a fox who could not reach some grapes hanging temptingly above him. The fox consoled himself with the rationalisation that they were sour anyway; hence the saying 'sour grapes'. Rationalising is the process of coming up with good, acceptable, but false explanations for something that has happened. Essentially this defence mechanism is a self-deception that cushions us against disappointment, anxiety or other intolerable feelings.

Displacement

Sometimes we cannot express the feelings we have towards the person who provoked them. A junior teacher may feel angry with his head of department but fear losing his job if he expressed this anger. Instead he may displace this anger on to his pupils and take it out on them. Children often displace feelings of anger or hostility they have towards their parents on to their toys. When we use the phrase 'kick the cat' we are talking about displacement.

Regression

When people are ill they often become childlike in their behaviour, perhaps being more tearful or demanding than usual. Nurses are very familiar with this when dealing with patients whose ego is threatened with feelings of intense anxiety. Children often regress or revert to earlier behaviour patterns of temper tantrums, bed-wetting and so on when a new baby comes into the family. This mechanism is prompted by a wish to return to an earlier time when life is remembered as being less stressful, less difficult.

Sublimation

Often referred to as the most healthy of the defence mechanisms, sublimation is the process of channelling unacceptable drives into more acceptable activities. Freud saw culture as a sublimation of our deepest urges. Sexual and aggressive energy can be redirected into creative projects such as painting and music.

Resistance

When we try to make someone aware of their unconscious processes they often come up with all kinds of difficulties. These represent the ego's attempt to prevent disturbing material from coming into awareness thus protecting the person from anxiety. Typically people will change the subject, bring in red herrings to the conversation, develop headaches or any other physical symptom that will divert attention away from the disturbing material. We will be examining resistance further when we discuss psychodynamic practice.

Other defence mechanisms

We cannot describe all the defence mechanisms here; there are too many. Other mechanisms include fixation (being stuck at an early level of development – we will be describing this later); identification (acting and behaving like someone else); and reaction-formation (going to opposite extremes to hide unacceptable feelings, for example, being celibate to hide strong sexual urges or taking risks to mask fear).

How does our personality develop?

Human beings are born in a physically and emotionally immature state; we are therefore dependent on others and have to go through a developmental process. Freud believed that the basic structure of personality is acquired during the first five years of life; in the words of William Wordsworth, 'The child is father of the man'. Normal development has three interrelated strands according to Freud: psychosexual development; the development of the ego and super-ego; and the development of the defence mechanisms by the ego.

   Freud placed great importance on biological drives and in his theory of personality development he focused on the drive to reproduce, or the sex drive, believing it to be central to human nature. The basic pattern of these psychosexual stages is biologically determined but the way that parents respond to their child's needs and impulses has a powerful influence on the development of the personality.

The five stages of development

Freud described five stages of development: oral, anal, phallic, latency and genital. These stages are referred to as 'psychosexual' because they relate to the mental aspects of sexual phenomena. Passing through each stage successfully (meaning with few tensions or conflicts remaining) requires an adequate amount of gratification – not too much and not too little. This requires the ability on the part of the parental figures to recognise the stage their child is passing through in order to be responsive to the specific needs of that stage.

The oral stage

The oral stage lasts from birth until the child is about one year old. The centre of pleasure is the mouth which the child uses not just for eating but also for exploring through sucking and biting. The pleasure derived from these activities is said by Freud to be sexual and we need to remember that the word 'sexual' here refers more to sensual pleasure and not the everyday use of the word. You may have seen a baby nursing at the breast and noticed the pleasure it derives from this activity.

The child at birth is governed purely by the id. Freud believed that the new born has no ego with which to relate to the outside world. Other psychodynamic schools, for example the object relations approach, believe that a primitive ego is present at birth which begins to develop as the child reacts with its environment. As the id strives to find immediate satisfaction of its needs (the pleasure principle) it soon discovers that in reality not all needs can be met (the reality principle) and the child's ego begins to develop, exerting some control over the impulses of the id in response to this realisation.

The anal stage

After the first year, Freud stated that the focus of pleasure shifts to the anus; satisfaction now comes from the process of elimination and retention of faeces. During this stage which lasts into the third year, toilet training is an important aspect of the child's social world and poses the first conflict between the id and reality. The child obtains pleasure from its bowel movements and also from playing with what it regards as part of itself. However, parents have other ideas, regarding the faeces as smelly, messy and definitely something to be flushed away. The child is faced with a choice of either meeting the demands of the id, which has been the dominant force in its life up to this point, or meeting the demands of its parents. If the child listens to the urges of the id, it risks the possible negative reactions of its parents. On the other hand if it obeys the parents, it has to deny the demands of the id.

The ego starts to exert more authority over the id and although the resolution of this conflict may take some time it can be relatively trauma free. Much depends on the handling of the situation by the parents.

This is the age commonly known as the 'terrible twos' as the child struggles to become his or her own person. The child begins to be more aware of itself as separate from mother; the sense of self develops and the battles are not only over toilet training but also over other activities such as eating and dressing as the child begins to assert its own will. This struggle with the parents is important for the development of a sense of autonomy and control.

The phallic stage

Children between the ages of three and six years old become curious about sexual matters. The focus of pleasure shifts to the genital area. Children become more aware of gender differences not only anatomically but also in the social expectations as regards male and female roles.

Freud believed this stage to be of particular importance in the development of a healthy adult personality. The child develops sexual feelings for the opposite sex parent. He described how boys unconsciously desire their mothers and therefore are jealous of their fathers and wish to get rid of them. Fantasising about the death of his father causes anxiety in the child and he fears he will be punished by being castrated. The satisfactory resolution of this conflict requires the development and use of two defence mechanisms: identification and repression. The child identifies with his father by absorbing his father's values and standards; attempting to become almost his clone. Through this identification process the super-ego begins to develop by forming a set of rules about what are proper and improper feelings, thoughts and actions. At the same time the boy has to repress his sexual desire towards his mother, transforming it into acceptable love. If unsuccessfully resolved, problems can arise later.

This major conflict is referred to as the Oedipus complex after the Greek legend about a young man called Oedipus. The term 'complex' simply refers to the elements of the mind which have become repressed. Oedipus was abandoned by his parents, a king and queen in Greece, because it was prophesied he would kill his father and marry his mother. The boy was raised by shepherds in another country. Later he returned to his birth place, still unaware of his origins, met and killed his father in an argument and then married his mother.

Freud later developed the female equivalent of the Oedipus complex, often called the Electra complex (after Oedipus' sister). The same sense of attraction and rivalry is experienced though now the mother is the rival and the attraction is towards the father. Since the mother is typically a very important love object in a child's experience the combination of jealousy and hatred along with love leads to conflict. As with boys, girls also resolve the conflict through identification and repression. The girl realises that neither she nor her mother has a penis whereas the father does. The girl does not therefore experience castration anxiety but rather feelings of having already lost her penis; Freud called this penis envy. Believing that both she and her mother have been castrated enables her to identify with her mother and adopt the sex-role behaviour modelled by her. At the same time feelings for her father are repressed. Freud believed that the resolution of this complex was harder for girls and therefore could result in greater submissiveness and lower self-esteem. Not surprisingly this theory has never been a popular one with women and has led to considerable controversy especially regarding Freud's notion of penis envy.

Most individuals manage to develop a balance between the drives of the id, the ever censoring super-ego and the pressures from the external environment.

Latency stage

Freud had little to say about this and the next stage of development. From around the age of six until about twelve he deemed the sexual drive to be relatively inactive. The resolution of the Oedipus complex requires repression of the drives of the id and the energy is redirected into new activities. Children become more interested in other people and develop social and intellectual skills. School, friendships, sport and other leisure activities now provide opportunities for satisfaction of the drives of the id.

Genital stage

With the onset of puberty the sexual impulses of the id begin to resurface with the hormonal and physical changes in the body. The balance between the id, the ego and the super-ego is disrupted. The focus of the sex drive moves from the individual's own body as a source of satisfaction to seeking relationships with others involving mutual gratification. The person now turns from earlier selfish absorption to a sense of caring and responsibility towards others. This is an important stage in social development.

Most psychodynamic approaches today place less stress on Freud's theory of psychosexual stages and emphasise instead the quality of family relationships. For example, in object relations theory the importance of early relationships in shaping personality rather than the satisfaction of sexual impulses is stressed. These relationships are with parts of the infant's own body such as the thumb, with parts of the mother's body (or other caregiver) and with non-human objects such as comfort blankets. These ideas are complex and we cannot do them full justice here. Freud's ideas continue to form the basis for all psychodynamic thinking. Psychodynamic and psychoanalytic counsellors and psychotherapists believe that in order to understand the adult personality it is necessary to understand how that personality developed throughout childhood.

How our problems develop and how we maintain them

Since we all experience conflict in our lives, we can all potentially suffer from psychological disturbance. A healthy personality is one in which the ego is developed enough to be able to adapt continually in order to maintain harmony and balance between the opposing forces of the id, the super-ego and the external world. Problems arise when the ego is too weak to cope with this conflict.

Conflict and the stages of development

Psychological disturbance is the result of severe psychological conflict. Freud believed that neuroses are acquired as a result of conflicts experienced up to the age of six although symptoms may not appear until much later in life. It is during these first six years of life that we are particularly dependent on others. If the ego is overloaded with the tension between the strong drives of the id and the punitive super-ego it can break down. As the drives of the id surge towards the surface they are expressed in disguised form as symptoms. The specific nature of these symptoms will depend on what kind of thoughts and impulses have been repressed and on the inborn strengths and weakness of the particular individual.

Disturbances in adult life have their roots in childhood experiences which have disrupted the developmental process. Passing successfully through the various stages of development results in a mature adult with a well-developed ego capable of handling the demands of its three masters: the id, the super-ego, and the reality of the environment. Such people have the resources to deal with the inner conflicts that are part of the normal human condition.

Failure to resolve the conflicts of each stage can result in the infant becoming stuck at that stage. Freud called this fixation and thought it occurred as a result of either too much frustration or too much gratification. Both make it difficult for the child to move on to the next developmental phase. Personality traits associated with each stage can be identified; confusingly they are often opposites. For example, someone fixated at the oral stage can show either excessive passivity and dependence or can show exaggerated independence.

At the oral stage, satisfaction of the impulses of the id are totally dependent on others. The decision to wean a child too early may lead to frustration of oral gratification which can result in a self-centred and demanding personality as an adult. The term 'oral fixation' is often used in everyday language to describe people who are overly dependent on oral habits such as pipe smoking to relieve tension and anxiety.

During the anal stage, toilet training may be too severe and punitive. Rather than lose their parent's love, the child complies with their demands but this can lead to a weak sense of self, since it is the parents who take control and not the child's developing ego. The ego does not learn how to resolve the conflict between the child's belief that shit is a prized product to be relished and enjoyed and the idea that toilet behaviour is somehow dirty and should be kept a secret. On the one hand the child is praised for producing its faeces and may therefore even present it to the parent as a gift – only to be met with disgust. The child may become excessively concerned with cleanliness and order thus bringing praise and attention from the parents. The phrase 'anal retentive' is often used for adults who show obsessive preoccupation with order. Fixation at this stage can also show itself in a preference for messiness.

Freud believed that the Oedipus complex is at the root of most psychological problems. We are not aware of the existence of our complexes; they are not under our control. Although repressed, complexes still have emotional charge, they are still active and like a dormant volcano can, without much warning, come to the surface and cause problems.

At the centre of the Oedipus complex is the tension between the id and the super-ego. Into this also come the punishing reactions of the same-sex parent which might be real or imaginary as the child experiences sexual longing for the opposite-sex parent. The child's impulses are driven into the unconscious where they continue to exert an influence. If the conflict is not resolved, problems of sexual conflicts, anxiety and guilt can arise later in life. The ego, unable to deal with the tension, breaks down and the repressed emotions and desires surge to the surface. However these forbidden desires are not allowed to express themselves openly but emerge in disguised form as symptoms.

Sometimes a failure to resolve this complex results in the individual not being able to separate from the parents in adult life. A man who seems to be always arguing or picking a fight with his boss, his doctor or anyone else seen to be in authority is showing fixation at the phallic stage; he is still trying to dominate the father figure. On the other hand a man who was unable to challenge his father in the phallic stage may become overly submissive in adult life. Women fixated in this phase may show preferences for older men or may try to dominate men, thus symbolically castrating the father who rejected her.

Modern psychodynamic writers tend to place less stress on the psychosexual nature of child development and more on the quality of the relationships the child has with parents and family. Erikson (1965), for example, suggests that in the first year of life the child either learns to trust the world or it acquires a basic sense of the world as untrustworthy depending on whether or not its needs are met. This learning experience then affects the type of relationships the individual makes in later life. Bowlby (1969) has focused more on the effect loss of attachment has in childhood, it can shape the person's capacity for forming close attachments later in life.

Jennifer's parents went out one evening when she was two leaving her with her aunt. Because of a serious car accident they did not return home for two months; Jennifer was too young to understand what had happened. In later life, whenever someone important to her went on holiday or even away for a single night, she experienced a sense of impending doom and became very anxious, often to the extent of panicking.

Anxiety

We all experience periods of anxiety but it is when the ego, warned by these feelings of anxiety, is unable to deal with the situation and becomes overwhelmed that anxiety becomes pathological.

Freud distinguished between three kinds of anxiety: reality anxiety; neurotic anxiety; and moral anxiety. Sometimes there is a real threat in the environment and if we did not feel some anxiety our ego would not be warned and would therefore not react. Reality anxiety is therefore essential to our survival but if the individual is unable to take appropriate action, the anxiety may become too much and incapacitate the person.

Neurotic anxiety occurs when the id's impulses are dominating the personality and threaten to take over; the individual becomes afraid of losing control and being punished by the super-ego or by outside agents like the parents. Since the drives of the id are largely unconscious, the person is unlikely to be aware of the cause of the anxiety and will therefore report general feelings of fear.

Moral anxiety is felt when the super-ego is too strong and produces strong feelings of guilt and shame. The anxiety is related to a fear of punishment by one's own conscience.

Role of the defence mechanisms

We have already described the defence mechanisms we all use to protect us from anxiety. Everybody needs and uses defence mechanisms; they are essential to our existence. When they are carried to extremes, however, they cause us problems. Defence mechanisms do not remove the conflict; the distressing ideas are simply removed from consciousness. In the unconscious, they do not cease to exist but go on exerting an influence on the person's behaviour. Keeping the conflicts outside our awareness maintains our problems by preventing resolution. The psychological disturbance finds expression in the form of various symptoms.

Marina's mother collapsed one day and was incontinent and sick; she had suffered a stroke. While her father took her mother to hospital, Marina had to clear up her mother's mess. When she visited her mother she felt repulsed when she touched her and was unable to hug her. Following her mother's death a few days later, unable to deal with the sense of loss and the feeling of guilt resulting from the conflict of loving her mother and yet being unable to touch her before she died, she repressed these feelings (remember this is an unconscious process — Marina would not have been aware that this was what she was doing). Subsequently she developed severe obsessional symptoms. She began washing every surface in the house over and over again, she washed her hands frequently and if anyone brushed up against her she had to have a shower and wash all her clothes.

She displaced the urge to assuage her guilt, to cleanse her 'wicked soul', onto the need to wash her hands and her house numerous times a day. When asked why she felt the need to wash so much, she said that every time she cleaned herself or her house, she felt it was a new start but she had to keep doing it because she kept getting contaminated again and again. The defence mechanisms of repression and displacement were alienating her from the conflict that needed resolution; she was dissociated from her true feelings. She no longer had any idea what her 'sins' were but continued to believe she had to wash them away. When asked about the death of her mother, she denied having any feelings left other than a sense of missing her.

Freud stated that psychological problems were maintained by the benefits provided by the defence mechanisms. He used the terms primary and secondary gain. Primary gain is entirely intrapsychic, that is it is related only to the individual itself. Marina's defence mechanisms were enabling her to avoid facing the loss of her mother and the sense of guilt resulting from her feelings of disgust. The distress of the obsessional behaviour was more tolerable than the pain of recognising the underlying conflict; thus the defence mechanisms which were initially useful to ease her pain were maintaining the disturbance.

Secondary gain develops later, once the symptom is established and is related more to the outside world. In Marina's case her obsessions provided her with a reason to be dependent on her partner for money since they prevented her from working. If she were to give them up then she would have to face up to responsibilities in the outside world.

THE THERAPY

The psychodynamic approaches are sometimes called the 'uncovering' therapies. They all aim to help the client take the lid off that seething cauldron and bring the contents of the unconscious into conscious awareness. The idea is that if we know what it is that frightens or upsets us and can understand the underlying conflicts, we can then change our behaviour. By making links between the past and the present, clients can be helped to combine the previously unknown parts of themselves into their present and future selves, thus becoming more integrated individuals.

Distinctive features

It is the emphasis on the importance of the unconscious that distinguishes this approach from all others. Throughout therapy the counsellor attempts to understand the unconscious links between the client's past and present, between the client and the therapist, and between the internal and external 'worlds' of the client. The internal world of the client consists of the relationships between parts of the self, within the psyche. The external world concerns the relationships with others.

The emphasis on the unconscious is linked to the belief that everything that occurs in therapy is significant; nothing is accidental or too small for attention. The way clients are referred and their reactions to this, their expectations of counselling, punctuality, mode of dress, posture, all of these are examples of what the therapist will note and consider important information about the person.

Another distinctive feature of this approach is the use of interpretation by the therapist as a way of making conscious that which is unconscious. As we will be discussing in this section, transference within the therapeutic relationship, and resistance to the uncovering process are analysed and understood by the therapist followed by interpretation to the client. The interpretation of dreams also contributes to this process of uncovering.

Assessment

The assessment of clients is believed to be an essential process in the psychodynamic approaches. It serves two purposes. Assessment helps the counsellor decide whether the client is likely to benefit from the approach and it provides the valuable information which the counsellor uses to gain a preliminary and tentative understanding of the client's problems.

In order to build up as complete a picture as possible of the causes of clients' problems and current conflicts, the counsellor uses the first session to acquire as much information as possible. The following list indicates the areas the counsellor is interested in.

1   Factual material. The family history and the current life situation of the client.
2   Presenting problems and duration. What is the problem that has brought the client to counselling and how long has it lasted?
3   Precipitating factors. Why has the client come for help now, what has happened in the recent past, what was the trigger?
4   Current conflicts and further problems that often emerge in later sessions.
5   Underlying conflicts and past problems. What has happened in the past that is related to current difficulties?
6   Goals. What does the client want to achieve?
7   Method of referral. How did the client come to counselling, have they been sent, was it their own idea, was it to please their partner?
8   Appearance of the client and manner.

(Taken from Jacobs, 1988)

From the information gained counsellors decide whether it is appropriate to work with the clients or refer them elsewhere. This decision is made by taking into account the knowledge they have gained in the assessment process, their own experience and the time they have available. The ability of a client to understand problems from a psychological perspective (often referred to as psychological mindedness) is another important factor in consideration of the suitability of a particular client for psychodynamic psychotherapy. It is believed that the prospects of a successful outcome are greatly improved if this is present. This psychological mindedness is difficult to define. It is considered to be present if the client can relate their history readily, without too much prompting and with some understanding of how their history may relate to their current problems. Some awareness and acceptance of the existence of an unconscious mental life is also a factor, as is the ability to use their imagination. In the first session the psychotherapist may offer a simple interpretation in order to assess whether the client has the capacity to step back and reflect on and use the interpretation to further their self-understanding.

Goals

Bringing the unconscious thoughts and feelings into conscious awareness helps individuals make sense of their current problems, of past memories, and of dreams. Through the understanding of the causes of their difficulties current conflicts can be resolved. Therapy is aimed at enabling the person make sense of the way they relate to others and also to the different parts of themselves. Becoming consciously aware of parts of ourselves that we previously did not know about enables us to integrate these alienated parts into our sense of self.

Successful therapy does not necessarily mean that the person's emotional problems are 'solved', but by promoting understanding the person is thought to be more able to confront their problems more directly. Freud once said that the psychoanalyst's task is to replace neurotic misery with ordinary unhappiness (Breuer and Freud, 1895). Making the unconscious conscious means that conflicts and repressed memories previously under the drives of the id can now be under the control of the ego. 'Where the id was, there ego shall be' (Freud, 1933: 80). Part of therapy is aimed at strengthening the ego and re-educating it not to use defence mechanisms in a maladaptive way. For example, repression as a defence mechanism is established when the ego is weak; once the ego is strengthened repression is no longer appropriate as a way of dealing with experiences. Psychodynamic counselling also aims to alter the super-ego so that it represents less punitive moral standards.

Therapeutic relationship

Therapist style

From the description of the assessment process it might seem that a psychodynamic counsellor's role is somewhat similar to that of a detective: gleaning information from all possible sources and deducing the solution. All the therapist has to do is to ferret around in the person's unconscious and make clever interpretations. Although there is some truth in this impression, the therapist's role is far more complex.

The therapeutic relationship has to be established in which the client can feel safe to reveal and explore the contents of their unconscious mental life. Descriptions of psychodynamic approaches often refer to the three rules that guide the counsellor's attitude and style. The 'rule of abstinence' is a deliberate holding back from responding to the client in the way that most people would consider normal social interactions. The 'rule of anonymity' refers to the fact that psychodynamic counsellors reveal nothing of themselves in order for the client to see the counsellor in their own particular way. The 'rule of neutrality' refers to the attitude that psychotherapists take to all clients in that they are committed in a caring way to discover the truth and they show respect for their clients' independence. The psychodynamic therapist therefore reflects on what the client says, and does not offer advice but rather tries to help the client understand themselves more fully. By remaining neutral and not seeking to influence the client, the process of free association is helped.

The psychodynamic counsellor has to be constantly alert, allowing their attention to focus on all aspects of the session: what the client is actually saying (the manifest content) and what the client is not saying (the latent content), noting at the same time any resistances to certain topics and the client's body language. Freud has described this as an attitude of 'evenly suspended attention'.

Transference

'Transference' was simply the term Freud gave to the situation where a person treats another person as if they were someone else from their past. The 'rule of anonymity' allows the transference to develop; clients can see an anonymous psychotherapist as a mother or father figure, as a sibling or any other significant person in their life.

Katy's mother was a dominant woman who made all Katy's decisions for her: choosing her clothes, what she liked to eat, even her friends. When Katy reached her teenage years she began to resent this and consequently left home at the age of 16. One day a friend noticed her toothpaste and commented that it did not contain fluoride. Katy immediately saw this as a criticism and berated her friend for interfering 'How dare you tell me what toothpaste I should buy?'. Katy had transferred her deeply buried resentment of her mother on to her friend.

Initially Freud thought that transference was something that only occurred between the client and the therapist. However he came to recognise that it is present in all human relationships. Transference can be positive. When we fall in love we often see the other person as perfect: these are strong feelings that echo the early mother–baby relationship. Usually more realistic perceptions eventually take over and the relationship then either breaks up or develops into a more authentic one.

Countertransference

If clients can be influenced by unconscious feelings and attitudes from their past relationships, so too can counsellors and psychotherapists. In Freudian theory, countertransference refers to those times when therapists treat their clients as if they were someone else. At the time it was regarded as a neurotic disturbance in the therapist. Therapists' own emotional difficulties and unconscious conflicts were believed to prevent them from practising effectively.

A psychotherapist experienced quite strong feelings of anger towards one of her clients, George, for no apparent reason. In a subsequent discussion with her supervisor she came to realise that features of George's face reminded her of her very domineering father. She realised that her anger did not belong to George but that she was transferring onto him her feelings towards her father which she had not resolved.

Today, countertransference also refers to the feelings experienced by a counsellor towards her client which may enhance understanding. This can occur when the feelings are evoked by the client through some kind of unconscious communication. These feelings experienced by the counsellor may be shared by others who come into contact with the client and can therefore be an important source of information about how the client relates to others.

> James was telling his therapist of the problems he has maintaining close friendships. As he went through his story he spoke very slowly, with great deliberation and his therapist experienced feelings of irritation towards him. Realising that if they were not in a therapeutic relationship she would probably express this irritation or break off the conversation, the therapist gained insight through her own feelings into how James makes others feel.

Psychodynamic counsellors need to pay attention to inner feelings and conflicts in order to differentiate between those that are evoked by their clients' problems and those evoked by their own unresolved emotional difficulties.

The therapist's responsibilities

Psychodynamic counsellors and psychotherapists regard various aspects of the therapeutic process as important and as their particular responsibility.

The setting

The provision of a physical environment in which clients can talk freely without being distracted by things in the room or noises outside is important. Most people associate Freud and psychoanalysis with the couch. Nowadays most psychodynamic counsellors provide a room which contains furniture and decor which is neutral, not revealing anything of themselves, with the chairs arranged so that the client and counsellor can look at each other without being directly face to face, which can be threatening to the client. In the types of settings in which counsellors work these days the provision of an ideal setting is not always possible. For example, those working in doctors' surgeries often have to do so surrounded by the paraphernalia of medicine and the general noise created by nurses, doctors and patients. Even in these circumstances the reactions of the client to intrusions is monitored as being another source of information about them.

The client, Marina (see pp. 41–2), always moved her chair so that she could sit at right angles to her counsellor. During the counselling process this was interpreted to her as being symbolic of her reluctance to allow the counsellor near her inner world. As she began to gain an understanding of the roots of her obsessive symptoms so she also began to turn the chair towards the therapist.

Boundaries and the contract

The way that clients use the time offered to them and respond to the boundaries set is important in this approach. What could be regarded as accidental can be examined and interpreted in the session. For example, if a client arrives late or too early for a session this is sometimes seen as significant and it would then be addressed by the therapist, although as Freud once said, 'Sometimes a cigar is just a cigar'! Contracts are often agreed with clients with respect to the length of therapy; either a set number of sessions or a finishing date is agreed. Sometimes a more open-ended arrangement may be made but even then the ending or termination of therapy is carefully planned.

The psychodynamic counsellor takes great care to maintain time boundaries so that clients can feel secure in the knowledge that a set time each week is theirs. The sessions start and end on time and any alteration to the regular arrangement is discussed, giving the clients as much notice as possible. The way clients respond to these changes can be used to help them understand the links between past and present.

The psychodynamic counsellor also pays attention to the boundaries relating to the relationship with their clients. When clients try to break these boundaries, for example, by flirting with the counsellor, asking personal questions repeatedly, phoning up with spurious queries, and so on, this becomes the focus of the session and can be used therapeutically.

The respect for boundaries provides a safe environment for clients to explore feelings which they sometimes experience as overwhelming. The environment or space that the therapist creates for the client is often referred to as a holding environment which highlights its function as providing containment for a person's difficult feelings. This is seen as similar to the form of holding a mother gives to her distressed child. By providing a safe psychological space it is hoped that the client can then admit to their disturbing thoughts and feelings without avoidance or suppression. Often clients have been brought up in homes where the environment was unpredictable and the mother did not provide the containment needed by the child.

Techniques

Free association

Free association is the fundamental rule for clients. They are encouraged to say whatever comes into their heads however irrelevant, distressing, or irrational it may seem. This includes thoughts, feelings, fantasies, memories and images. The idea is that by giving free rein to the mind, by not censoring what emerges, that which is repressed will come into conscious awareness. In normal conversation we often hold back our thoughts, sometimes we do this consciously but often we do not realise until after the event that we have been holding back. In psychodynamic counselling clients are encouraged to be open to their inner experience. Since mental events are not regarded as random but determined by unconscious processes, anything that comes into mind must be the result of thoughts of which we are not aware. Through the process of free association these hidden unconscious thoughts gradually come into awareness.

Throughout this process the counsellor will try not to influence what the client says by obeying the rule of neutrality. Sometimes the counsellor will use basic techniques such as prompting the client for associations. For example, in response to a client stating angrily, 'I don't like hypnosis' the counsellor might ask 'what does hypnosis mean to you' to encourage the associations linked to that word. Sometimes simply repeating the important word such as 'hypnosis?' is enough of a prompt.

Throughout the process of free association the counsellor listens carefully, observing at the same time any non-verbal clues such as fidgeting in the chair, identifying thoughts and feelings that the client is conveying and is perhaps unable to express.

Interpretation

Using the information gained from the assessment session, the process of free association, dreams, slips of the tongue and from the transference relationship with the counsellor, the psychodynamic counsellor begins to form a series of ideas or theories about clients that explain their behaviour. Interpretations are often regarded as a magic, mystical insight by those not familiar with this approach, but really they are simply explanations offered to the client and are aimed at bringing into conscious awareness what the client is unconsciously communicating. Counsellors speculate about the causes of clients' problems and may offer them in a tentative way to the client. For example, the counsellor might have said to Marina 'Could it be that you are turning your chair away from me, just as you also turned away from your feelings about your mother?'

Working with resistance

Interpretations are used to help clients understand how they use defence mechanisms including resistance. Clients often resist the process of free association because revealing distressing, hurtful material is not easy. For example, Susan had sexually abused her brother when they were both children. Her deep feelings of guilt meant that she resisted for some time before revealing the true story of what happened; it was too painful for her to face. She was too afraid of what would emerge and of the counsellor's reactions.

During free association the counsellor takes note of 'sticking points': places where the client suddenly changes direction away from the difficult memory, or looks uncomfortable. Usually this happens when the disturbing unconscious ideas are near the surface. To be good detectives the counsellor listens with an attitude which Freud called 'glechschwebende Aufmerksamkeit' usually translated as 'free-floating attention'. The counsellor listens without any conscious effort to reflect on what the client is saying, but just lets all the information sink in. In this way, while listening to the client's free association the counsellor becomes aware of the presence of resistance. They then move out of the 'free-floating' state to reflect on why the client might be using resistance and what it is that the client may be guarding against. When counsellors believe they have a possible interpretation it is offered to the client explaining how they arrived at the interpretation. If it is accurate and given at the right time, resistance will diminish. Resistance is not an all-or-nothing phenomenon but is more like the brakes on a bicycle that are applied or released gradually.

Anything that prevents the work moving towards uncovering and understanding is seen as a resistance. We have already mentioned the resistance to revealing repressed material. Resistance can also be related to secondary gain; clients simply do not want to give up the benefits related to their problems such as attention and care. Sometimes the super-ego provokes an unconscious and powerful sense of guilt with a need for punishment and clients remain ill because they feel they deserve no better. This is a very difficult form of resistance to overcome.

Working with transference

Another type of resistance relates to the transference situation. The neutrality and anonymity of the counsellor means that the client does not have a clear picture of who the counsellor really is. This makes it possible and easy for them to transfer feelings and thoughts they have towards others onto the counsellor. They can then relive the type of parent–child relationship they may have actually had or may have wished for. Often the client transfers the bad experience they had with one or both of their parents on to the counselling relationship. The psychodynamic counsellor observes the transference, encourages and explores it with the client. Thus the client experiences again the old emotions from the past and attaches them to the therapist such as the fear of rejection, hostility, or perceiving the therapist as threatening. Such negative transference feelings often emerge later in the counselling process and are always important to work with.

There is a difference between positive transference and therapist idealisation. The latter can impede therapy. For example the clients may regard their therapists as wonderful people, putting them on pedestals and as someone who is to be pleased or even seduced. These reactions are often an expression of the clients' problems in relationships generally and need to be explored and understood.

In this story there are three relationship links between Paul and others: those in the past between himself and his mother and grandmother; those

Paul's mother was seriously ill when he was a child and his grandmother, who lived a few doors away, became his substitute mother. Because his mother was so unreliable, Paul became very dependent on his grandmother and would go running around to her house in tears whenever the slightest thing went wrong. This reliance on her to solve his every problem continued into his early twenties. His grandmother then died of cancer and Paul came to a psychodynamic counsellor very distressed. Initially he developed positive transference feelings, seeing the counsellor as trustworthy and 'able to understand me perfectly'. He developed a strong dependence on the counsellor, bringing all his problems to her each week, telling her all the little stories he used to tell his grandmother, clearly expecting the counsellor to offer him comfort and advice. He tried to fit the counsellor into his neurotic pattern of dependence. At work, after his grandmother's death, he tried to transfer his feeling of dependence onto his colleagues, in particular his personnel manager. Although initially sympathetic, they soon became frustrated with his clinging behaviour and began rejecting him. In early sessions with his counsellor he expressed anger towards those colleagues he felt had let him down. Later he also became quite angry towards the counsellor, transferring his feelings of anger at his mother's apparent rejection on to the counsellor. She encouraged this transference and eventually was able to interpret it to Paul. For some time he resisted her explanations of the transference, refusing to understand what was going on. Gradually he was able by re-experiencing his feelings to understand and work through the dependency. He lived out the past in his attitude to the counsellor without realising it; the analysis and interpretation by the counsellor brought the unconscious and repressed material into the open.

in the present with his counsellor; and those in the present or recent past with his colleagues. These points of connection with others can be represented in the form of a triangle (Malan, 1979). Often called the 'triangle of insight' or the 'triangle of person' it gives a clear picture of the links that can be made (see Figure 2.1). Paul's counsellor was able to interpret the link between his past relationships with his mother and grandmother and with the transference relationship with her: the T/P link. In this story the link between his attempts to relate to his colleagues in the same way he used to relate to his grandmother clearly demonstrates the O/P link. Finally in his angry feelings towards his counsellor we can see evidence of the O/T link. Paul was able to make some of these connections himself, others required interpretation by the

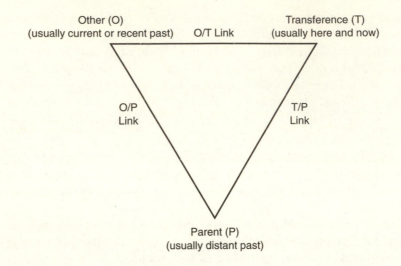

Figure 2.1 The triangle of person
Source: Malan, 1979

counsellor. Eventually he was able to understand himself and work through his experiences.

Interpretation of dreams

As we have discussed, psychodynamic counsellors believe dreams are windows that provide us with a glimpse into the unconscious. Clients are asked to describe the manifest (actual) content of the dream. The words and images of the dream can then be focused on and the client is asked to free associate on each in turn in order to discover the latent (underlying) content. The dream can then be interpreted using these free associations along with other material the client has previously brought to the session. The interpretations of dreams is a much more personal matter than many realise; it is not simply a process of looking up the symbols in a book.

Dreams are particularly significant in Jungian therapy. Jung believed that dreams revealed more than just repressed wishes. He said, 'Dreams may contain ineluctable truths, philosophical pronouncements, illusions, wild fantasies, memories, plans, anticipations, irrational experiences, even telepathic visions, and heaven knows what besides' (Jung, 1931: 147). He also believed dreams act in some way to compensate for extreme conscious attitudes. For example, someone who sees her father as an ideal person, kind, thoughtful, in every way perfect, may dream of him as a hostile destructive person. Dreams are often related to current problems with which the dreamer is struggling. For example, before an important meeting, a businesswoman may rehearse the event in a dream.

Working through

Through the process of interpretation, clients gain considerable insight into their problems and experiences. They gradually become aware of the factors and forces which previously lay repressed in their unconscious. Often a client will say, 'Oh I see what you mean' or 'yes it is all very clear to me now', indicating to the therapist that they have achieved an emotional awareness and insight into their dynamic mental processes. They gradually become aware of the various factors and forces which previously lay hidden in the unconscious.

However, a single moment of insight resulting from one interpretation is unlikely to lead to permanent change. Psychodynamic therapists recognise the importance of constant repetition of interpretations. If the interpretations are 'ringing bells' for the client, the psychotherapist will continue to express them every time a fresh example is presented in the session. In this way the client is helped again and again to recognise and gradually integrate the material previously warded off. The repeated interpretations are not presented like a 'broken record' that has got stuck. One of the therapist's tasks is to find new ways to present the interpretations by, for example, changing the language used, shifting the perspective, or varying the examples in the material the client presents in the session to illustrate the ideas. In this way the client is helped to recognise the same conflict in a number of different situations in the present and in the past. The process of repetition also enables the therapist to refine the interpretations as more information is revealed in the sessions. The initial interpretation is like a first draft. Through the process of working through, this draft is developed and polished as more information about the client's attitudes and feelings is revealed, resulting in a more sophisticated and accurate version.

In the example above, Paul spoke of his anger to his colleagues, his doctor and later his therapist, thus providing her with a number of opportunities to repeat and refine the interpretation of transference.

The ending of therapy

Not long before he died, Freud wrote a paper called 'Analysis Terminable and Interminable' in which he debated whether it is possible for psychoanalysis ever to be completed. In theory it probably never can, but in practice therapy does come to an end, limited by time, the skills of the counsellor, the defences of the client and financial constraints. This will inevitably mean that there will always be loose ends; a reflection of the reality of life. A definite date for the last session usually raises a whole range of issues for the client. It may trigger memories of past endings and losses which were distressing or difficult. The client may then relive past endings with the counsellor, repeating patterns of behaviour and defences used to protect them from negative feelings such as anxiety and depression.

Paul (see p. 51) became demanding of the counsellor's time when a date for their last session was fixed. He became distressed again, asking for extra sessions, and he tried to prolong each session by bringing up distressing material in the last few minutes. The psychodynamic approach regards the working through of issues like these as an important part of the therapy. Knowing that Paul was repeating a pattern of behaviour he had used with his grandmother, the counsellor was able to explain and interpret his reaction to the approaching last session. These interpretations helped Paul to gain insight into his reactions and through the repetition of them he was enabled to work through this dependence.

How the child experiences the process of gradual separation and movement away from total dependence on its mother to autonomous existence plays an important role in the way that separations and losses will be experienced later in life. The ending of therapy provides the client with the opportunity to explore, confront, understand and change reactions to loss and endings.

CLOSING COMMENTS

In his day Freud moved where others 'feared to tread'. He spent many years developing and refining his theories; a development and evolution that has continued since his death. Psychoanalytic theory and practice has left its mark on society today and on the development of counselling and psychotherapy world-wide; yet much of what Freud said has been either ignored or misunderstood perhaps because his theories are rich and complex. Many people have fragments of Freud's teaching in their minds without understanding how they fit together in a coherent system of thought and analysis.

In this chapter we have only been able to present a brief description of the principles and concepts underlying psychodynamic practice. We have only skimmed the surface of Freud's complex theories and we have not been able to address the various schools that have evolved out of his work. The psychodynamic family is vast; shelves in libraries and book shops are filled with books by and about its past and present members. A bibliography is provided for the reader interested in furthering their understanding and knowledge about this approach.

REFERENCES

Bowlby, J. (1969) *Attachment and Loss. I. Attachment.* London: Hogarth Press.
Breuer, J. and Freud, S. (1895) *Studies on Hysteria.* Standard Edition of the Complete Psychological Works of Sigmund Freud, Vol. 2. Edited and translated J. Strachey (1955), London: Hogarth Press and the Institute of Psychoanalysis.

Ellenberger, H. F. (1994 [1970]) *The Discovery of the Unconscious. The History and Evolution of Dynamic Psychiatry*. London: Fontana Press.

Erikson, E. (1965) *Childhood and Society*. Harmondsworth: Penguin Books.

Freud, S. (1900) *The Interpretation of Dreams*. Standard Edition of the Complete Psychological Works of Sigmund Freud, Vols 4 and 5. Edited and translated J. Strachey (1953), London: Hogarth Press and the Institute of Psychoanalysis.

Freud, S. (1901) *The Psychopathology of Everyday Life*. Standard Edition of the Complete Psychological Works of Sigmund Freud, Vol. 6. Edited and translated J. Strachey (1960), London: Hogarth Press and the Institute of Psychoanalysis.

Freud, S. (1905) *Three Essays on the Theory of Sexuality*. Standard Edition of the Complete Psychological Works of Sigmund Freud, Vol. 7. Edited and translated J. Strachey (1953), London: Hogarth Press and the Institute of Psychoanalysis.

Freud, S. (1905) *Jokes and their Relation to the Unconscious*. Standard Edition of the Complete Psychological Works of Sigmund Freud, Vol. 8. Edited and translated J. Strachey (1960), London: Hogarth Press and the Institute of Psychoanalysis.

Freud, S. (1914) *On the History of the Psychoanalytic Movement*. Standard Edition of the Complete Psychological Works of Sigmund Freud, Vol. 14. Edited and translated J. Strachey (1957), London: Hogarth Press and the Institute of Psychoanalysis.

Freud, S. (1920) *Beyond the Pleasure Principle*. Standard Edition of the Complete Psychological Works of Sigmund Freud, Vol. 18. Edited and translated J. Strachey (1955), London: Hogarth Press and the Institute of Psychoanalysis.

Freud, S. (1923) *The Ego and the Id*. Standard Edition of the Complete Psychological Works of Sigmund Freud, Vol. 19. Edited and translated J. Strachey (1961), London: Hogarth Press and the Institute of Psychoanalysis.

Freud, S. (1925) *An Autobiographical Study*. Standard Edition of the Complete Psychological Works of Sigmund Freud, Vol. 20. Edited and translated J. Strachey (1959), London: Hogarth Press and the Institute of Psychoanalysis.

Freud, S. (1926) *Inhibitions, Symptoms and Anxiety*. Standard Edition of the Complete Psychological Works of Sigmund Freud, Vol. 20. Edited and translated J. Strachey (1959), London: Hogarth Press and the Institute of Psychoanalysis.

Freud, S. (1927) *The Future of an Illusion*. Standard Edition of the Complete Psychological Works of Sigmund Freud, Vol. 21. Edited and translated J. Strachey (1961), London: Hogarth Press and the Institute of Psychoanalysis.

Freud, S. (1930) *Civilisation and its Discontents*. Standard Edition of the Complete Psychological Works of Sigmund Freud, Vol. 21. Edited and translated J. Strachey (1961), London: Hogarth Press and the Institute of Psychoanalysis.

Freud, S. (1933) *New Introductory Lectures on Psychoanalysis*. Standard Edition of the Complete Psychological Works of Sigmund Freud, Vol. 22. Edited and translated J. Strachey (1964), London: Hogarth Press and the Institute of Psychoanalysis.

Freud, S. (1937) *Analysis Terminable and Interminable*. Standard Edition of the Complete Psychological Works of Sigmund Freud, Vol. 23. Edited and translated J. Strachey (1964), London: Hogarth Press and the Institute of Psychoanalysis.

Hartmann, H. (1939) *Ego Psychology and the Problem of Adaptation*. New York: International Universities Press.

Jacobs, M. (1988) *Psychodynamic Counselling in Action*. London: Sage.

Jones, E. (1961) *The Life and Work of Sigmund Freud*. Edited and abridged in one volume by L. Trilling and S. Marcus. New York: Basic Books.

Jung, C. (1931) *The Practical Use Of Dream Analysis*. In Sir H. Read, M. Fordham, and G. Adler (eds) (1966) *C. G. Jung The Collected Works*. Vol 16. 2nd edn. London: Routledge and Kegan Paul.

Kohut, H. (1977) *The Restoration of the Self*. New York: International Universities Press.

Malan, D. H. (1979) *Individual Psychotherapy and the Science of Psychodynamics*. London: Butterworth.

FURTHER READING

Bateman, A. and Holmes, J. (1995) *Introduction to Psychoanalysis. Contemporary Theory and Practice*. London: Routledge.

Brown, D. and Pedder, J. (1991) *Introduction to Psychotherapy*. 2nd edn. London: Routledge.

Hinshelwood, R. D. (1994) *Clinical Klein*. London: Free Association Books.

Jacobs, M. (1986) *The Presenting Past*. Milton Keynes: Open University Press.

Klein, J. (1995) *Doubts and Uncertainties in the Practice of Psychotherapy*. London: Karnac Books.

3 The person-centred approach

INTRODUCTION

> I take no action and the people are transformed of themselves;
> I prefer stillness and the people are rectified of themselves;
> I am not meddlesome and the people prosper of themselves;
> I am free from desire and the people of themselves become simple like the
>   uncarved block.
>   Tao Te Ching by Lao Tzu (551–479 BC) translated by D. C. Lau (1963)

The quote above was one of the favourite sayings of Carl Rogers, the founder of the 'person-centred' approach. He believed that we all have the innate ability to discover and develop our own inner resources and that we can use these resources to grow and mature into physically and psychologically healthy human beings. We know better than anyone else what is best for our development. The term 'person-centred' indicates that the person of the client is always at the centre of therapy and not the techniques or expertise of the therapist. The sensitivity and quality of the relationship between the therapist and the client is of critical importance. If certain crucial elements are present in this relationship then clients will be enabled to find their own way forward, and will be equipped to overcome future problems as well as current ones.

Person-centred counselling aims to help individuals free themselves from the constraints and obstacles that are currently preventing them using their innate ability to discover their way forward. The idea of 'constraint' in this setting is illustrated by Sir Edmund Gosse in his autobiographical *Father and Son*. In describing his upbringing in a fundamentalist sect he writes:

> Certain portions of my intellect were growing with unwholesome activity, while others were stunted, or had never stirred at all. I was like a plant on which a pot has been placed, with the effect that the centre is crushed and arrested, while shoots are straggling up to the

light on all sides. My father himself was aware of this, and in a spasmodic
way he wished to regulate my thoughts. But all he did was to try to
straighten the shoots, without removing the pot which kept them
resolutely down.

Gosse, 1974: 146

The person-centred approach would say that if the pot is removed and other
elements are thereby released the plant will grow and develop almost as if the
constraint had never been there.

This approach to counselling and psychotherapy has gone through several
name changes. Rogers first called it the non-directive approach to emphasise
the role of the counsellor as a facilitator rather than an adviser. Later he began
to call it client-centred and then when the approach began to be applied to
other areas such as education, the term person-centred was employed. Many
practitioners today still prefer to use the label client-centred therapist in
order to distinguish themselves from those applying this approach in other
areas.

CARL ROGERS

Family background and early life

Like Sir Edmund Gosse, Carl Rogers had a strict fundamentalist upbringing.
He was born in Oak Ridge, a small village on the outskirts of Chicago in
1902, the fourth of six children. His parents believed in a fundamentalist
brand of Christianity. They were Congregationalists. Rogers' mother often
quoted the verse 'All our righteousnesses are as filthy rags in Thy sight, oh
Lord' (Isaiah 64:6), expressing her belief that human beings were essentially
sinful and that even their best efforts were worthless. Much of what might be
considered part of a normal childhood was regarded as evil: parties, theatre,
dancing, card games, and even fizzy drinks were frowned on. Reading for
relaxation and interest was regarded as self indulgent and sinful.

Rogers has described his parents as 'in many subtle and affectionate ways,
very controlling of our behaviour' (Rogers, 1961: 5). As God's elect, they saw
themselves as different from others; certain behaviours, thoughts and feelings
were not acceptable. Rogers did not confide in them because he feared that his
private thoughts and feelings would be judged.

His parents did not mix with people in the community. When Carl was
twelve they bought a farm, partly to protect their family from the corruption
of town life – 'Come out from among them and be ye separate' (2 Corinthians
6:17). Rogers has described this 'unconsciously arrogant separateness'
(Rogers, 1980: 28) as characterising his behaviour throughout his school life.

There were two conflicting messages here: to adopt Gosse's simile, it was as
if there were two heavy pots distorting Rogers' early development. On the one

hand he was taught that he was born worthless and inferior and on the other that he was also somehow superior to others outside the faith and should not mix with them. Carl was lonely as a child and had little opportunity to make friends; he buried himself in books to console himself. Through his reading he created a fantasy world of adventure and excitement.

The family work ethic required all the children to take a share in the chores on the farm. Rogers developed a taste for working on the land, experimenting to find out what helped plants and crops grow on his own designated plot. Rogers extended his reading to include scientific books on agriculture from which he learnt how to set up and conduct experiments. He also became interested in the many species of moths that he found in the surrounding woods, becoming quite an expert and even breeding them in captivity. These early lessons in scientific enquiry laid a basis for his later research into counselling and psychotherapy.

University life

Rogers enrolled at the University of Wisconsin in 1919 to study agriculture. By the end of the first year he had decided to become a Christian minister. He changed the focus of his study to history, believing this to be more relevant to his change of career. Freed from the control of his parents he began to develop genuine friendships for the first time and to find a more personal and less judgmental form of Christianity for himself. The metaphorical pot on his inner growth was beginning to be displaced.

In 1922 he was chosen to go to China for an International World Student Christian Federation Conference. On this trip he discovered that Christians could hold views very different to those he had learned as a child. A new world opened up to him, not only culturally but also emotionally and intellectually. He described the trip as 'eye opening' and said that it was a 'tremendous relief to quit worrying about whether you believe what you are supposed to believe' (Kirschenbaum, 1979: 25).

In 1924, shortly after Rogers graduated in history, he married his childhood sweetheart Helen. In the same year he enrolled in the Union Theological Seminary. A group of students including Rogers set up a seminar in which they were free to explore their own questions and doubts about their beliefs and this enabled Rogers to develop further his own philosophy of life. While studying theology he found himself attracted to the psychology courses given at the Teachers' College, Columbia University just across the road from Union Seminary. After attending some of these courses, in the autumn of 1926 he decided to move his studies totally to Teachers' College and began a degree in clinical and educational psychology.

Rogers was granted a fellowship at the Institute for Child Guidance, New York for the academic year 1927–28. This provided him not only with useful experience but also with a salary – a much-needed boost to his income, for in 1926 his son David was born and in 1928 his daughter Natalie.

Early career and professional development

Rochester 1928–39

In 1928 Rogers was offered the post of psychologist in the Child Study Department of the Society for the Prevention of Cruelty to Children in Rochester, New York. His work here involved diagnosing and planning treatment for delinquent and deprived children sent by the courts, schools and other agencies. He gained a reputation as one of the major authorities on children and youth. In 1931 Rogers finally received his doctorate from Columbia University.

Ohio 1940–44

In 1939 Rogers published his first major book, *The Clinical Treatment of the Problem Child*. Perhaps as a result of this, he was offered a full professorship at Ohio State University. Here he lectured, ran workshops, wrote numerous articles and established a counselling service on the campus. His second book *Counseling and Psychotherapy* was published in 1942. What was striking about this book, apart from its innovative ideas, was the fact that over one third of it consisted of a transcript of an electronically recorded series of sessions with a client called Herbert Bryan. These recordings were made on 78-rpm discs which had to be changed every three minutes – a far cry from today's easily transportable cassette machines. Over eight hundred records were cut and painstakingly transcribed. These recordings provided Rogers and his students with the opportunity to study therapeutic processes in detail.

Chicago 1945–57

In 1945 he moved to the University of Chicago as professor of psychology and set up a counselling centre there. In 1951 his book *Client-Centered Therapy* was published. Rogers became an influential figure in psychotherapeutic circles gaining respect as a therapist, a theorist and as a researcher. In 1956 he received the Distinguished Scientific Contribution Award – the American Psychology Association's highest honour. He was also elected as the first president of the American Academy of Psychotherapy and was invited to be a visiting professor at a number of prestigious universities.

Wisconsin 1957–63

In 1957 Rogers moved to the University of Wisconsin as professor of psychology and psychiatry. Up to this point he had used his approach with mildly disturbed or 'neurotic' individuals. At Wisconsin his pioneering spirit made him eager to explore the possibilities of using the client-centred approach (as it was called then) with more disturbed people including schizo-phrenics.

In 1961 his book *On Becoming a Person* was published. This was a time when interest in the third force in psychology was growing and campaigns for civil rights, for the rights of women and of ethnic communities were gaining public attention. The ideas of the client-centred approach, with the emphasis on helping individuals reach their full potential, meshed well with these developments.

California 1964–87

In the summer of 1963, at the age of 61, Rogers decided to leave academic life and went to La Jolla, California as a resident fellow of the Western Behavioral Sciences Institute. Here he found freedom from the bureaucratic entangle-ments of academic life. In 1968 with other people he formed the Center for the Studies of the Person where he remained as a resident fellow until his death in 1987 at the age of 85.

Carl Rogers the person

Carl Rogers was a man who put his theories and beliefs about his approach to therapy into practice in his personal life. Students have described him as a great listener, someone who seemed to learn as much from them as they did from him. Those who worked for him were encouraged to develop and use their own inner resources and not to look to him for instruction.

He was a man of great warmth and he cared for others but he could seem distant and reserved. This may have been a result of his isolation and inhibi-tion as a child. Feeling awkward in social settings was something from which he never really escaped. Rogers once said that he was at his worst when he was expected to be a 'leading figure' or an 'exciting person' (Kirschenbaum and Henderson, 1990: 187).

His childhood love of watching plants grow continued throughout his life. He enjoyed creating the right conditions for their growth – just as he did with people. 'My garden supplies that same intriguing question I have been trying to meet in all my professional life: what are the effective conditions for growth?' (Rogers, 1974: 115). He also enjoyed photography and making artistic and unusual mobiles.

Rogers often expressed amazement at the impact his work had on the field of psychotherapy and counselling. He once said, 'I certainly do not attribute it to any special genius of my own, and most assuredly not to any far-sighted vision on my part' (Rogers, 1974: 115). He had no idea that his attempts to be more effective with his clients would lead to such an influential approach to counselling. Recognising that the process of learning continued indefinitely, Rogers believed and hoped that the person-centred approach would continue to grow and develop after his death.

DEVELOPMENT OF THE PERSON-CENTRED APPROACH

Initial approach to therapy

At Teachers' College Rogers studied psychology based on behaviour theory with a strong emphasis on psychological testing as a way to study and understand people. This approach appealed to his scientific interests. During his year at the Institute for Child Guidance he was exposed to a very different school of thought. He found its dynamic Freudian views 'in great conflict with the rigorous, scientific, coldly objective, statistical point of view then prevalent at Teachers' College' (Rogers, 1961: 9).

At the Child Study Department in Rochester he found a way of combining elements of these radically different viewpoints. He described the clinic once as being rather like a garage. A problem child was brought in and using the scientific, behavioural approach an expert made a diagnosis and decisions were then made as to how the problem could be corrected. The first step in therapy was an interpretation of the problem in the Freudian tradition by the therapist. Once a person understood their past and present behaviour, change would occur.

Dissatisfaction

Rogers' main concern was continually to strive to find more effective ways of helping his clients. As a result of inevitable failures, he became increasingly disillusioned with the use of interpretation. One of his clients was a young pyromaniac. Believing at that time that delinquency was often based on sexual conflict, he traced the boy's desire to set fires back to his sexual impulse to masturbate. Once this interpretation was made Rogers believed the case was solved. The boy was put on probation, but shortly afterwards he began to light fires again. This incident was one of several which alerted Rogers to the possibility that interpretation in the psychodynamic style was not an effective therapeutic tool.

The key case

Rogers began to experiment with more subtle and gentle interpretations hoping that this would enable his clients to accept his explanations. One day he was interviewing the mother of a very troublesome boy. Using her own evidence, he gently tried to convince her that her own early rejection of her son had caused his problems. But the mother refused to accept this interpretation. Rogers gave up and suggested that they end the contact. The mother agreed but before she left she asked him if he counselled adults for their own problems. When he told her that he did, she sat down and began to tell him of her despair and sense of failure about her marriage.

Rogers listened with amazement. This was very different from the formal case history that he had taken from her about her son. He left the direction of the conversation to her and made no attempt to interpret. This approach proved to be successful and the experience had a profound impact on Rogers' thinking.

Transition

Rogers began to realise that:

> it is the client who knows what hurts, what directions to go, what problems are crucial, what experiences have been deeply buried. It began to occur to me that unless I had a need to demonstrate my own cleverness and learning, I would do better to rely upon the client for the direction of movement in the process.
>
> Rogers, 1961: 11–12

The crucial step from diagnosis and interpretation to simply listening had been taken. On 11 December 1940 Rogers presented a paper at the University of Minnesota on 'Some newer concepts in psychotherapy' (Rogers, 1942). He criticised the directive approach in use in Minnesota, and described an alternative method. He believed he was summarising the viewpoints of other therapists: more emphasis on feelings, on the present rather than the past and a greater reliance on the individual's own drive towards health. He stressed the therapeutic relationship as the experience where growth can take place. He later said that person-centred counselling had been born that day, although he originally called it non-directive counselling.

To Rogers' surprise his speech created quite a stir; he received both criticism and praise. Realising that he was creating something new he decided to develop his ideas further in a book called 'Counseling and Psychotherapy: Newer concepts in practice' (Rogers, 1942). Rogers was the first to use the term 'client' when referring to persons seeking help. He wanted them to assume responsibility for their own problems. The term 'patient' suggested that they were sick and needed expert help. Setting the counsellor up as an 'expert' only made the person more dependent. 'Client' suggested team work and equality instead and removed the idea that the person was crazy or inferior.

The publication of his book brought increased respect for Rogers amongst his students and others outside the university, but there was further criticism within his own psychology department. The idea that clients could know more about their inner selves than psychologists did had little appeal to the professionals. Undaunted by such negative reaction Rogers continued to develop and change his thinking, making use of his experiences with clients and his observations of other non-directive counsellors.

Final developments

The development of the person-centred approach we know today went through three crucial stages.

Stage one – non-directive counselling

The first stage was known as non-directive counselling. Clients were encouraged to release their emotions when talking about their problems. Interpretation and the giving of advice were to be avoided. Rogers believed that insight gained had to be achieved by the client and that it should not be imposed by anyone else. His own negative experience as a child probably played a part in this. The role of the therapist was to provide the right conditions for client growth to take place by conveying 'acceptance' and 'understanding' through the reflection of feelings. Later Rogers was to refer to this as 'unconditional positive regard'.

Stage two – the importance of the therapist's attitude

By the late 1940s Rogers began to realise that the techniques of the approach were being over-emphasised. Therapists seemed to be following a set of rules: 'don't interpret', 'don't give advice', 'repeat what the client has just said'. He began to use the label 'client-centred' instead of 'non-directive' which implied passivity. He realised that the therapist's attitude was of primary importance. The therapist had to believe that the means of change and release from constraint lay with the client and could not be imposed. The therapist's function was to enter and seek to understand as completely as possible the client's inner world and to provide gentle and delicate support. Later, Rogers called this 'empathy'.

Stage three – the therapist's feelings

But what if the psychotherapist cannot feel genuinely accepting or understanding of a particular client, either permanently or at a particular time? In 1949 Rogers was seeing a very disturbed client. He felt trapped by her dependence on him and he did not like her. Eventually 'I got to the point where I could not separate my "self" from hers. I literally lost the boundaries of myself' (Kirschenbaum, 1979: 191–2). He recognised that the relationship with this client was destructive to himself and unhelpful to her, but he was unable to break the link. Finally, realising he was on the edge of a breakdown himself, he referred her to a psychiatrist.

Rogers entered into a therapeutic relationship with another colleague and discovered deep unresolved problems within himself. He had to acknowledge that it had always been difficult for him to allow himself to feel that someone cared for him, accepted him and prized him (Rogers, 1980). It was years since he had heard his mother say that all his 'righteousnesses are as filthy rags' but he still had buried feelings of being unlovable and repulsive. Contact with this difficult client had re-opened these old wounds. Through the therapy with his colleague he came to accept and value himself. He learned to receive and give love without fear.

Out of this came the recognition that therapists should pay attention to their own feelings in the therapeutic relationship. Rogers believed that if he had been honest with his client this would have been more effective. By pretending to understand and accept her, he was actually harming her. The therapist needs to react genuinely in the relationship. Later, Rogers called this 'congruence'.

In the last two decades of his life Rogers became more interested in the broader social implications of the person-centred approach. For example, he became involved in interracial and intercultural groups such as the militant Catholics and Protestants of Northern Ireland. The client-centred approach extended its influence also into education, organisational change and society in general. As a result Rogers felt it was no longer appropriate to use the term 'client' in these settings and came up with the term 'person-centred' in order to do justice to the expansion of his ideas into ordinary day-to-day life.

Since Rogers' death in 1987 there has been a gradual drifting apart of other professionals working in the area. The approach has become less influential in the United States of America particularly in academic and professional circles. Perhaps this is partly because of the rapid increase of other approaches and the resulting competition between them. Also medical insurance companies insist on diagnoses before payment is made. Formal assessment and diagnosis go against the philosophy of this approach.

In the United Kingdom and in other countries in Europe counsellors working in higher education and in voluntary organisations have not felt these pressures. The approach is flourishing and an association, several agencies and many training programmes for person-centred therapy have been established. There has been a tendency in some circles to regard its emphasis on the therapeutic relationship as a starting point for other approaches. So trainees will be taught basic person-centred ideas, especially the three core conditions of congruence, unconditional positive regard and empathy. On to this basic training is then added the theories and techniques of the approach in question, for example cognitive-behavioural, multimodal or psychodynamic. Of course the minute this happens these students are no longer studying person-centred therapy; indeed they have moved away from the basic tenet that the client knows what is best and that the provision of the core conditions is not only necessary but also sufficient to bring about change. The notion of a person-centred psychodynamic counsellor, for example, is a contradiction in terms.

THE THEORY

Overview

Carl Rogers originally felt no need to devise explicit, precise theories – in fact he was suspicious of them. Trying to fit the person to the theory often meant that the client's experiences and perceptions were ignored or misunderstood. But to foster the continuing development of the person-centred approach he realised that some theorising was necessary. He regarded all theories as provisional and expected his theories to be developed by others in response to new evidence from research and clinical experience. Theory stimulates further creative thought but only if it can be seen for what it is: 'a fallible, changing attempt to construct a network of gossamer threads which will contain the solid facts' (Rogers, 1959: 191).

When Rogers explained his theories of personality and therapy he always recognised his debt to others. He referred to 'our theoretical thinking' in his writings, acknowledging the enormous contribution made by those he worked with.

He had no particular mentor but he did recognise that he had been influenced by other therapists, notably Otto Rank. Rank had been a disciple of Freud but he broke away from him in 1925 and developed his own approach. Rogers took from Rank the emphasis on the therapeutic relationship and the idea of the therapist as 'supporter' rather than 'director'.

There are certain key terms and phrases in Rogers' work which occur frequently in books about person-centred counselling. It is important that these do not become mere jargon, emptied of the freshness of meaning that he gave to them. Some may seem unfamiliar or unusual – we have attempted to make them comprehensible and familiar.

Person-centred therapy is one of the humanistic approaches. Instead of focusing on the childhood origins of the client's problems, person-centred therapy focuses on the present: the 'here and now' experience. The emphasis is on the person's capacity for personal growth, awareness, feelings, and human potential.

Personality theory

Rogers was brought up to believe that human nature was corrupt and worthless. Even when people did achieve good things this did not come from within themselves but from God working in them. It is remarkable that from this pessimistic view of humanity he developed such a positive and optimistic theory of personality. His ideas were a radical challenge not only to religious ideas but also to Freud's views that human nature was destructive and irrational.

Actualising tendency

Plants have an innate tendency to grow from a seed towards their full potential, flowering and bearing fruit. Rogers believed that the same is true of human beings. The person-centred approach calls this instinctual drive the 'actualising tendency'. The word actualise means to make real, to bring into existence. This strong drive continues throughout life as we move towards the fulfilment of all that it is possible for us to achieve and become. None of us ever lives long enough to know our full potential. We are always in a state of 'being and becoming'.

The actualising tendency is common to all living things; it 'maintains and enhances' them (a phrase frequently used by Rogers and others writing about his approach). Maintenance carries the idea of guarding and keeping alive; there are astounding examples of living things – plants, animals and human beings – surviving the most hostile and terrible conditions. Enhancement indicates growth and development; for human beings it is the creative fulfilment of the personality, the satisfaction of physical and psychological needs.

Rogers often explained his ideas through the plants and animals of his childhood years. He described a vivid image from his childhood of a potato storage bin kept in the cellar of the Rogers' house. Despite the hopelessness of their situation, deprived of water, soil and light, the potatoes sprouted pale spindly shoots. Even though they had no chance of becoming normal healthy plants, the potatoes continued to strive to grow. Rogers often remembered these potatoes as he dealt with the individuals he met on the back wards of the state mental hospitals. He saw their apparently bizarre, abnormal behaviour as an instinctual striving towards becoming themselves.

The 'street children' of Rio de Janeiro are a human example of the same drive towards survival and fulfilment, often living in sewers on scraps of food. Their determination to stay alive and to reach a fuller state of life is a remarkable example of the effects of this drive. Actualisation, however, involves more than just physical growth and survival. It includes the reduction and satisfaction of psychological needs, the need for love and safety, the desire to learn and to be creative. Rogers believed that the actualising tendency is the only motive needed to account for all our behaviour, whether to fill an empty stomach, to produce children, or to become independent and healthy.

Emotion

There are two main groups of emotions: the unpleasant and/or excited feelings, and the calm and/or satisfied feelings (Rogers, 1951). The first group are experienced when people are seeking to satisfy their needs and seem to have the function of focusing behaviour on the current goal.

Matthew is playing when a large Alsatian dog approaches. Having once been bitten by a dog, he perceives the animal as dangerous and feels fear. This emotion quickens his reaction as he seeks to satisfy his need for safety – he runs away. As soon as he perceives he is safe, he will experience relief, an emotion from the second group. The intensity of the emotions we experience is related to the relationship we perceive as existing between our behaviour and our need to 'maintain and enhance' ourselves. If Matthew perceives his behaviour of running away as making the difference between life and death, the intensity of his fear and his satisfaction at escaping will be greater than if he perceived it as saving him from a nasty scratch.

Experience, perception and behaviour

At any given moment there is a range of experience available to our awareness. While you are reading this book the sun might be shining, you might have a headache from concentrating and your child might be laughing in another room. You might be so absorbed in enjoying what you are reading that you are not aware of any of these experiences. Nevertheless they are potentially available to your conscious awareness and can become conscious if your attention is drawn to them – for example, if your child's laughter changes to crying. The range of experiences potentially available to conscious awareness is sometimes called the 'phenomenal field' or 'experiential field'. Each of us lives in this private world of experience and we are only consciously aware of a small portion at any one moment.

Rogers maintained that in order to understand behaviour we need to realise that each of us perceives reality in a different way. There is therefore no absolute reality. For example, a teacher, Mr Rasit, will be perceived by each of his pupils in different ways. Angela may regard him as firm and reasonable but Barry may see him as bossy and unfair. Each of these pupil's behaviour with regard to this teacher will therefore be different. Angela is likely to be friendly, do her homework, answer questions in class whereas Barry is likely to be argumentative, surly, and refuse to answer questions. Reality for each of these pupils is a matter of individual perception based on past experience plus theories about the future. Barry's perception of Mr Rasit may have been distorted by the memory of another firm teacher who was unfair to him. He may have the idea that all teachers are the same and that Mr Rasit will also treat him unfairly.

Perceptions are not fixed however and we are constantly changing them in the light of our experiences. If Mr Rasit punishes Angela and she experiences this as unfair, her perception of him may well change and become closer to Barry's. As both teacher and pupils get to know one another better, their perceptions of each other can constantly change. Prejudice may be defined as the process of holding on to original perceptions even when experience contradicts them. A psychologically healthy person will change and adapt their perceptions in the light of experience. In this way our perceptions can become more reliable guides to true 'reality'.

What determines our behaviour is not objective reality (whatever that is) but our own subjective awareness of the world around us and of ourselves. Barry and Angela react and behave according to their perception of reality.

Internal frame of reference

A person's subjective world, consisting of all memories, sensations, perceptions and meanings that are available to consciousness, is sometimes referred to as the internal frame of reference. Rogers stresses that this private world can only be fully known to individuals themselves. You are the only one who can ever really know how you are perceiving the experience of reading this book. We may have an idea of your experiencing but the depth and exact nature of your perception are only potentially known to you. The term person-centred reflects this emphasis on the subjective view of individuals. In order to understand the behaviour of another person it is necessary to get as close as possible to seeing the world through that person's eyes, through their frame of reference.

Organismic valuing process

In order to satisfy the actualising tendency (the drive to grow physically and psychologically), we need to know what is of value to that growth. Person-centred theory calls this ability to weigh up and value experiences positively or negatively, the organismic valuing process. The term organism refers to the totality of the individual as being 'more than the sum of its parts'. All humanistic psychologists tend to focus on the whole person rather than isolating different processes such as behaviour, thoughts, or feelings. If we listen to our 'organismic valuing process' we will know what will help us move towards our potential. If we are hungry, for example, we will rate food highly and move towards it. Once the hunger is satisfied, food loses it high value status.

The self and the self-concept

The idea of a 'self' is central to Rogers' theory of personality. He never explicitly made a distinction between the self and the self-concept, but such a distinction is implicit in his writings. Rogers noticed that clients often expressed their problems in terms of their self. For example, they might say, 'I don't know who I am', 'I don't seem to be able to be me', or 'I don't let anyone see my real self, I hate my self'. This self is the real inner life of the person and is reflected in Shakespeare's 'To thine own self be true' (Hamlet I.iii.78). It is present from birth and refers to the awareness a person has of something that is 'him' or 'her' – an awareness of what is enjoyable, painful, exciting and of what he or she can and cannot do. Infants learn about the 'real self' through their own experiencing. For example, a child playing on the floor notices his feet for the first time and incorporates them into his sense of self: 'I have feet'. This knowledge of the self develops independently of interaction with others.

Unlike the real inner self, the self-concept develops through interactions with others: 'you are a brave boy', 'aren't you an observant child', 'why are you always so naughty?'. We will be discussing later how this self-concept is acquired and how conflict between the self and the self-concept causes problems for the person. The development of the self is often referred to as self-actualisation and is therefore a subsystem of the actualising tendency.

How does our personality develop?

Rogers does not suggest that personality develops through any set stages or that development ever ends. He always stressed the possibility of continual unfolding towards fulfilment of our potential. We are pre-programmed to move forwards and, provided conditions are favourable, we will continue to do this throughout our lives. The person-centred approach regards the development of normal personality as the result of certain innate characteristics modified by the individual's experience and their social environment.

Innate characteristics of the human infant

Rogers believed that the actualising tendency and the organismic valuing process are both present at birth. He believed that the child really does 'know what is best'. In infancy it is not affected by what other people think or by self analysis. If you observe a child, you will find that it prefers and seeks out experiences such as exploration, manipulation of objects, social communication with significant other people through crying, gurgling, or screaming – in fact any behaviour that will enhance its growth. It will reject any experience that does not assist the actualising tendency.

The child reacts with the environment as it perceives it. A loving grandmother might pick up her grandson in an affectionate way but if he sees her as strange and threatening, that is his reality. A child has a need for safety and in response to his own perceived reality and motivated by the actualising tendency he will show distress and hold out his arms to his mother. Through experience of his grandmother he may change his perception of her and therefore also his behaviour. This process of testing reality and changing perceptions continues throughout life.

Although the real inner self is present at birth, infants are not aware of themselves as separate beings. They do not seem to know where their bodies end and the world begins. They are unable to differentiate themselves from the things and the people around them. As they interact with their environment and the significant people around them they gradually acquire this sense of being a separate entity. This awareness which is at first non-verbal will guide behaviour. Later the child will express self-awareness with statements such as, 'I don't want to do that', 'that's my toy', or 'let me do it'. There is now a recognition of physical and emotional separateness. This is the beginning of the process of self-actualisation.

Development of the self-concept

As the child interacts with significant others it becomes aware of their evaluations. Sometimes these evaluations will be positive, 'clever girl' and others will be negative, 'naughty girl'. The perception of self acquired in this way is known as the self-concept. Sometimes the self-concept matches the person's inner sense of self. Often though there is a mismatch and then a conflict can arise as the desire to actualise (develop and maintain) the self-concept works against the need to actualise the real self.

Need for positive regard

As the awareness of self surfaces, the child develops a need for love and acceptance – or positive regard. It was irrelevant to Rogers whether this need is inherent or learned, the fact is that it is there and could have a strong influence on the developing child. The child's behaviour is shaped by the need for approval and it will therefore do things to please its parents even to the extent of ignoring its own inner feelings.

Rogers gave the example of a young infant who found it satisfying to hit its baby brother. The pleasure derived from this may be consistent with the child's sense of itself as loveable. At this early age the infant has no perception of the brother's frame of reference (that is what the brother experiences when he is being hit). When the parents see this behaviour they may disapprove of it and give the message that the behaviour is bad and the child is not loveable. This is inconsistent with the infant's own valuing process (which values the behaviour highly) and with its sense of self as loveable. This is an example of how conflict can arise between the inner self (I am loveable) and the self-concept (I do bad things and am unloveable).

Introjection

One way the child can resolve the inconsistency is to deny any awareness of the satisfaction gained by hitting his brother thereby maintaining the sense of self as loveable. The parental attitudes are taken on as if based on the child's experience. The internalisation of the values and beliefs of significant others is a process known as introjection. In the example above, in order to introject (or take on board as if they were his own) the values of his parents, the young infant would have to deny and distort its own experience of satisfaction.

Fully functioning person

There is a delicate balance here. The child is driven to follow its growth tendency by satisfying its physical and psychological needs but it also needs positive regard. If it can reconcile these two needs and if the self-concept it acquires is in tune with the real inner self, the child will grow into a 'fully functioning person'. This is an ideal concept, a hypothetical person who has reached their full potential.

A fully functioning person is one who is open to experience. He or she would not be unduly concerned with the opinion of others and therefore could allow all experiences to be consciously perceived. This person would have such a clear idea of the path to their own fulfilment (the actualising tendency) that their behaviour would be entirely effective in protecting their own interests (maintenance) and in seeking their own physical and psychological goals (enhancement). They would only do those things that continued to allow them to be truly themselves. Such a person would be able to trust their own ability to know what is good and bad for their development (the organismic valuing process) and they would accept responsibility for their own behaviour. They would fully accept themselves for who and what they are and this acceptance would be based on their own valuing process and not on the praise and opinions of others. This self acceptance would mean that the person would not need to be defensive and would also accept others for what they were and this would lead to good relationships with them. Such a clear perception and understanding of one's self and one's healthy way forward would not be selfish or anti-social; the fully functioning person would have escaped from jealousies and rivalries and would respect the rights of others because of the rewarding character of reciprocal positive regard.

How our problems develop and how we maintain them

Clearly none of us are fully functioning people, although some seem to be nearer this goal than others. Although we all have the potential to become psychologically healthy this does not always happen. Sometimes significant people in our childhood deprive us of what we need and our development is therefore blocked and distorted. The normal growth of the potatoes in Rogers' cellar was blocked by deprivation and Edmund Gosse's young plant was distorted by the pot of prohibition and suppression.

Blockage of the actualising tendency

Interruptions of the actualising tendency distort and inhibit the normal growth of the personality. These blockages usually occur through the overwhelming need for positive regard. If positive regard is conditional upon 'good' behaviour it will cause conflicts between the self and the self-concept. This leads to anxiety and confusion. Rogers has described the need for positive self regard as 'pervasive and persistent' (Rogers, 1959: 223). The satisfaction of this need is so strong that it will override the organismic needs.

Jane, aged three, lived with her parents in a small flat. One day she discovered that pulling the books off the bookcase in the hall was a satisfying experience. In terms of her organismic valuing process, she valued it highly, it was a good thing to do. Her mother, tired of endlessly picking up the books, had other ideas and scolded the child angrily. Jane was now faced with a conflict. Her actualising tendency was driving her to continue the behaviour since it satisfied her need to explore. The conflict between Jane's self (perceived by her as loveable) and the self-concept imposed by her mother (as unloveable because of her behaviour) created a sense of incongruence, a disturbing mismatch. The love and approval of her mother seemed to be conditional on her denying herself this enjoyable experience.

Conditions of worth

Rogers used the phrase 'conditions of worth' to describe the way a person has positive self regard only when approved of by parents and significant others. If her mother's love and approval was conditional on Jane stopping her book-throwing behaviour Jane would have to introject (take on as if her own) her mother's values. By denying or distorting her pleasure when pulling books off the shelf she would then be able to maintain self-regard (one's view of one's own worth). The healthy way of resolving this conflict would require Jane to retain her own evaluation which in this case could be 'I enjoy doing this. I also enjoy pleasing my mother, her distress when I behave like this is dissatisfying to me'. Her behaviour would then become a balancing of these two needs – sometimes she will behave to satisfy her need to please her mother and sometimes she will satisfy her own pleasure playing with the books.

Silencing the organismic valuing process

If Jane has to continue to distort her own experience in the need for positive regard, eventually the voice of her real inner self will be silenced. When this happens she will cease to trust her organismic valuing process (the inner instinct that knows what is best for her) and her personal growth will be stunted.

Internalising the values and beliefs of others leads to a negative self-concept since the standards set are usually unrealistically high. Cut off from their own sense of value and inner resources, individuals continually strive for the conditional positive regard they feel they need. They fail and a vicious circle begins. They begin to behave as others perceive them. In our example, if Jane is constantly being told off by her mother and perceives that her mother's love is conditional upon good behaviour, she will fail more and more. Jane will become fearful; she will never know whether her next action or utterance will bring condemnation or praise from her mother. As she starts school she will see herself as a failure and behave accordingly and will be unlikely to succeed at her studies. This will further reinforce her sense of worthlessness.

The child now has two valuing processes governing behaviour: the organismic valuing process and the conditions of worth process. Individuals are deceived into believing that decisions based on the latter are actually based on their own valuing process. If many significant conditions of worth are imposed the psychological consequences can be severe.

Introjected values

Rogers has suggested that introjected values (beliefs, values and attitudes of others taken in as if our own) are learned in the home, at school, in church, from society and even from the government. For example, at school children are often taught that only by getting grade A will they be acceptable and valuable as human beings. Introjected values from government might be the 'Me first, self next, what's left I'll have' attitudes of Thatcherism. Children brought up like Edmund Gosse and Carl Rogers internalise the beliefs that only by adhering strictly to the beliefs of fundamentalist Christianity can they have any self-worth.

Maintaining our problems – the denial and distortion of experience

Individuals who are highly dependent on the evaluations of others for their sense of self-worth will seek to preserve their self-concept at all costs. If there is a conflict between their self-concept and their inner experiences a state of 'incongruence' (mismatch) is said to exist. The individual may then use a defence mechanism to protect themselves from the anxiety and confusion they feel. Depending on the situation the experiences are either selectively accepted into consciousness, denied or distorted.

Elizabeth is a university student studying psychology. Evaluations and judgements by her parents and school have given her a sense of poor self-worth. Her self-concept is that 'I am not intelligent, I only got into university because they needed to fill the places'. When she receives a good mark for an essay, she distorts the experience by saying that 'the teacher must have been tired when she marked it, she didn't really read it'. An essay with a low mark however is focused on and used to reinforce her self-concept. Positive comments or feedback would create conflict between her low self-worth and her experience – so Elizabeth ignores or distorts them. Even when she was awarded a first class honours degree she dealt with this incongruence by saying 'it was only because all the other students had not worked at all and a certain percentage had to get firsts'.

This type of denial is partly conscious. A more profound and significant type can occur where the experience is not permitted to enter conscious awareness at all. It is as if the perception is prevented from being represented in the mind. Freud referred to this as repression. Rogers (1951) gave the example of an adolescent boy brought up in an over solicitous home. His self-concept is that he loves and is grateful to his parents. But he may actually feel intense anger at the subtle control being exerted over him. (At this point one wonders whether Rogers was speaking of his own childhood.) The boy experiences the physiological changes that accompany anger but his conscious self prevents these changes from being perceived and brought into awareness. It is as if the mind is thinking, 'I cannot allow myself to feel this . . . whatever it is . . . because I am a grateful boy and only feel love and gratitude'. To maintain his self regard and the positive regard from others the boy disowns his anger. Thus the awareness of the physiological changes is denied and confusion and anxiety are avoided. Alternatively he might distort the perceptions so that they are more consistent with his self-concept as loving and grateful, and might perceive the sensations as a 'bad headache'.

Defence mechanisms protect the person from distress. They also maintain the psychological disturbance because they preserve the person's alienation from their organismic self and their actualising process. Some individuals do this so successfully that they are totally unaware of their psychological disturbance and are unlikely to enter a psychotherapist's room. They often come across as self-assured and confident but the person-centred approach would still classify them as disturbed because they have usually completely lost touch with their inner selves. Sometimes others close to them will complain of their lack of 'real' feelings. These individuals are often those who suffer most following a traumatic incident such as the Kings Cross fire in London, or the Oklahoma bombing. Under such conditions the carefully constructed edifice comes tumbling down. They had seen themselves as someone who is always in control, not emotional but stable, calm human beings. Suddenly they are forced into contact with their inner selves and feel fear, confusion, anger and helplessness for the first time perhaps since they were little children. Their world literally falls apart and they disintegrate.

THE THERAPY

In his seminal speech at the University of Minnesota in 1940 Rogers said:

> Therapy is not a matter of doing something to the individual or inducing him to do something about himself. It is instead a matter of freeing him for normal growth and development so that he can again move forward.
>
> Rogers, 1942: 29

Both Edmund Gosse and Carl Rogers achieved this freedom by moving away from the atmosphere at home that restricted them. The person-centred approach states that liberation from blockages of the actualising tendency can also be achieved through the therapeutic relationship. As individuals recover from deprivation and restriction they once again are able to listen to their own inner voice (the organismic valuing process) and reject the conditions of worth imposed by others. Discrepancies between their real self and the self-concept can then be resolved. Rogers believed that in the therapeutic relationship, clients experience, perhaps for the first time, acceptance and understanding rather than evaluation. They are then freed to recognise and acknowledge their real self.

Distinctive features

The person-centred approach challenges the notion of professionalism and claims that the personal qualities of the therapist are more important than degrees or qualifications. Regarding the therapist as an expert with special knowledge implies a power imbalance in the relationship with the therapist as an authority figure. The person-centred approach regards it as essential that individuals realise they can trust their own experiencing and the validity of their own perceptions. This could not happen if the client perceives the counsellor or psychotherapist as all knowing, the expert with all the answers.

What distinguishes this approach from all others is the emphasis on the quality of the therapeutic relationship with no reference to techniques. It is a process-oriented approach. If certain necessary conditions are present, then changes will occur in the client and the process of growth can take place. Rogers listed what he regarded as 'The necessary and sufficient conditions of therapeutic personality change' (Rogers, 1957: 95):

1   Two persons are in psychological contact.
2   The first, whom we shall term the client, is in a state of incongruence, being vulnerable and anxious.
3   The second person, whom we shall term the therapist, is congruent or integrated in the relationship.
4   The therapist experiences unconditional positive regard for the client.
5   The therapist experiences an empathic understanding of the client's internal frame of reference and endeavours to communicate this experience to the client.
6   The communication to the client of the therapist's empathic understanding and unconditional positive regard is to a minimal degree achieved.

The first two are really conditions that have to exist before therapy begins. The next three we have already met; they will be further described in the next section. The final condition relates to the client's perception of the counsellor's attitudes and is discussed under the section 'Conveying the core conditions'.

Assessment

No formal assessment is used in the person-centred approach. All clients are regarded as being out of touch with their actualising tendency. No other diagnosis is seen as necessary. Rogers believed that prescribed assessment procedures often miss what the client's experiences are. This is illustrated by the key case described earlier when Rogers missed the difficulties the mother was experiencing. In taking a formal case history often only what the counsellor regards as important and relevant is considered. This is contrary to the belief that the client is at the centre of the therapeutic process. Rogers regarded psychological diagnoses such as depression or anxiety to be detrimental since the process of assigning such labels places evaluation in the hands of an expert. This is likely to work against clients taking responsibility for self-understanding and working towards change by getting in touch with and trusting their own valuing processes.

Unlike most other approaches to psychotherapy, the first meeting with the client is not used to take a history or make a formal diagnosis. Nevertheless, person-centred therapists consider carefully whether they can be of help to a particular client. Brian Thorne (1996) believes that those who have most to gain from person-centred therapy are those who really want to change, are prepared to recognise their responsibility in the therapeutic process and are prepared to take the necessary emotional risks. Once the counsellor and client have agreed to work together, therapy begins immediately, the counsellor has no agenda but allows the client to choose the content of the session.

Since person-centred therapists do not set themselves up as experts they do not have the attitudes of other professionals who often believe that they have the answers to all their clients' problems. Person-centred therapists recognise their limitations and acknowledge that these limitations lie more in themselves and in their ability to provide the necessary conditions for change and growth than in the approach itself. During the initial sessions counsellors will ask themselves whether they are the right person to help this particular client. If not then referral to another counsellor is made.

Goals

Since the client-centred approach believes that psychological difficulties are caused in the main by blockages of the actualising tendency (the innate drive towards maintenance and growth), it follows that the main goal of therapy is to release the individual from any constraints and restrictions. The counsellor's aim is to provide the conditions necessary for this to occur through the therapeutic relationship. If successful the client is enabled to explore in safety their inner experiences long denied or distorted which are inconsistent with their self-concept. There is no final result, no end state but rather a continuing process of change which hopefully will continue after therapy has ended as the person moves towards becoming a more fully functioning person. Specific goals relating to the clients' presenting problems are not indicated, since it is expected that freeing the actualising tendency will enable the client to resolve them.

Therapeutic relationship

Therapist style

In the person-centred approach the relationship between client and counsellor is regarded as equal. The therapist does not seek control or authority over the client by diagnosing, evaluating, directing the content of the sessions or by using techniques to intervene in some clever way to bring about change. The focus of the relationship is always on the client's concerns.

Some critics of person-centred counselling have described it as a soft option where the therapist adopts the passive role of 'simply' listening and grunting at appropriate moments. Perhaps these people do not understand that person-centred counsellors have to invest much of themselves in the process. They cannot rely on their diagnostic skills, their brilliant techniques and interventions, their role as provider of a 'cure', or hide behind being regarded as an expert. They have instead to become involved in the world of their clients, seeking to understand it from the client's point of view. They have to believe in the worth and value of each client. Rogers saw the therapist as a companion to clients on their journey as they enter into and explore their inner worlds.

Congruence

There is no value in psychotherapists presenting acceptance, warmth and understanding if inwardly they are feeling irritation, dislike, and boredom. Rogers believed it was better for the therapist to express such feelings, if persistent, in the session. He believed the client will sense them anyway and to hide them would interfere with the therapeutic process. Just as congruent triangles match each other exactly in size and shape so should the counsellors' outward responses match their inner feelings. Counsellors need to be fully aware of their feelings during the session and 'to live these feelings, be them in the relationship and . . . communicate them if appropriate' (Rogers, 1962: 417).

Other terms for congruence that have been used include genuineness, realness, openness, authenticity and transparency. All these words capture some aspect of this condition. Rogers particularly liked the word 'transparent';

the counsellor is so open in the relationship that the client can see right through to the real person. By truly being themselves, counsellors are giving the strong message to their clients that being true to their inner selves is not only all right, but is actually a good thing. The client will learn also that the counsellor is to be trusted, any responses can be accepted as honest. This trust is earned through the counsellor being genuine in the relationship and not commanded through any 'expertise'. By being prepared to be open about feeling confused, helpless, irritated or mistaken the counsellor demonstrates self-acceptance despite these 'weaknesses' and gives a powerful message to the client. Congruence gives the client experience with a genuine egalitarian relationship and not a one-sided relationship with distant professionals who may seem to be merely 'doing their job'.

Sometimes incongruence can occur because therapists are not aware of their underlying feelings. Rogers called this 'creeping incongruence' stating that it can be very difficult sometimes for the counsellor to realise what is happening. He stressed the importance of supervision and the therapist's own personal growth as a way to deal with this. Other blocks to being congruent include the counsellor's personal difficulties which might be in the same area as the client's problems. Or the counsellor may be unwilling to admit to feelings regarded by some as weak, perhaps because they want to project an image of a well-adjusted, normal, stable and expert therapist.

There are dangers inherent in being congruent. By becoming more involved in the therapeutic relationship the counsellor's own fears and needs may get confused with those of the client. Rogers stressed that congruence is not a question of the counsellor having to 'blurt out impulsively every passing feeling' (Rogers, 1962: 418). The session would otherwise become counsellor-centred instead of person-centred. Congruence is rather a state of being. Feelings only need to be expressed when they are persistent and of great strength and when communication of them assists the therapeutic process.

Unconditional positive regard

Many clients who come for counselling believe that others will only love them and approve of them if they behave, think and feel in the 'right' way. Often they have only ever experienced conditional positive regard. Unconditional positive regard means that the counsellor offers the person respect, acceptance and caring whoever they are at that point in their lives. It is free from any conditions of worth. It is a non-judgemental attitude which indicates an appreciation of individuals *as they are* regardless of their attitudes or how they might be behaving. Rogers often used the word 'prizing' to convey that this attitude is more than mere acceptance.

John was experiencing extreme anxiety. While talking about his family it became clear that he had not seen his sister for many years. He then revealed that she had accused him in front of the whole family of sexually abusing him when they were children. As he spoke of this he became quite indignant at this false accusation for in his eyes they had been engaging in normal sexual exploration 'which every child does, don't they?' Despite her own attitudes to childhood sexual abuse, the counsellor offered John respect and made it clear to him that she accepted and prized him as a human being whatever his behaviour. As John began to realise that he was not going to be judged for what had happened between him and his sister he was gradually able to let go of his denial and distortion of what had actually happened. Through facing up to the sexual abuse he was eventually able to admit the truth to his family, especially his sister, and eventually obtained their forgiveness.

In this example if the counsellor had not been able to offer John unconditional positive regard but instead had been judgemental of him it is unlikely that he would ever have been able to resolve this conflict. Person-centred counsellors' acceptance extends to the full range of their clients' attitudes, feelings and behaviours even when clients' value systems are completely different from their own. Individuals like John need the respect and acceptance of another person if they are to discover again their potential to 'maintain and enhance' themselves. By providing a safe place where John knew he would not be rejected he was able to look at the dark side of himself. As human beings, counsellors are fallible and therefore have limits. If John's counsellor was not able to show him respect and acceptance then he should be referred to another counsellor. Unconditional positive regard must be genuine and unaffected by the differences in belief systems between client and counsellor.

Unconditional positive regard is important because it undermines clients' beliefs that they are only valued if they behave as required by significant others. It also breaks into the cycle of the defensive behaviour of clients by making it redundant; there is no longer any need for the client to shy away from his inner self. He learns it is possible to be truly himself and still be accepted. The counsellor must sometimes patiently wait, continuing to value the person for some time before earning the trust of the client and being allowed behind the defensive shield. John had to be absolutely sure that his counsellor would not reject him when she 'knew the awful truth' about him before he would explore what happened in his childhood.

Empathy

If your friend came to you in floods of tears because her cat had just died, you would possibly feel for her and try to offer comfort. At the same time you might feel puzzled at her sadness, it was after all only a cat and she had only had it three weeks. This kind of response is called sympathy because there is a lack of understanding of your friend's distress; you are be viewing and judging the event from your own private subjective world (your internal frame of reference). Empathy is different; it is a way of being which is all about entering into and understanding another person's private world as they perceive it. Rogers regarded it as extremely important.

> It involves being sensitive, moment by moment, to the changing felt meanings which flow in this other person, to the fear or rage or tenderness or confusion or whatever that he or she is experiencing. It means temporarily living in the other's life, moving about in it delicately without making judgements; it means sensing meanings of which he or she is scarcely aware, but not trying to uncover totally unconscious feelings, since this would be too threatening.
>
> Rogers, 1980: 142

In our example, in being empathic with your friend you would try to understand what the cat's death meant to her, how she perceived the loss. It might be, for example, that she had invested a lot of love in her cat because it gave her affection unconditionally as animals do, perhaps unlike the people in her life. In order to fully understand her you would need to put to one side your own way of perceiving the world in order to sense and respond to your friend's way.

Empathy is the process of understanding another person 'as if' you were that person. Rogers described it as a way of laying aside our 'own views and values in order to enter another's world without prejudice' (Rogers, 1980: 143). If the 'as if' quality is lost then the process can become one of identification when the counsellor is no longer understanding an event from the client's frame of reference but from her own experience of a similar event.

Susan's father had just died following a painful and protracted illness. Susan does not focus on this in the next session but chooses to talk about her difficulties with her partner. The counsellor, who lost her own father in similar circumstances, identifies with Susan's loss and suggests to her that she must be grieving and feeling quite distressed. This is not from Susan's frame of reference, however. Susan is feeling sad about her loss but during her father's illness has worked through this and was able to say good-bye to him. She now feels relieved that his pain and suffering are over. An empathic counsellor would be able to 'stand in Susan's shoes' and sense the feelings she has about this event. From where Susan is standing the lack of a grief reaction is understandable.

Research has shown clearly that when clients experience their counsellors as deeply empathic, they are helped to explore their inner selves more profoundly and constructive change is more likely to occur. Clients who have long felt alienated suddenly find themselves being able to feel connected to another human being; one who is really trying to understand them. As they realise that their 'strange, abnormal' feelings and thoughts are understood by the therapist they feel less isolated. This will assist disclosure and exploration of further 'odd' thoughts. Sometimes these discoveries will be unsettling to the client; 'I never knew I was capable of feeling courageous about something'. As these new beliefs about themselves are accepted the client's behaviour will change.

Empathy is non-judgemental. It would not be possible for you to understand your friend's grief at the loss of her cat if you are all the while thinking that she is being rather pathetic. Such an evaluation would block the empathic state of being. As clients sense the non-judgemental nature of the therapeutic relationship they are further encouraged to look at previously denied or distorted aspects of themselves. Prejudices and personal theories about why a client is behaving in a certain way, a need to be liked by the client or the need to see clients improve each session can also block the development of empathy.

There are inherent dangers in being empathic. Counsellors sometimes find that they experience the same feelings as the client but when this happens they need to hold on to the 'as if' quality so that the emotions remain under control. Clients need to know that however chaotic their inner lives may seem, the counsellor remains a reliable companion and not somebody who will become overwhelmed or disintegrate in the presence of this chaos. This requires that person-centred counsellors feel secure enough in their own identity so as not to get lost as they move into their clients' worlds.

Sometimes the counsellor is able to catch hold of what the client is currently and consciously feeling. At other times the counsellor steps gently into the client's world and sensitively listens for faint glimmerings of feelings on the 'edge of awareness'. Eugene Gendlin, who was one of Rogers' students and later became the director of his research into the use of the person-centred approach for schizophrenics, made an important contribution to the understanding of the empathic process (Gendlin, 1981). He stressed this idea of sensing the underlying feelings and responses of which the client is not yet aware. Here also dangers lurk, for if these underlying feelings are expressed too soon the client can become frightened. Rogers has described this as 'blitz therapy' which has a destructive rather than a constructive outcome.

The interaction between the three core conditions

Although we have discussed each of the core conditions as if they were separate entities, in practice they need to be combined. Unconditional positive regard is facilitated by the process of empathy for example. Both empathy and unconditional positive regard need to be genuinely felt by the therapist. Each condition facilitates the development of the other.

Impossible to achieve and exclusive to the therapeutic relationship?

This may all sound a bit idealistic to the reader; as if the three core conditions have to be fully present for all clients all of the time. In reality this is not what happens. No-one can be one hundred per cent genuine or empathic. What the person-centred approach advocates is that the nearer the psychotherapist reaches this goal the more change and growth will occur.

Rogers also believed that each of the core conditions is important in everyday relationships. They are not exclusive to the therapeutic relationship but they are of special importance to it.

Conveying the core conditions

It should be clear to you by now that person-centred counsellors use no specific techniques. Therefore this section looks at the sixth condition in Rogers' list of 'necessary and sufficient conditions for change': the communication to the client of the core conditions provided by the therapist. There are no clearly set out or established ways of conveying these attitudes although many training courses try to categorise skills such as reflection of feelings and content, or summarising what the client has said so far. These skills are not used exclusively by person-centred counsellors but also by most other approaches.

In this section we have chosen to illustrate ways of communicating each of the three core conditions. The reader should once again bear in mind that there is much overlap among these conditions.

Conveying congruence

If the client has had long experience of significant people in their lives being dishonest, less than open, or giving mixed messages then it will be very hard for them to believe that here is someone who is truthful, honest and open.

Being congruent in a therapeutic relationship can feel very risky for the counsellor. What do you say to a client when feeling dislike or boredom? Clients are often adept at perceiving mixed messages where the words of the counsellor, intended to convey warmth and interest, do not match the body language or tone of voice.

Ivor, recently separated from his wife, has spent three sessions talking about the problems his parents, friends and colleagues at work were having. The psychotherapist became aware of her own feelings of irritation and boredom at this long litany of other people's lives. She asked him about his relationship with his wife and children from whom he is separated.

IVOR: Oh well you know, it's good. The kids are with me every other weekend and my wife and I are quite good friends now.

He then returned to a long description of what his children were doing at school. The counsellor's feelings of irritation persisted.

COUNSELLOR: Can I stop you there for a moment?. . . You know this room to me feels kind of . . . filled with all these people in your life. I feel a bit irritated I guess because I am having a problem wondering . . . where are you in all of this?

IVOR: (pausing thoughtfully then shaking his head) My god you're right, it's like I don't exist, like I don't care how I feel about all this, just sort of keep my head busy so that I don't . . . oh god my kids, I can't bear to be without them.

Breaking down at this point, Ivor was subsequently able to explore how he did feel about the separation and the resulting loss of his children. He also came to realise that this pattern of ignoring his own feelings was how he had always related to people and that he did so in the belief that other people preferred him to be strong and silent about his feelings.

Notice that the counsellor did not say 'you are being so irritating' but 'I feel a bit irritated' thus taking responsibility for her feelings. In everyday life we have a tendency to blame other people for the way we feel. 'He makes me so angry' or 'stop making me feel guilty' are typical examples. We cannot know whether another person is boring, irritating or confusing, we can only know how we feel about talking with them, how we perceive them. It cannot be an absolute truth that Ivor is boring but he may be behaving in a boring way at a given point in time. Because the counsellor acknowledged the feelings as her own, Ivor did not feel judged but instead was facilitated by her comments to view his behaviour and see for himself what he was doing.

Counsellors need to be sufficiently aware of all the possible reasons for their feelings. In this next example the counsellor is feeling confused and interrupts the client.

Indira, a college student, is telling her counsellor all about her difficulties with her parents who are insisting on her having an arranged marriage. In fact she has a boyfriend although she has not told her parents about this.

INDIRA: They just don't seem to understand, you see in my country it's all normal, but I am in love with Peter and I don't see why . . . but it's my religion so I suppose I ought to comply with their wishes. I mean they want me to get an education, do something useful but I know that once I go to India that will be it and well I do believe in arranged marriages, you know it's my faith but well I live here now and then there's Peter, as well as my studies and they aren't easy, I'm afraid they are suffering 'cos my tutor said . . .

COUNSELLOR: Can I stop you there for a moment? I am aware that I am feeling rather confused, I am not able to follow your story very well and I am wondering if it would help us both if we concentrated on one aspect of the situation. What do you think?

INDIRA: Yes, I guess I am feeling a bit confused too. Perhaps I should start with my parents and my relationship with them.

In this illustration an alternative explanation for the counsellor's confusion is that it is the result of being unable to concentrate due to tiredness. This would lead to a different response.

> COUNSELLOR: Can I stop you there for a moment. I am aware that I am feeling very confused. I feel uncomfortable saying this because I know it is because I am tired and I did not concentrate as well as I should have done while you were talking. I think it would help if you could clarify one or two things.

Clients are often very observant and Indira is likely to have noticed her counsellor's loss of concentration. If the counsellor had tried to cover it up instead of acknowledging it this would have had a detrimental effect on the trust that Indira was developing towards her counsellor.

Conveying unconditional positive regard

This is perhaps the hardest attitude to hold and convey. People sometimes ask 'how can you feel unconditional positive regard towards someone who has abused their own child?' Behind this question lies a misunderstanding. Unconditional positive regard does not mean approval of the client's behaviour. It is the caring and the desire to understand that is unconditional. The person-centred counsellor attempts to accept clients as people of worth, while not necessarily liking some of the things they do or believe. It is often the hardest condition for the client to believe in after perhaps a lifetime of regard being dependent on what they do, think or feel.

Each counsellor has their own particular repertoire of responses which can be verbal or non verbal. Often a gentle touch on the arm, maintaining eye contact or a warm smile can say far more than the spoken word.

> Ian came to counselling feeling very depressed. Repeatedly throughout the early sessions he said: 'I don't know why I am here, I am so ugly, you must find it very difficult to look at me, it is all my badness coming out. There is no point to this. It is a fact, I am ugly, this cannot change. No one can accept this face of mine, it tells you what I am.'
>
> Eventually the counsellor said to him: 'I feel very sad. I sense that you want me to agree with you, that you are ugly and totally bad. But I cannot do that although I acknowledge that that is how you see yourself. I do not see you as an ugly bad person but as someone who has never been accepted for who you really are, a valuable human being.'
>
> Following this response Ian looked straight at the counsellor for a few seconds. The counsellor maintained eye contact, then as tears began to form in Ian's eyes, she leant forward towards him reaching out her hand tentatively. To her surprise (he had already told her he would not let his

parents touch him as a child) Ian took hold of her hand. He said very quietly: 'You almost sound as if you care, no one has ever been like that before, you're looking at my terrible face and you do not hate me for it.'

He then withdrew his hand and sat for some time in silence with his head bowed deep in thought. Respecting his need for space to be with himself the counsellor sat still. Eventually he looked up and said: 'I don't know whether to believe you really but I feel now that maybe, just maybe there is a chance for me.'

Conveying empathy

In the early days the emphasis on reflection of feeling as a way of communicating empathy led to this being known as *the* technique used in the person-centred approach. As long as the counsellor is repeating back to the client what their feelings are, then they were regarded as being person-centred. This attitude is, sadly, still prevalent today. Having been on the receiving end as a client of one of these parroting counsellors one of the authors recalls being intensely irritated by having her last words simply repeated back to her. The counsellor believed he was conveying that he understood by picking up on her feelings and on the content of her story and mirroring this back to her. In practice the author did not experience this as an attempt to really understand or be interested in what she was saying. It all sounded too much as if the counsellor were on 'automatic pilot'.

MARIA: Yeah I'm feeling pretty cheesed off really with my boss, he keeps making lewd remarks to me, you know kind of personal ones directed at me.

COUNSELLOR: (attempting to reflect content and feeling) So your boss keeps making these personal comments and you feel quite annoyed with him.

MARIA: (with annoyance) That's what I just said.

A more empathic response would have been:

COUNSELLOR: (picking up tentatively) Lewd remarks? Sexual?

MARIA: Yeah, I mean sexual nudge nudge wink wink remarks like the other day he said when I was wearing a short skirt, 'mmm we all know how you're feeling today then don't we lads, I reckon she wants it' and he made a kind of face you know, sort of leering. Like I'd worn the skirt on purpose 'cos I was feeling randy or something.

> COUNSELLOR: I notice you're clenching your fist as you describe what happened, as if you're more than cheesed off, but really angry, even hurt, how dare he insult you. Is that right?
>
> MARIA: Yes yes, that's it, insulted, yeah too right insulted, I mean I'm not some tart flaunting it, how dare he see me in that way, yeah it does hurt, that's right. And I am angry, yeah. I really want to get on in this job, I'm good at it and I like working there but if this goes on, well I don't see how I can stay.

By picking up on the 'lewd remarks' and by tentatively introducing the word 'sexual' the counsellor has made it acceptable for the client to explore further what it is about the situation that really annoys her. Also the counsellor identified and responded to the hurt associated with being insulted and again tentatively checked this out with the client. Person-centred counsellors do not *tell* clients how they feel but share in a tentative manner their own understanding of how the clients are feeling. If the counsellor has fully understood, the client's response is often 'yes that's it, that's exactly it'. By being tentative the counsellor is respecting the client's right to disagree and explore their feelings and thoughts further.

> Taking this conversation a bit further, at the end of her last response Maria's voice dropped almost to a whisper as she said 'I don't see how I can stay'. Noticing this the counsellor responds with:
>
> COUNSELLOR: You don't see how you can stay . . . I sense you feel scared at that thought, is that right?
>
> MARIA: (thoughtfully) Mmm scared, well, no that's not quite it, it's more like feeling helpless, there's nothing I can do it seems. I mean I don't think I'd find it too hard to get another job but, well, I suppose it's more sad than scared 'cos I'd be losing something I've really worked for.
>
> Here Maria tries out the word scared 'for size' by repeating it to herself before rejecting it in favour of feeling helpless and then sad. If the counsellor had declared 'you are scared' the client would have found it very difficult to disagree and may even have believed the counsellor, thinking 'yes I must be scared, the expert says so and she should know'.

It can be very hard to perceive situations through the client's eyes. While reading about Maria you may have experienced thoughts such as 'why doesn't she just tell him to get lost', or 'why doesn't she just leave and get another job'. Such thoughts would have been from your frame of reference and not hers. Empathic thoughts would be of the order 'it seems really hard for you to be assertive with this boss', 'the thought of getting another job seems too upsetting at the moment'. To be truly empathic these thoughts would have to be expressed in a tentative way in order to check out whether you have understood her correctly.

CLOSING COMMENTS

In this chapter we have given you a taste of the most important theoretical and practical aspects of the person-centred approach along with a glimpse into the life of the man who developed it. Just as Rogers found a way to explore his inner world freed from the constraints of his fundamentalist background, so this approach seeks to help people free themselves from whatever blockages are currently preventing them from going on their own journey towards personal fulfilment. On this journey the counsellor or psychotherapist acts as a companion, not as a guide. The person is thus empowered and has control over and responsibility for what happens in therapy. The counsellor's function is to provide the conditions in which the person can feel safe enough to step out of their uncomfortable present way of being, which is at least familiar if chaotic, into an unknown place within themselves. Changing Gosse's metaphor a little, by regarding the pot on the plant as a pile of stones instead, the goal of therapy is to enable the person to begin lifting these stones off one by one, as they dare to move towards being in touch with their inner selves again and the drive which urges us on to become fully functioning people.

Inevitably we have only been able to give an overview of this approach. If you are interested to know more, we have included a list of recommended reading at the end of this chapter. You can go on your own voyage of discovery and explore further the remarkable contribution Carl Rogers has made not just to the world of therapy but also to other diverse areas of human existence, for example, the Person-Centred Encounter Groups which Rogers developed towards the end of his life. These are groups of people who come together to share and explore each other's life experiences with a 'facilitator' present, whose role is to provide a safe psychological climate to promote self understanding and change.

In his final years Rogers became preoccupied with world peace and the promotion of international understanding. The person-centred approach rejects the notions of power so inherent in our society: men having power over women; white over black; heterosexual over homosexual; and adult over child. He travelled extensively to areas of the world where tension and conflict were prevalent such as Northern Ireland, South Africa and Russia. His book *A Way of Being* (1980) contains papers he wrote on his vision of how a future world could be. His greatest achievement in this regard was to bring together leaders of seventeen countries to a conference held in Austria on the 'Central American Challenge'. Without his knowledge, Rogers was nominated for the Nobel Peace Prize in 1987; before the final decision was made, he died.

REFERENCES

Gendlin, E. T. (1981) *Focusing*. (2nd edn.) New York: Bantam Books.

Gosse, E. (1974) (First published 1907) *Father and Son. A Study of Two Tempera- ments*. London: Oxford University Press. Thanks are due to William Heinemann Ltd for permission to reprint the extract on pp. 57–8.

Kirschenbaum, H. (1979) *On Becoming Carl Rogers*. New York: Delacorte Press.

Kirschenbaum, H. and Henderson, V. L. (eds) (1990) *The Carl Rogers Reader*. London: Constable.

Rogers, C. (1939) *The Clinical Treatment of the Problem Child*. Boston: Houghton Mifflin.

Rogers, C. (1942) *Counseling and Psychotherapy*. Boston: Houghton Mifflin.

Rogers, C. (1951) *Client-Centered Therapy*. Boston: Houghton Mifflin.

Rogers, C. (1957) 'The necessary and sufficient conditions of therapeutic personality change'. *Journal of Counseling Psychology*, 21(2), 95–103.

Rogers, C. (1959) 'A theory of therapy, personality and interpersonal relationships as developed in the client-centered framework', in S. Koch (ed.), *Psychology: a Study of Science, Vol III. Formulations of the Person and the Social Context*. New York: Harper and Row.

Rogers, C. (1961) *On Becoming a Person*. Boston: Houghton Mifflin.

Rogers, C. (1962) 'The interpersonal relationship: the core of guidance'. *Harvard Educational Review*, 32, 416–29.

Rogers, C. (1974) 'In retrospect: forty-six years'. *American Psychologist*, 29(2), 115–23.

Rogers, C. (1980) *A Way of Being*. Boston: Houghton Mifflin.

Thorne, B (1996) 'Person-centred therapy', in W. Dryden (ed.) *Handbook of Individual Therapy*. London: Sage.

FURTHER READING

Mearns, D. and Thorne, B. (1988) *Person-Centred Counselling in Action*. London: Sage.

Thorne, B. (1992) *Carl Rogers*. London: Sage.

4 The rational emotive behavioural approach

INTRODUCTION

> Men are disturbed not by things but by the views which they take of them.
>
> Epictetus AD *c*. 55–*c*. 135

Albert Ellis, the founder of rational emotive behaviour therapy, often quotes this line from the Stoic philosopher Epictetus to emphasise the basic premise of this approach to counselling and psychotherapy. Rational emotive behaviour therapy maintains that our emotional problems and counterproductive behaviour are largely the result of 'crooked' unhelpful thinking. It is not events that cause our problems, but the way we think about them. Ellis calls our unhelpful thoughts 'irrational beliefs' and says that they are at the core of much emotional disturbance. Rational beliefs on the other hand are flexible, helpful ways of thinking and enable us to be psychologically healthy.

Ellis maintains that we consciously or unconsciously 'choose' to disturb ourselves by having irrational beliefs. If we take responsibility for our problems and work hard to change the 'crooked' thinking that underlies them to more rational ways of thinking, we improve our chances of resolving our difficulties. The quote from Epictetus continues:

> When we meet with difficulties, become anxious or troubled, let us not blame others, but rather ourselves, that is our ideas about things.

A woman is travelling by train to an important meeting. The train is seriously delayed. If she has the unhelpful irrational thought, 'I *must* not be late for this meeting, it will be so awful if I am. I am so stupid I *absolutely should* have left earlier', she is likely to end up feeling very anxious and will probably not function well in the meeting. Alternatively if she thinks to herself, 'I would prefer to be on time, but

I don't have to be, it's not the end of the world', she will just feel concerned and thus more able to deal with the meeting. The railway company may be responsible for her late arrival but they are not responsible for her anxiety.

The pioneering work of Albert Ellis had a great influence on the development of the cognitive-behavioural approach to counselling and psychotherapy. Rational emotive behaviour therapy was the first of the cognitive-behaviour therapies. When Ellis began using the approach in 1955 he called it 'rational therapy' (RT) to emphasise the role of thinking in the creation and maintenance of emotional problems. His opponents accused him of following eighteenth-century rationalism; a philosophy that emphasises the importance of reason and intellect above all other aspects of human experience and ignores the role of emotion. To counter this in 1961 he changed the name of the therapy to rational-emotive therapy (RET).

From the beginning, Ellis emphasised the important role that behaviour plays in the maintenance and remediation of psychological problems. He believes that we cannot simply change our attitudes and beliefs just by talking about them, we need to put changes into practice. In 1993 he wrote: 'So, to correct my previous errors and to set the record straight, I shall from now call it what it has really always been – rational emotive behaviour therapy (REBT)' (Ellis, 1993: 258).

ALBERT ELLIS

Family background and early life

Albert Ellis was born on 27th September 1913 in Pittsburgh, Pennsylvania. The family moved to New York when he was four years old where he has lived ever since. He does not believe that the events of his childhood shaped his personality, but he has acknowledged that certain elements in his early life sowed the seeds for the later development of rational emotive behaviour therapy. During his childhood he experienced considerable adversity but

> I always seemed to have been the kind of person who, when unhappy, made an effort to think about and figure out ways to make myself less unhappy. In a way I was a born therapist for myself.
>
> Palmer *et al.*, 1995: 55

Albert and his younger brother and sister were brought up in a family which today would probably have been referred to the social welfare agency. Both his parents neglected their children. His father was a travelling salesman and even when he was at home, he took very little notice of his children. Albert's mother, although physically present, was absent in an emotional sense. Ellis described her as 'quite unequipped to deal adequately with either marriage or child-rearing, she was much more immersed in her own pleasures . . . than she was in understanding and taking care of her children' (Ellis, 1991: 2). Albert looked after his younger siblings, taking care of all the household tasks. He was often left in charge while his mother was out socialising. Ellis later said that he did not think that this parental neglect had any serious adverse effect on him. 'I decided not to hate my mother for her ineptness and used it instead to twist her around my little finger and even in some ways to exploit her' (Ellis, 1991: 3). When Albert was twelve years old, his parents divorced and he saw even less of his father who provided very little financial support.

When he was five he developed tonsillitis and a serious streptococcal infection. He was admitted to hospital for emergency surgery. Between the ages of five and seven he was frequently in hospital, mainly because of nephritis which developed after the surgery. In hospital weeks would pass without a visit from either of his parents. With the stoicism of the ancient philosophers he later admired, Ellis has never acknowledged feeling homesick or miserable during this long period of illness. He did, however, become concerned for his health and avoided childhood games, being drawn instead towards more intellectual activities. He developed an enthusiasm for reading and by the age of eight had read all the volumes of an encyclopaedia, the *Book of Knowledge*. By the time he was sixteen he had read many of the philosophers including Epictetus, Spinoza, Kant and Bertrand Russell.

Ellis did well at school and enjoyed his time there except when he was asked to speak publicly in class, when he 'sweated and sizzled with anxiety and desperately looked for (and sometimes managed to cleverly find) some way out' (Ellis, 1991: 3). He did not resolve his shyness until he was older. Instead he managed to structure his world so that his social difficulties did not interfere.

At the age of twelve, Ellis decided he was going to be a famous novelist. He recognised that while he was working towards this goal he would have to support himself. He decided to train as an accountant. After leaving the New York High School of Commerce at the age of sixteen, he entered the Baruch School of Business and Civic Administration graduating in 1934 with a degree in business administration. The great depression that began in 1929 disrupted his plans. His mother lost all her savings and the family became very poor. Ellis had to find any work he could and took a number of low paid jobs.

While studying accountancy he became interested in psychopathology (the scientific study of mental disorder) and read books by Freud, Jung, Adler and others, pursuing what had become a hobby: the psychology and philosophy of happiness. Ellis joined a radical political group and as one of the leaders was expected to speak in public against war and fascism and for revolutionary democracy. He had read that if we make ourselves do what we are afraid of doing we can overcome our fears (a method known as 'in vivo desensitisation'). He forced himself to speak over and over again in public and found that he could overcome his fear and that he had a real talent for public speaking. This could be viewed as Ellis's first experience as a rational emotive behaviour therapist with himself as his own client. He later said:

> Once I deliberately made myself uncomfortable, I became comfortable and finally began to enjoy it. . . . So by telling myself cognitively that nothing terrible would happen if I did speak poorly and was disapproved of for doing so and by acting against my phobia, I made a 180-degree circle and completely overcame it.
>
> Dryden, 1991: 135

His reading, especially Freud, also helped him with his sexual hang-ups, and his shyness with women. Having successfully used in vivo desensitisation to overcome his fear of public speaking, he decided to use it again to overcome his other problems. He went to the Bronx Botanical Gardens every day and forced himself to approach any woman sitting there and talk to her. In one month he approached 100 women in this way and spoke to them all. He only made one actual date – and she never turned up. Despite this failure, he overcame his fear and became more proficient at talking with women generally.

Having got over his shyness with women, Ellis found that he preferred their company since they talked more readily about their problems than men. His new ease with women enabled him to have a number of intimate relationships. His first wife, Karyl, had emotional problems which initially attracted him. But he discovered that he could not trust her and decided on their wedding night that he would divorce her. His next important relationship he once described as 'one of the greatest romances in human history' (Palmer *et al.*, 1995: 57). This relationship failed because her socialising interfered with his work. His second marriage to a dancer called Rhoda failed for similar reasons. In 1964 he met his current partner, Janet Wolfe and this relationship is still going strong. He once commented that his life 'would be greatly bereft of laughter, warmth and intimacy without her' (Dryden, 1989: 541).

Ellis wrote many novels, plays, and poems in his early twenties but none were published. Realising that he was not going to be the Great American Novelist, he turned to non-fiction. His first attempt, 'The art of never making yourself desperately unhappy' was not successful either. He decided to concentrate instead on writing about his liberal ideas on sex and love, believing that they would be more attractive to publishers. He read hundreds of books on love, sex and marriage and wrote a book called *The Case for Sexual Promiscuity*. This provocative title and the book's contents were too controversial for the publishers and Ellis again found himself in the position of 'failed writer'. His friends meanwhile, had begun to regard him as an expert in the field and came to him for help with their own sexual and marital problems. He enjoyed helping them, using with them the therapeutic skills he had first employed on himself.

University life

He was advised that if he wanted to make a profession out of helping people, which he discovered he was good at, he should gain some professional quali-fication. So, in 1942 he chose to study for a master's degree in clinical psychol-ogy at Teachers College, Columbia University. Following his graduation a year later, he published a seminal paper, 'The sexual psychology of human hermaphrodites' (Ellis, 1945). He continued to study for a PhD and wanted to write his dissertation on the love relationships of young women. Again he was frustrated in his goals, this time by two influential professors who were completely opposed to this topic. Ellis was ahead of the sexual revolution that was to come and these senior faculty members were afraid of the bad pub-licity his research into sex would generate. Instead he changed the focus of his dissertation to a study of the use of personality questionnaires.

Early career and professional development

In 1943 he started a private counselling practice offering sex and marital therapy. Over the next fifteen years Ellis became one of the USA's leading sex-ologists, publishing a number of popular books including *Sex without Guilt* (1958), *The Art and Science of Love* (1960), *Sex and the Single Man* (1963a) and *The Intelligent Woman's Guide to Manhunting* (1963b). These all became best sellers. He was often criticised for his liberal views on sexuality and for his support for gay liberation. When the sexual revolution of the 1960s came, Ellis was one of its leaders.

In the late 1940s he taught at Rutgers and New York University and was appointed the senior clinical psychologist at the Northern New Jersey Mental Hygiene Clinic. By 1950 he had been made chief psychologist of the entire New Jersey State Department of Institutions and Agencies. By the end of this year he had published nearly fifty articles and reviews and had a book, *The Folklore of Sex*, in press (1951). The Commissioner of the Department, Sanford Bates, was appalled by the sexual liberalism expressed in this book and succeeded in forcing Ellis to leave his post.

Since 1951, Ellis has devoted his time to his private practice, his writing, lectures, workshops and the development of his ideas concerning his approach to psychotherapy. His first book on REBT, *How to Live with a Neurotic*, was published in 1957. He has now published well over fifty books and six hundred articles on REBT, sex and marriage. In 1959 he founded a non-profit-making educational organisation now called The Albert Ellis Institute.

During the 1980s REBT had considerable influence on psychotherapy and counselling in the United States. In a survey carried out in 1982 Ellis was rated second among the most influential psychotherapists. Carl Rogers came first and Sigmund Freud third. In 1985 he received the American Psychological Association's Award for Distinguished Professional Contributions to Knowledge. REBT was also having an impact in countries and continents all over the world.

Albert Ellis, the person

Albert Ellis is now in his mid eighties but this has not stopped him working thirteen hours a day. He thrives on challenge; without it he easily becomes bored. Social chit chat, going on holiday, even going to see films or plays all have the potential to bore him, since they do not provide him with the necessary challenge for his tremendous energy. He is a very task focused person and has little time for the niceties of socialising. As a result he has few close friendships. First impressions of Ellis are often of a cold and blunt person, too self-assured, even arrogant. But anecdotes from his colleagues and trainees give a picture of a generous and supportive man.

Ellis has always been a controversial figure. He has experienced powerful opposition and censorship from many different quarters. Several of his books were banned from public sale, he has been refused teaching positions in various universities and was even investigated by the FBI. Undaunted he persisted with his main goal in life and his chief source of satisfaction: the growth of rational emotive behaviour therapy.

DEVELOPMENT OF RATIONAL EMOTIVE BEHAVIOUR THERAPY

Initial approach to therapy

When Ellis began working as a sex and marriage therapist, he found it helpful to give his clients information about sexuality, relationships, the raising of children and other related issues. He observed that clients often held unhelpful beliefs about these matters. His informative and authoritative approach worked well and was one of the earliest attempts by a therapist to use a cognitive approach to psychological problems.

However, Ellis recognised that this method had its limitations. Underlying sexual and marital problems were the problems that the individuals were having with themselves.

> If people are to be helped to live happily with each other they had better first be shown how they can live peacefully with themselves.
>
> Ellis, 1994: 1

Ellis decided to train in psychoanalysis and began seeing clients using the orthodox psychoanalytic techniques of free association, dream analysis and resolution of transference difficulties through interpretation (see chapter 2 for an explanation of these terms). At this stage he still believed, like Freud, that people became disturbed as a result of their childhood experiences and that to achieve change they had to understand what had happened to them.

Dissatisfaction

Despite his early success as a psychoanalyst, he gradually became dissatisfied with this method. Although his clients usually gained insight into the origins of their difficulties, their emotional problems persisted. Many of his clients found free association too difficult, others rarely dreamed or could not recall their dreams, and he found the long silences in psychoanalysis frustrating both to him and to his clients. When his clients complained that he was not helping them, he

> dutifully and cleverly interpreted that they were, by their refusal to go along peaceably with the analytic rules, demonstrating in the transference relationship with me their past difficulties with their parents. They thereby resisted getting better.
>
> Ellis, 1994: 3

While he enjoyed 'detecting', as he privately called the process of making connections between his clients' childhood experiences and their current problems, he had to admit to himself that he often got it wrong. Why was it necessary for the therapist to be so passive in the process that it often took months before the client was 'ready' for his interpretations? Why couldn't the therapist speed the process by asking pointed questions and by showing his client what he clearly discerned himself?

From about 1950, and as a direct result of his increasing dissatisfaction with psychoanalysis, Ellis began to experiment with other methods. He abandoned the ubiquitous couch and began working with his clients face to face seeing them once a week rather than the three to five times required by classical psychoanalysis. Using a more active and 'superficial' approach, giving interpretations much earlier in the process than Freudian therapists advocate and by giving information and advice, Ellis found that his clients got better more quickly and with more long-lasting results than with psychoanalysis. He was still dissatisfied, however, as his clients did not sustain their gains, and often slipped back.

He became interested in behavioural learning theory, recognising that psychoanalysis and behaviour theory both emphasised the role of learning and conditioning in early life. He decided that people could be helped by encouraging them to take action; insight alone was not enough. He began to add cognitive and behavioural techniques to his psychoanalytic procedures. He published two monographs on his experiences: 'New approaches to psychotherapy techniques' and 'Psychotherapy techniques for use with psychotics' (1955a, 1955b). He still believed that clients' activities and relationships were driven by unconscious motivations and that if they understood these and could change and practise new ways of behaving they would get better.

Despite all the changes he made, Ellis still found that many of his clients seemed to cling tenaciously to their unhelpful ideas and thoughts and remained emotionally disturbed. He asked himself, 'Why do highly intelligent human beings, including those with considerable psychological insight, desperately hold on to their irrational ideas about themselves and others?' (Ellis, 1994: 9). By now Ellis was realising that the theory of early childhood experiences and learning to explain emotional disturbance was inadequate. Something essential was lacking.

The key case

About this time Ellis was seeing a 37-year-old woman. She spent most of the time fighting with her husband, she was not doing well at work and she believed that the world was against her. Ellis discovered that her parents had taught her to be suspicious of the world; that she had a right to demand a good life whether or not she worked for it; and that unless she did what they asked of her and did only what they approved of, then she was useless and ungrateful. Since it was impossible for her to behave in a way that *always* pleased them, she grew up believing that she was worthless and inadequate. Love and acceptance were conditional on her doing as they asked.

During two years of therapy with Ellis, the woman gained an understanding of why she felt so hostile towards her husband: she was demanding from him the unconditional acceptance she had not received from her family. She also understood how her parents had indoctrinated her with a sense of inadequacy. Ellis decided to give her homework assignments. She was to try to remember that her husband was not her father and she should therefore act towards him in a different way and she should try to do her best at work even though she still might fail. Over the next six months her relationship with her husband improved, they fought less and at work she was rewarded for better performance. But she still believed that essentially she was worthless. Nothing Ellis could say and none of the insights she gained could shift these false beliefs. She said:

> I know I'm doing better of course. . . . But I still feel basically the same way that there's something really rotten about me, something I can't do anything about, and that others are able to see.
>
> Ellis, 1987: 151

Ellis asked her what evidence she had to support the belief that she was 'really rotten'. Finding none, she asked him how she could continue to believe it without any proof. Ellis was momentarily baffled. Her question reflected his own thoughts. Then it came to him that the simple reason was '. . . because, well, you're human' (Ellis, 1987: 152). This was the turning point. Human beings have no difficulty in holding wrong ideas about themselves especially if these have been reiterated from childhood. The woman needed a new, more realistic way of thinking, and would have to practise using it.

The woman was able to work on her new self-statements and told Ellis two months later:

> Whenever I find myself getting guilty or upset, I immediately tell myself that I am saying some silly sentences to myself to cause this upset; and almost immediately . . . I find this sentence. And just as you have been showing me, my belief invariably takes the form of 'Isn't it *terrible* that . . . ?' or 'Wouldn't it be *awful* if . . . ?'. And when I closely look at and question those sentences, and ask myself 'How is it *really* terrible that . . . ?' . . . I always find that it isn't terrible or wouldn't be awful, and I get over being upset very quickly.
>
> Ellis, 1987: 157

Transition

Ellis tried this approach with other clients with similar successful results. He believed that he had discovered why people become disturbed and why they persistently remain so. The ability to use language, which differentiates us from animals, enables us not only to talk to others, but more significantly, to talk to ourselves. We tell ourselves that things are awful and terrible when in fact they are perhaps bad or irritating. We also tell ourselves that what we want is what we MUST have – a desire becomes a necessity. He began to see that our psychological problems are not merely the result of early experiences or of learning but that we keep on re-indoctrinating ourselves through our self-talk. The way we think becomes our personal philosophy of life. If that philosophy is based on false premises then psychological problems are the result.

Ellis turned his back on the psychodynamic way of thinking and returned to the hobby of his youth: philosophy and in particular the philosophy of happiness. He had discovered that our cognitions, our ways of thinking, are central to almost all our problems. By the beginning of 1955, Ellis was calling himself a rational therapist. In 1956 he gave his first paper on his new approach at the American Psychological Association convention in Chicago. He published his first article 'Rational psychotherapy and individual psychology' in 1957 and outlined twelve basic irrational beliefs that people use to upset themselves. For many years his approach was associated in many therapists' minds with the identification of irrational beliefs and with showing clients how to identify, challenge and change them.

Final developments

Despite opposition from other schools of therapy, Ellis continued to develop his approach adding various emotive and behavioural techniques to his repertoire. In 1962 he revised and published earlier papers and articles in his seminal book *Reason and Emotion in Psychotherapy*; this book was later revised and updated in 1994. During the 1960s other cognitive-behaviour theories were developed by people like Aaron Beck (1967), Donald Meichenbaum (1977). Ellis's approach became more acceptable and influential.

Rational emotive behaviour therapy has not stopped developing since its inception in 1955. During the late 1960s and early 1970s Ellis made several important additions including: differentiating between types of negative emotions; the use of dramatic and forceful methods to challenge clients' beliefs; and an emphasis on the primacy of 'crooked' thinking in the form of absolute 'shoulds' and 'musts'. In the early 1970s Ellis condensed the original twelve irrational beliefs into three major ones. He also began to develop his ideas about people's reluctance to tolerate any discomfort (later called discomfort disturbance). We shall be discussing all of these concepts later in this chapter.

THE THEORY

Overview

In *Reason and Emotion in Psychotherapy*, Ellis writes that the basic principles of rational emotive behaviour therapy are not new (Ellis, 1994). He 'frankly adopted and adapted them from many thinkers' (p. 53). Ancient Greek and Roman philosophers such as Epicurus, Epictetus and Marcus Aurelius, and some ancient Asian philosophers such as Confucius, Gautama Buddha and Lao-Tsu, believed that people are largely responsible for their own emotional disturbances. Although Ellis has been influenced by the Stoic philosophers, he says that he 'is hardly a Stoic . . . REBT favors self-actualisation and maximum pleasure *as well as* self-discipline and a moderate degree of Stoicism' (Ellis, 1994: 65).

Modern philosophers who have influenced Ellis include Immanuel Kant and his ideas on the power and limitations of cognition. Philosophers of science such as Karl Popper and Bertrand Russell helped Ellis see that we develop hypotheses about ourselves, other people and the nature of the world in order to put purpose and meaning to our existence. Our own philosophy of life is based on these theories which Ellis refers to as 'beliefs'.

Ellis has also been influenced by the work of general semanticists who stress the potent effect that language has on thought. We structure our thoughts by the language we use and our self-talk has a powerful effect on our emotions. A number of important psychotherapists have also influenced the development of REBT. Alfred Adler is often referred to as the first therapist to use cognitive methods. His motto, 'Omnia ex opinionone suspensa sunt' (Everything depends on opinion) underlines the main thrust of his and later Ellis's argument that a person's behaviour is determined by his ideas. Of the behaviourists, Ellis acknowledges the influence of John Watson and Burrhus F. Skinner. His own successful attempts to cure himself of his fears using behavioural methods have also influenced the form of psychotherapy he has developed.

The theory underlying REBT has emerged from several disciplines. Its stress on cognition and the need for action classifies it as a cognitive-behaviour therapy. Unlike other forms of cognitive-behaviour therapy, however, it has a distinct philosophic emphasis.

Personality theory

Our goals and purposes in life

Although primarily classified as a cognitive-behavioural therapy, REBT is also regarded as a humanistic-existential approach. As humans we attempt to give our lives meaning and purpose. REBT focuses upon our experiences and values, and believes like Rogers that we have self-actualising potentialities – that is that we strive beyond survival towards fulfilment (see chapter 3 for fuller description). Rational emotive behaviour theory regards human beings as basically hedonistic. Ellis uses this word to describe the happiness he believes we can all achieve if we work hard enough. We are happiest when we are actively working towards achieving our goals. If we think, feel and behave in ways which assist us to achieve our basic goals and purposes, then we are living rationally. The opposite is living irrationally and involves thinking, feeling and behaving in ways that block these goals and purposes.

Human beings are fallible and imperfect; however hard we try we will make mistakes and sabotage our attempts to achieve our goals. Sometimes we do this by satisfying our short-term goals at the expense of our long-term goals. Achieving long-term goals often means experiencing discomfort in the short term; something humans seem reluctant to tolerate. We are naturally short-term hedonists.

Enlightened self-interest

REBT has been accused of encouraging people to be selfish. But Ellis does not advocate the pursuit of our own happiness at the expense of others. He qualifies this self-interest by the use of the word 'enlightened'. Although most of the time we put ourselves first, the interests and goals of others, especially those we love, will come a very close second. We live in a social world and if we act responsibly our actions will lead to a better world in which we can live.

The ABCs of REBT

The REBT theory of personality is best explained using Ellis's now famous ABC model that explains the relationship between thinking, emotion and behaviour.

The 'A' stands for Activating events. As we work towards achieving the goals and purposes of our life we constantly experience external and internal events. External events are events and situations that occur outside ourselves. They can be actual events such as a knock at the door, or seeing a neighbour across the road or they can be events we believe have happened but may not have done, such as thinking 'there is a burglar at the door'. Although it could be argued that all thoughts are internal events because they occur inside the person's head, in cases like this they are classified as external events since the thought is about something external to us. Internal events are events that occur inside us. Again these can be actual events such as having a headache or they can be events which we believe have happened but may not have done, for example thinking 'I have a brain tumour'.

The 'B' stands for the evaluative Beliefs we hold about the activating event. These can be rational or irrational. The 'C' stands for the emotional, behavioural and cognitive Consequences of those beliefs.

A   Activating events – external or internal
B   Beliefs (evaluations) – rational or irrational
C   Consequences – emotional, behavioural, cognitive

Cognitions at A

Rational emotive behaviour therapy identifies four types of cognition: descriptions, interpretations, inferences and evaluative beliefs. The first three types of cognition can all be activating events in the ABC model and are thus best placed under 'A', whereas the fourth type of cognition is placed under 'B' and we shall describe it later.

In the remainder of this section we illustrate the ABC model with the story of a young woman, Tania, who is standing by a window with her back to a young man, Larry. He is in love with her but does not know how she feels about him.

Descriptions

Descriptions are the simplest type of cognition. What we see, taste, touch or hear we describe without adding anything to it. The description can be accurate or inaccurate. In our example, Larry might describe the external event correctly, 'Tania is standing by the window', or incorrectly, 'Tania is sitting by the window'. If at the same time he notices the internal event that his hands are sweating, he might describe this as 'my hands have gone clammy'.

Interpretations

Interpretations add something to what our senses are telling us; they go beyond the data that are available. They are not evaluative and our emotions are not involved at all. For example Larry might think, 'Tania is looking out of the window'. Since he cannot see her eyes, this is a hunch on his part, she could have her eyes closed, or she may be looking at the floor. It is therefore an interpretation about an external event. Like descriptions, interpretations can be accurate or inaccurate. He might also interpret the internal event of his sweating hands and think 'Must be the curry I had for lunch'. This may not be correct since sweating can be due to other factors.

Inferences

An inference goes one step further. Again, this type of thought goes beyond what our senses tell us, but this time emotions are involved and the thought is partly evaluative. Larry might make the inference 'Tania is looking out of the window *because she does not like me*'. This may or may not be true, she may be looking at some children at play outside. We make inferences when our emotions are involved but these inferences do not fully account for the precise emotions experienced. Emotions are the result of the fourth type of cognition, evaluative beliefs at B in the ABC model.

Cognitions at B

Evaluations – rational and irrational beliefs

Evaluative beliefs usually involve the person making some kind of judgement about the activating event. They can be either rational (helpful) or irrational (unhelpful) and account for the precise emotions experienced. Whether a belief is rational or irrational can be assessed on four dimensions as illustrated in the table below.

Table 4.1　Characteristics of rational and irrational beliefs

Rational beliefs are:	Irrational beliefs are:
Flexible and often expressed as preferences, desires, wishes, likes or wants	Rigid and dogmatic and often expressed as 'musts', 'shoulds', 'oughts'
Consistent with reality	Not consistent with reality
Logical – the second part of the belief follows on logically from the first	Illogical – the second part of the belief does not follow on logically from the first
Pragmatic – they help the person achieve their goals	Not pragmatic – they usually interfere with the person's goals in life

In our example, Larry might have had the following thought sequence which we illustrate using the ABC model:

A　Larry is looking at Tania, standing by the window [actual external event]
　　He thinks:
　　　　She is standing by the window with her back to me [description]
　　　　She is looking out [interpretation]
　　　　This means she doesn't like me [inference]
B　　I would like her to like me, but she doesn't have to [rational preference]
　　　　If she doesn't it is bad but not terrible [evaluative, rational anti-awfulising belief]
C　Larry feels sad [emotional consequence]
　　And leaves the room [behavioural consequence]
　　He thinks:
　　　　I wonder why Tania doesn't like me, but perhaps I am reading the signals wrong [cognitive consequence]

Ellis seems rather fond of making up words. 'Awfulising' refers to the irrational belief that if something doesn't happen it will be absolutely awful, nothing could be worse. The rational alternative is an 'anti-awfulising' belief when the person concludes that an event is bad but not so bad that they can't stand it.

In this example, Larry is holding rational beliefs. Larry's beliefs are flexible because he allows for the possibility that his wishes may not happen by expressing them as a preference rather than as a MUST. They are consistent with reality, since Larry can prove that it is bad but not terrible if Tania doesn't like him. They are logical because he recognises that just because he wants something it does not follow that he absolutely MUST have it. They are pragmatic since, whether his wishes are fulfilled or not, although he might feel sad he will not feel disturbed about the outcome. Therefore his beliefs do not interfere with his goals in life.

If Larry were to have irrational beliefs at B the emotional, behavioural and cognitive consequences would be different:

A   Larry is looking at Tania standing by the window [actual event]
    He thinks:
        She is standing by the window with her back to me [description]
        She is looking out [interpretation]
        This means she doesn't like me [inference]
B   I want Tania to like me therefore she absolutely MUST like me ['mustur-batory' irrational belief, making demands on someone else]
        If she doesn't like me it will be awful and I can't stand it [evaluative belief – awfulising and I-can't-stand-it-itis]
C   Oh I feel so depressed [emotional consequence]
    He goes home and sits in his room doing nothing for days [behavioural consequence]
    He thinks:
        Tania doesn't like me, nobody likes me [cognitive consequence – over-generalization]

In this example Larry's belief is irrational because it is expressed as an absolute MUST and is therefore not flexible. There is no universal law that states that Tania MUST like Larry so this belief is not consistent with reality. He makes the logical error of believing that just because he wants her to like him it follows that she MUST or SHOULD like him. Ellis refers to irrational beliefs of this kind as 'musturbatory' thoughts. 'I-can't-stand-it-itis' and 'mustur-batory' are further examples of Ellis's invented words. The latter usually raises a few eyebrows! Later in the chapter we will be discussing how mustur-batory thoughts contribute to emotional disturbance. (Ellis also refers to 'I can't-stand-it-itis' as low frustration tolerance, described later in this chapter.) The conclusion Larry comes to is that if he does not get what he demands it will be awful and he won't be able to tolerate it at all. This conclusion is not pragmatic since the emotional, behavioural and cognitive consequences of holding this belief will interfere with his life goals.

Some 'shoulds' are not irrational. For example, the word 'should' may be applied to a recommendation: 'you should put your money in the bank to keep it safe'. There are also conditional shoulds, for example, 'if I work hard on this chapter I should be able to get it completed in time'. Then there is the deserving should: 'he should go to prison for life for what he has done'. There is only one kind of should that is irrational, the absolute should. Absolute shoulds have derivatives such as 'it's terrible, I can't stand it' and they lead to unhealthy negative emotions.

Cognitions at C

In the two examples above we have included cognitive consequences of the evaluative beliefs at B. How these cognitions can easily become distorted is described later in this chapter.

Emotion

In the ABC model the 'C' often stands for emotional consequences. The feelings we experience are largely determined by the beliefs we hold and therefore are under our control. If we change the belief we change the emotion. Ellis qualifies this by acknowledging that in some cases spontaneous emotional outbursts occur without any previous thought. For example, if someone makes a sudden loud noise behind you, you may instantly experience acute fear. These kinds of emotions seem to be biologically rooted; they serve a survival function.

REBT theory distinguishes between healthy and unhealthy emotions. Emotions can also be negative and positive. Most positive emotions, such as happiness, are seen as healthy although mania while experienced as positive is actually quite unhealthy. Some negative emotions are also regarded as healthy although they can be intense and unpleasant. For example, it would be healthy and appropriate to experience intense sadness on the death of a parent. Healthy negative emotions enable us to change what can be changed and adjust to events that cannot be changed. If in our example, Tania decides that she cannot return Larry's affections, he cannot change that situation. He may feel sad and this sadness is healthy because it will enable him to process and digest the event and find a way of adjusting to it.

Unhealthy negative emotions get in the way of change where change is possible, or prevent us from adapting to events that cannot be changed. If Larry experiences depression this will prevent him from adjusting to the situation – and most likely will affect Tania's opinion of him. He will tend to think and act in ways that will defeat him in his overall goal of finding happiness. Unhealthy emotions include anger, anxiety, depression, guilt and shame. The healthy emotions that contrast with these are annoyance, concern, sadness, remorse and disappointment.

Behaviour

The 'C' in the ABC model can also stand for behavioural consequences. REBT theory holds that a person's behaviour is largely determined by the beliefs they hold about themselves, others and the world. Useful behaviour tends to result from rational beliefs, unproductive behaviour from irrational beliefs.

Our behaviour usually has some purpose. For example, we might act in a certain way to change the unpleasant feelings we are experiencing. Ellis forced himself to speak in public in order to overcome his unpleasant feelings of anxiety. Or we might act in a certain way to elicit a desired response from someone else. Unable to get any response from Tania, Larry might start crying in the hope that Tania will feel guilty for ignoring him and offer him comfort. People tend to behave in specific ways in response to their emotions and beliefs. For example, some people when they experience fear tend to withdraw from the situation rather than face the fear. This 'action tendency' helps the person avoid discomfort in the short term but it is unhelpful in the long term because it prevents the person from dealing constructively with their fear. Ellis avoided social contact with women for a long time thus avoiding discomfort. If he had persisted with this action tendency, he would not have overcome his fear and would perhaps never have had a satisfactory intimate relationship with a woman.

The interaction of cognition, emotion and behaviour

The reader might have got the impression from the above that REBT theory holds that our senses, thoughts, feelings and behaviours are separate from each other. The ABC model outlined above appears deceptively simple. Something happens (A), we have a belief about it (B) and as a result we act, feel or think in a certain way (C). This hides the complexity of the reality. In fact none of the four fundamental processes – sensing, behaving, thinking or feeling – occur in isolation. When we sense something, we have the tendency to do something, have thoughts about it and experience feelings. For example, if a girl sees a pound coin lying on the pavement, she will tend to bend down and pick it up. She is also likely to feel pleased about her find and to think about what she will spend it on. If she decides to spend it on sweets she will then move in order to go to the shops, think about what she will buy, and feel excited. Her thoughts contribute to her emotions and to her actions. Similarly her emotions have an effect on her thoughts and behaviour and her behaviour will have an effect on her thoughts and feelings. If she changes one of them, the others will tend to change too. If she thinks, for example, about her mother's instructions to come straight home, her emotions may change from happiness to guilt as she continues on her way to the shops. As a result she may change her behaviour and go home after all.

How does our personality develop?

Ellis has yet to develop a detailed coherent theory of how our personality develops. This is probably because he believes it to be more useful in therapy to concentrate on the present aspects of our behaviour and personality rather than on how they originated and developed. The current theory focuses on the interaction of innate characteristics and environmental influences.

Innate characteristics

Humans are born with two biologically based tendencies. Ellis believes our tendency to think irrationally is innate because of the ease with which humans think crookedly. Even people who have been rationally raised tend to take their wishes and desires and easily turn them into demands on themselves, on others and on the world. The tendency to think irrationally can be clearly seen in young children.

The second biologically based tendency is that we all have the ability to exercise choice to work towards changing our thoughts. We are not slaves to our innate tendency to think irrationally. This optimistic view of human personality underlies the practice of REBT, as we shall see later in the chapter.

Ellis has stated that probably 80 per cent of the diversity of human behaviour has a biological base and the remaining 20 per cent rests on environmental influences (Ellis, 1976). Humans have the biological ability to learn from experiences and from other people as soon as they are born. Unlike other animals, we have a well-developed cortex that enables us to respond and modify our behaviour according to environmental influences.

Environmental influences

Ellis suggests that a number of environmental factors influence and maintain our personality. We are born into families and are usually reared in social groups: the family; school; the wider society. In these groups we learn ways of behaving, thinking and feeling, and the rules of the culture into which we have been born. We can be influenced through our relationships with other people, through specific teaching by parents, teachers and others and also through books and the media. Ellis recognises the effect that rewards and punishment have on us. These come from people around us and also from within ourselves as we rate our behaviour as either 'good' or 'bad'.

Stages in development

When they are born infants display rational behaviours such as sucking and crying. These behaviours are largely instinctive and enable infants to satisfy their needs for food and comfort. Ellis (in Dryden, 1990) has suggested that during the first two years of life a child begins to develop its capacity to be a 'scientist', to formulate ideas, expectations and theories about itself, other people and the world. These theories become more specific as their cerebral cortex develops and probably centre around the idea that since pleasure is good and pain is bad, they want more pleasure and less pain. This rational belief has healthy emotional, behavioural and cognitive consequences. However they can also develop irrational beliefs such as 'Pain is bad, I must never experience it. It is so bad I can't stand it'. As we shall see later this intolerance to the inevitable pain and discomfort of life – which Ellis calls low frustration tolerance (LFT) – leads to emotional disturbance.

Shortly after developing ideas about comfort and discomfort and as they begin to be able to use language, Ellis believes that children develop a sense of self or ego. They begin to see themselves as either good or bad – often helped by the attitude of their parents to them. Ellis argues that humans are particularly open to influence as children by the teachings of parents, other members of the close family, school teachers, cultural and societal norms and by their peers. A child's first thoughts may be along the lines of 'I like to be loved and approved of', a wish that turns into a 'must'. They (the parents or significant others) 'absolutely should' give me the love and approval I 'must' have. As the sense of self develops the child then adds on to this 'If I am not loved and approved of there must be something wrong with me, I am bad. I deserve to be punished'.

Sometimes parents and other significant people in a child's life use language in an unfortunate way. For example, a mother might say to her son 'You MUST be a good boy and eat your vegetables'. Children can easily understand this to mean that unless they carry out these 'demands' from their parents then they will not be loved and approved of. In fact, the parent usually means 'I would like you to eat your vegetables but if you don't I will still love you'. The child takes the preference too seriously because of the language used by the parent and turns it into an ever-to-be-obeyed command. Ellis sees human beings as born 'musturbators' since even when the parents and teachers express their wishes as preferences the child will still often turn these into 'musts'.

How our problems develop and how we maintain them

REBT theories on the origins of our emotional problems are an extension of Ellis's ideas about the way we all tend to think. As the ancient philosophers believed, it is not what happens to us that upsets us but rather we upset ourselves by having irrational thoughts about our experiences.

Biological basis of human irrationality and disturbance

The strong focus on the biological origins of our emotional disturbances is a distinctive feature of REBT. It emphasises the power that our innate tendencies to think irrationally have over the power of environmental influences to affect our emotional state. By using the phrase 'biologically based', Ellis does not mean that our emotional problems and personality characteristics are as genetically fixed as our eye colour. We do not inevitably have a certain trait just because it is innate, and even if we do, change is always possible.

Individuals with an innate tendency to be anxious, for example, will more easily develop anxiety than individuals without this genetic predisposition. Such individuals are also more likely to have difficulty modifying the beliefs leading to this trait although change is nevertheless possible.

Ellis supported his belief in the biological basis of human irrationality by making a number of observations. He once wrote, 'do you know anyone who has remained perfectly free of all neurotic symptoms, never subscribed to religious dogma, and never surrendered to any foolish health habits? I practically defy you to come up with a single case' (Ellis, 1977: 15). He also noted that across social and cultural groups the same kinds of irrational beliefs can be found. Wherever we go in the world we will find examples of irrational beliefs in the form of absolutism, dogmas, religiosity and demandingness. 'Extremism tends to remain as a natural human trait that takes one foolish form or another' (Ellis, 1977: 17). Even when we manage to give up one irrational belief, we can take on another.

Environmental influences

Environmental influences, particularly familial and societal, contribute to emotional disturbance. As 'scientists' we are not critical enough of the messages we receive from those around us. If we were, advertising would not be as successful as it is and prejudices would not be so easily formed. There is an interaction between biology and the environment in that some are born more suggestible than others, therefore some humans become more easily emotionally disturbed than others. This idea explains why if two children are born into a psychologically damaging family, one can develop relatively unscathed while the other is emotionally damaged. Ellis cites the example in his own family. He has emerged from his childhood reasonably psychologically healthy, while his sister, who was innately more prone to have rigid and crooked thinking, was emotionally disturbed.

The ABC model revisited

The ABC model used to explain the relationship between activating events (A), the beliefs we have about them (B) and the consequences of those beliefs (C), has already been described earlier in this chapter. Here we want to focus again on the irrational beliefs we hold and the derivatives of these beliefs.

Evaluative irrational beliefs (B) are usually expressed in terms of dogmatic 'shoulds', 'musts', 'oughts' and 'got tos'. REBT states that such beliefs have a high probability of having unhealthy psychological consequences (C) which may prevent us from reaching our goals.

According to Ellis, there are three main irrational demands or musturbatory beliefs that people employ. The first are the demands about the self often stated in these terms: 'I must do well at school, if I don't then I am a bad person and not worthy of being loved' or, 'I should be a perfect mother, if I am not then I deserve all I get'. These beliefs can lead to anxiety, depression, shame and guilt.

The second basic must concerns the demands we place on others. 'You must be good to me, when you aren't I can't stand it, it is so awful. How dare you treat me like this, you are a bad worthless person and should be punished.' This is often linked to feelings of anger and hurt. The third basic must relates to the world and the conditions under which the person lives. 'The conditions under which I live must be as I want them to be, if they are not it is terrible, it's not fair, poor me.' This type of musturbatory belief can lead to feelings of self-pity, and hurt.

Out of any of these three 'musturbatory' beliefs can come irrational conclusions or derivatives. There are three main derivatives. The first two 'awful-ising' and 'I-can't-stand-it-itis' we have already met in the example of Larry and Tania. As a result of having the musturbatory belief that Tania absolutely MUST like him, he came to the conclusion that if she didn't this would be awful, a situation he would not be able to endure.

'Damnation' is the third derivative and refers to the tendency we all have to rate ourselves as bad or damnable if we do something we MUST NOT do or we fail to do something we ABSOLUTELY SHOULD have done. We also have a tendency to damn others or we conclude that life conditions are rated as rotten when they are not as they MUST be.

Cognitive distortions

In the second example, Larry's musturbatory beliefs influenced the way he processed information at C, so that he concluded that because Tania did not like him, nobody did. Humans have a tendency to distort incoming information in a variety of ways. Some examples follow:

All-or-none thinking

Sometimes individuals think in extreme terms. 'I MUST not fail at important tasks, I have failed my examination – therefore I'm a total failure at anything I try to do'.

Personalisation

We have a tendency sometimes to take our perceptions of an event that might have nothing to do with us and conclude that somehow what has happened is related to us. When Larry saw Tania at the window, the fact that she was not looking at him may have simply been that she was enjoying the view. He personalised the event and assumed that her actions had some personal significance for him and inferred 'she doesn't like me'.

Minimisation and maximisation

We sometimes evaluate an event as less or more important than it is. Students gaining good grades for their essays sometimes minimise their achievement, 'Oh it was only luck this time' and when they do badly will maximise their failure with 'It's terrible, I told you I can't write essays'.

Overgeneralisation

Sometimes we draw general conclusions from too few incidents. A lecturer who gets a bad reception from students on a couple of occasions may generalise 'I can't give good lectures'.

Perfectionism

Many people strive to be perfect in all that they do. The mother who says to herself 'I must be a perfect mother' may also say that since she does not always get it quite right she is a useless mother.

Family and group influences

The ABC model appears to explain our problems as if we lived in isolation. However, Ellis notes that we usually live in a family or a group of some kind. This group, or system, affects those that are in it. The existence of some-one who holds strong and frequently irrational beliefs with all the attendant emotional and behavioural consequences is likely to affect others in the system. We need to understand how our beliefs affect ourselves, how they affect others, how they affect the group as a whole and finally how that group affects us.

Two main types of emotional disturbance

Ellis believes that almost all emotional and behavioural problems can be loosely divided into two main categories: ego disturbance and discomfort disturbance.

Ego disturbance

Ego disturbance relates to the demands individuals make about themselves, others and life conditions. When they fail to live up to the demands they make about themselves, they rate themselves negatively. For example, 'I must be a kind unselfish person, if I'm not then I am bad'. If the demands are made about the present or the past, guilt or depression can be the result. If the demands on themselves are made about future events, ego anxiety can result as the person perceives that they may not be able to meet their self-imposed demands in the future.

We will be describing the healthy alternative to ego disturbance, that is, unconditional self-acceptance, later in this chapter.

Discomfort disturbance

When individuals make absolutist demands about their personal comfort and safety they are likely to experience emotional disturbance if these demands are not met. Because we are short-term hedonists, we sometimes will not tolerate frustration in the short term in order to achieve our long-term goals. For example, while you are reading this chapter, you may be experiencing some difficulties in grasping the concepts presented and feel some discomfort. If you have the demand that you should not experience any discomfort at all and that you can't stand it if you do, this could lead you to think 'what's the point, I'll never understand this' and give up the attempt. In the short term you might feel better because you have removed what you perceive as the source of your discomfort, but you will have sabotaged your long-term goal of understanding about REBT. On the other hand if you have the belief 'this is difficult and I would prefer to understand this without any difficulty but I can stand the short-term discomfort' you are more likely to persevere and achieve your long-term goal.

The three REBT insights

Ellis put forward a number of ideas to explain why we persist in having irrational beliefs. One idea is that we perpetuate our problems because we lack three major insights. The first one states that psychological disturbance is primarily determined by the musturbatory irrational beliefs we hold about ourselves, others and the world. People who consider that their disturbances are 'caused' by external events rather than by their own crooked thinking lack this insight. They try to change what is happening to themselves rather than their beliefs.

The second insight states that we remain disturbed by re-indoctrinating ourselves in the present with the irrational beliefs we hold. We may have acquired these beliefs in the past but it is because we *choose* to hold on to them in the present that we remain disturbed. People often focus on their 'awful' past, believing that these events are to blame for their disturbance. REBT states that neither our past history nor our present life conditions cause our disturbance although they may affect us in important ways.

Sometimes individuals have the first insight and/or second but lack the third. This insight states that in order to change our beliefs we need to work hard now and in the future to think, feel and act against our irrational beliefs. There are no short cuts, no magic wands – personality change requires persistent strong challenges to our crooked thinking and practice.

Low frustration tolerance

Low frustration tolerance is linked to discomfort disturbance. REBT holds that the major reason why people hang on to their problems is because they believe that they cannot tolerate frustration. They prefer to maintain the status quo, however painful, rather than carry out the tasks needed to bring about change. These tasks are seen as 'too uncomfortable to bear'. Ellis overcame his own low frustration tolerance and his public speaking phobia by forcing himself at the age of 19 to speak in public for a radical political group he had joined. By tolerating the initial discomfort he was able eventually to become a good speaker and even to enjoy it. Individuals who refuse to make themselves uncomfortable in order to achieve their goals of overcoming their emotional problems will remain disturbed.

Meta-emotional disturbance

Susy is a single mother, struggling to make ends meet. She frequently gets cross with her two children. She holds onto the irrational belief that she must be a perfect mother at all times and therefore should never get cross with them. So, when she does get irritable with them she feels guilty. By making herself guilty about her anger she adds a second problem to the first one. This way of perpetuating our difficulties used to be called 'Disturbances about disturbances' but is now referred to as meta-emotional disturbance.

Defences

REBT agrees with psychodynamic theory that people use defences to deny that they have any problems or that they need to take responsibility for their difficulties. For a description of these the reader should turn to chapter 2. REBT not only recognises defences to ward off threats to our ego but also defences to ward off threats to our sense of comfort. Ellis believes that by using defence mechanisms to prevent us taking responsibility for our problems we prevent ourselves from challenging and working to change our irrational beliefs.

Pay-off or secondary gain

Sometimes by hanging on to our irrational beliefs we get some kind of pay-off.

Jennifer had agoraphobia that prevented her from going out on her own. Eric, her husband, responded to this by being very loving and caring, enjoying her dependence on him. Jennifer was afraid that if she overcame her fears her husband would no longer pay her so much attention. Her emotional distress protected her from what she perceived would be an even more distressing and terrible situation.

REBT notes that it is the inferences and evaluations people make about the consequences of change that cause them to hang on to their disturbances.

Self-fulfilling prophecies

People have a tendency to behave in ways that go along with their own evaluations of themselves. For example, socially anxious people often behave in ways that discourage others from approaching them and talking with them, such as avoiding eye contact, standing hidden in the corner of the room, or answering in monosyllables.

THE THERAPY

Ellis believes that although most approaches to counselling and psychotherapy help clients with their difficulties, they lack efficiency, taking too long to achieve results. Rational emotive behaviour therapy aims to establish what the clients' problems are and to start work with them as quickly as possible in order to alleviate this suffering.

We can decide not to be slaves to our self-defeating tendencies but instead work hard towards changing our crooked thinking. This recurrent theme emerges again here as the basis on which rational emotive behaviour therapy is founded.

> It is unfortunate that they [humans] are so prone to create their own needless misery and disturbance by thinking crookedly, but it is fortunate that if they clearly see how they are doing this, and if they work hard to think differently, they can often, and sometimes quickly change some of the basic factors in their disturbances.
>
> Ellis, 1994: 54

Distinctive features

Unlike most other approaches to counselling and psychotherapy, REBT not only aims to help clients get over their current problems but also aims to help them achieve profound philosophical change. The ambitious aim is to help clients get better and stay better in the long term, rather than just feel better in the short term. Symptom relief is not enough. Ellis speaks of the pervasiveness of therapy and defines it as 'helping clients to deal with many of their problems, and in a sense their whole lives, rather than with a few presenting problems' (Ellis, 1980: 415). The relationship between REB counsellors and psychotherapists and their clients is also distinctive; they use a very active-directive approach with their clients and tend to use what Ellis calls 'force and energy' when assessing and challenging the clients' irrational beliefs.

Assessment

Counsellors and psychotherapists using REBT are not interested in gathering the minutiae of a person's existence and experience. Details of the person's past are considered not only non-essential but are seen as potential red herrings which divert both counsellors' and clients' attention away from the present emotional disturbances.

Basic information that is considered essential is collected through the use of a form Ellis devised called the Biographical Information Form. This enables therapists to gather information including the client's name, address, age, marital status, level of education achieved, occupation, number of siblings, whether the parents are still alive, and whether the client has had any previous therapy. The client is asked to list briefly the present and past main complaints, symptoms and problems and to state under what conditions their problems become worse or better. Further questions relate to their main social, love and sex, work or school difficulties and any medical or physical problems. Clients are also asked to list the things about themselves they would most like to change and finally they are asked to describe very briefly their relationship to their mother, father and siblings. This form provides basic information quickly without using up session time and is then available in a readily accessible form.

In addition REB counsellors and psychotherapists sometimes use a Personality Data Form (Ellis, 1968) that contains a number of typical irrational beliefs.

For example:

- I believe that it is awful to make a mistake when other people are watching.
- I believe that if one keeps failing at things one is a pretty worthless person.
- I believe that things are too rough in this world and that therefore it is legitimate for one to feel sorry for oneself.
- I believe that strong emotions like anxiety and rage are caused by external conditions and events and that one has little or no control over them.

The client is asked to indicate how strongly they believe in each statement. This form is useful because it quickly gives the therapist some ideas about which irrational beliefs are likely to underpin the client's problems.

One of the first questions the REB psychotherapist is likely to ask is 'What is your major problem at this time?' As the client begins to describe the problem, the counsellor breaks the problem down according to the ABC model and assesses each component. Since this assessment is part of the counselling process, we will describe it in more detail later.

One of the purposes of assessment in the early sessions is to decide whether clients are suitable for rational emotive behaviour therapy. Like all other approaches to counselling and psychotherapy, REBT is most effective with clients who are mildly disturbed but it has also been successfully used with strongly disturbed individuals. The more severely disturbed are much harder to help because they find it more difficult to accept the ABC model and because in some cases they find it much harder to think straight. For REBT to work the client has to understand that they really do upset themselves and that they are also capable of not doing so. By assessing the client's major problem in terms of the ABC model in the first session the counsellor is able to judge how difficult it is going to be to get the client to think rationally. Ellis has said that 'no matter how difficult I find them [clients] to be, I practically never give up; I just try to work harder and try to persuade them to work harder' (Dryden, 1991: 73).

Ellis does not think REBT is suitable for clients who are 'out of contact with reality, in a highly manic state, seriously autistic or brain injured, and in the lower ranges of mental deficiency' (Ellis, 1989: 222). Sometimes REB counsellors see these clients but the goals of therapy are more limited. For example, Ellis sees psychotic clients provided they are on medication to control their symptoms. He helps them to accept themselves despite their deficiencies.

REB counsellors and psychotherapists recognise the limitations of this approach. Both Ellis and Dryden have described clients they have been unable to help (Dryden, 1996; Ellis, 1991). Sometimes this is because the client refuses to carry out tasks that were agreed in the therapy session, or because the client refuses to accept responsibility for their feelings. Sometimes these failures are due to the limited skills of the practitioner for as Dryden once said 'REBT is easy to practise poorly'.

Goals

It is the ambitious goal of seeking deep, lasting philosophical changes which distinguishes REBT not only from most counselling approaches but also from other cognitive-behavioural therapies. These changes involve clients:

a) giving up their demands on themselves, others and the world, while sticking with their preferences;

b)   refusing to rate themselves, a process which would help them to accept themselves unconditionally;

c)   refusing to rate anything as 'awful'; and

d)   increasing their tolerance of frustration while striving to achieve their basic goals and purposes.

Dryden, 1996: 312

To give an example, here is an extract from a student's remarks in a session with her REBT counsellor.

> There is no way I can pass this exam, yet I simply must pass it, it will be just the end if I don't. But every time I say to myself, 'all you have to do is work' I just can't stick at it, I feel so sort of sick inside which only stops if I stop trying to revise. So I stop and go out instead. What doesn't help is that my tutor is such a hard marker where I am concerned, I mean he shouldn't treat me like that, it's not fair. Why should we have to go through such agony, it's awful.

In this extract the client demonstrates making demands on herself and others, she rates herself as 'worthless', rates the experience as 'awful' and demonstrates that she cannot tolerate frustration. If the therapist simply deals with the examination anxiety perhaps through relaxation exercises, or special tutoring sessions, the underlying philosophy the client holds will not change. The student will therefore be vulnerable to future upsets.

Sometimes if philosophic change is not possible the REB therapist will agree with the client to settle for less pervasive change. They might achieve some temporary relief from their symptoms or perhaps achieve some degree of philosophic change but not at a profound level.

Therapeutic relationship

Therapeutic style

Like most other approaches to counselling and psychotherapy, rational emotive behaviour therapy regards the therapeutic relationship as important. In line with the basic philosophy of not being dogmatic, REBT does not insist on one particular style of relationship. Nevertheless, an active-directive style is encouraged since it is regarded as the most effective and efficient. Ellis states that it is preferable that both counsellor and client are active throughout therapy. He has at times described the role of the counsellor as that of an authoritative, but not authoritarian, teacher. He has noted that 'My main activity, most of the time, consists of involved, concerned, vigorous *teaching*' (Ellis, 1973: 15). Clients are taught about the ABC model and once they understand the concepts, the counsellor can become less active, less of a teacher, as the clients begin to teach themselves. The role of the counsellor then becomes more actively encouraging. The ultimate aim is that clients learn to take responsibility for their own problems and learn how to be their own counsellor once therapy is completed.

The preferred therapeutic relationship is one where both client and counsellor accept themselves and the other as fallible human beings, where both are equal in their humanity although they may be unequal in terms of their expertise in and knowledge of personal problem solving.

REB counsellors often adopt a forceful style especially with clients who cling to their irrational beliefs with great tenacity, even when they have understood how these beliefs have contributed to their difficulties. Some clients expect therapists to be experts and therefore prefer a formal style, others might find such an approach difficult to relate to and would prefer a friendlier approach. This flexibility of style has not yet been adequately researched and it is therefore not really known which style is most effective and efficient. It is thought preferable for counsellors to consider their style carefully and not, for example, be forceful and active with clients who easily become passive in relationships, or be too directive with clients whose sense of independence is easily threatened.

Therapeutic conditions

One of the goals of REBT is to encourage the client to accept themselves unconditionally and not to rate themselves as bad or worthless. Therapists model this for their clients by unconditionally accepting them. This is one occasion when Ellis agrees with Christianity; 'Judge the sin and not the sinner'. In this respect REBT also agrees with Carl Rogers about the necessity for the core conditions of unconditional positive regard, congruence and empathy (see chapter 3) but disagrees that these conditions are sufficient. Even when clients act 'badly', that is in self-defeating ways, or describe anti-social acts they have committed, the REB counsellor deals with this in a non-judgemental fashion while at the same time not endorsing the clients' behaviour. The hope is that clients will begin to accept themselves as fallible human beings who sometimes behave well and sometimes badly but who are *never* essentially bad or good. Clients are encouraged to examine their behaviour critically and rate it as helpful or unhelpful, without rating themselves as bad or worthless. For example, it is preferable for the client to say of themselves, 'I have just stolen some money from my mother, this is unhelpful behaviour and it is better if I do not do it, but it does not mean I am damnable and worthless as a result'. This might sound like advocating bad behaviour but in fact the client is shown clearly how such an act is counterproductive to their overall goal of achieving happiness.

Rational emotive behaviour therapists are careful about showing too much warmth towards their clients. Being overly warm may reinforce the clients' demands for love and approval. Clients may *feel* better if shown the love and approval they believe they must have but they will not *get* better because the underlying irrational belief 'I must be loved and approved of and if I am not it is awful' remains unchanged. Too much warmth can also reinforce the clients' philosophy of low frustration tolerance by helping them avoid, for example, uncomfortable homework assignments. It needs to be stressed again here that this statement about warmth is again a preference and not a dogmatic must. Ellis recognises that in some cases therapist warmth is necessary, for example, with very depressed clients.

In chapter 3 we described the person-centred view on empathy. REB counsellors offer the same kind of emotional empathy (that is, communicating that they understand how their clients feel) but also offer philosophic empathy in that they demonstrate to their clients that they understand the beliefs that underlie the feelings.

To be an effective rational emotive behaviour therapist can be hard work. Counsellors need to be comfortable with structure and yet flexible enough to change their style to suit their clients. They also need to be comfortable with being active and directive in the relationship and with the idea of teaching their clients what they need to know. Therapists drawn to this approach tend to be philosophically inclined and they need to be comfortable with applying logic and the scientific method to the process of counselling. They need to be able to apply the REB philosophy to their own lives and have the ability to examine their own irrational beliefs. By applying the philosophy of unconditional self-acceptance and by demonstrating high frustration tolerance they can be good role models for their clients.

Techniques

The process of rational emotive behaviour therapy consists of a number of overlapping steps: assessment of the client's problems; teaching the theory of the REBT; disputing the client's irrational thoughts and, lastly, replacing them with rational alternatives. Ellis believes that the most effective and efficient way to achieve change is to encourage the client to use a variety of cognitive, emotive-evocative, imaginal and behavioural techniques. He believes that success is more likely if irrational beliefs are attacked from several different angles. REB counsellors also use a variety of styles including Socratic questioning and didactic teaching.

Since REBT recognises biological causes of certain forms of mental illness, such as manic depression, therapists encourage the use of medication when needed. They also pay attention to clients' physical well being, including nutrition, exercise and relaxation.

Socratic questioning

Socrates was a Greek philosopher (470–399 BC) who was responsible for teaching Plato (*c.* 428–347 BC), the best known of the ancient philosophers. Socrates chose to teach through the use of questions aimed at guiding his student to an understanding or to logical conclusions rather than through formal instruction. All cognitive approaches use the Socratic method to help their clients and REBT is no exception. The purpose is to encourage clients to think for themselves rather than simply accept the therapist's viewpoint. This method emphasises the collaborative nature of the relationship, and it prevents clients feeling that they are being told what to believe, act and feel. Research suggests that getting clients to come up with their own answers is a far more effective way of enabling them to remember what they have learned.

The didactic style

Sometimes clients are unable to grasp the connection between their thoughts and their emotions through Socratic questioning so the counsellor needs to be more didactic, and to teach the client. Also if clients' problems are the result of ignorance the giving of accurate information is essential. Ellis used this information-giving approach in his early days as a sex therapist to his friends.

Assessment of clients' As and Cs

The first stage in the therapeutic process is the assessment of clients' problems using the ABC framework. Clients often begin to describe their problem in terms of the activating event at A. REB therapists discourage long descriptions of what has happened. Clients may *feel* better as a result of talking but they will not *get* better. The relief is short lived.

> Many clients, some of them trained to do so by previous therapy, long-windedly and compulsively talk about their feelings, their feelings, their feelings. Although they had better fully acknowledge these feelings and freely express them in therapy, endlessly obsessing about them and whining about them will do little good and sometimes much harm.
>
> Ellis, 1991: 6–7

When describing A, clients are encouraged to be specific and precise about what happened and what their inferences were and not give unnecessary detail.

Gary, a young man aged seventeen is having problems with his anger. He has a very strict controlling father. In the first session the counsellor asked him what his main problem was.

GARY: My father is driving me up the wall.

This response is too vague, it does not enable his counsellor to assess the A or the C adequately and therefore makes it difficult to get at the irrational beliefs underpinning the problem. The counsellor asks the client to be more specific using Socratic questioning.

COUNSELLOR:　What does your father do that leads you to say 'he is driving me up the wall'?

GARY:　He won't let me go out and meet my mates in the evening. He's a control freak.

Gary is now being more specific. The counsellor may already be forming hypotheses about the client's irrational beliefs which might be 'He should not treat me in this way, he is an awful person'.

　　After assessing the A, the therapist usually makes a careful assessment of C. The consequences for the client of their irrational beliefs often indicate what kinds of evaluations are being made at B.

COUNSELLOR:　When your father stops you going out, how do you feel? What do you do?

GARY:　It makes me mad, god I get so angry with him, I even hit him the other day. I really don't want to do that, I want to find a way to make him stop trying to control me.

At this point, now that the counsellor has some idea about the A and C, she may ask for a specific example.

COUNSELLOR:　Tell me about a specific time that this happened.

GARY:　Last night, Chris rang and asked me to meet him down the pub. It was only 10 o'clock but Dad said I couldn't go. I mean I'm 17 I don't need him telling me what to do. He makes me so angry. I thumped him one and stormed out of the house. Now I know he hates me.

Notice that Gary is blaming his father for his angry feelings. The counsellor has now elicited the emotional consequence of anger, the behavioural consequence of 'storming out of the house'. There is also the false conclusion that his father hates him, Gary has no evidence to support this.

Teaching the B–C connection

Unless clients understand that their emotional problems are largely determined by their unhelpful beliefs they will not understand why the counsellor's next step is to assess those beliefs. In our example, Gary is blaming
his father for his problems and wants to find a way to 'make him stop
trying to control me'. It is important for him to accept the first REBT insight
that it is his irrational thoughts which are causing and maintaining his anger
and not the actions of his father.

Assessing the B

The next step is to assess the unhelpful thinking behind the client's emotional
and behavioural disturbances.

COUNSELLOR: OK so you say you were angry. When you were feel-
                           ing angry what was going through your mind, what
                           were you telling yourself to make yourself angry?
GARY: He shouldn't tell me what to do, he ought to leave
                           me alone.
COUNSELLOR: And if he doesn't?
GARY: He's a rotten person, I hate him, he's making my life
                           a misery and I just can't stand it anymore.

In this example the irrational beliefs that his father *should not* treat him
in this way, he is to be *damned* for doing so and the derivative that he,
Gary, *can't stand it* leads to the emotional, cognitive and behavioural
consequences that have brought Gary into counselling.

One of the drawbacks of this simple ABC model is that it obscures the fact
that assessing each part can be quite difficult. Clients are not always as helpful
as Gary appears to be. Often the inferences are linked together, and inferences
and evaluative beliefs are often connected in complicated chains interacting
with emotions and behaviours.

A student, Sarah, has come for help because she cannot get down to writing an essay. This is presented as a practical problem but she explains that she feels extremely anxious.

SARAH:	I get so anxious, my hands sweat.	Emotional consequence
COUNSELLOR:	What is it about writing your essay that you are anxious about?	Probing for inference about A
SARAH:	I won't be able to write a good one.	Inference 1
COUNSELLOR:	Well let's assume for the moment that you don't. What is it about writing a poor essay that you are anxious about?	Probing to see if this is the most relevant inference
SARAH:	I'll get a really low mark or even fail.	Inference 2
COUNSELLOR:	And if that is true?	Probing for relevance of inference 2
SARAH:	Well, that will just prove I am not good at writing essays.	Inference 3
COUNSELLOR:	Let's assume for the moment that that is true, what does that mean?	Probing for relevance of inference 3
SARAH:	I'll fail this course.	Inference 4
COUNSELLOR:	OK I can see that that is something you don't like the idea of but let's just imagine that it is true and you do fail what would that mean to you?	Probing for relevance of inference 4
SARAH:	I'm a failure, worthless, I should be able to do this and if I can't well I just couldn't stand it.	Irrational belief
COUNSELLOR:	OK let's just look back at what you have just told me, what would be most anxiety-provoking for you, being unable to write a good essay, getting a bad mark, realising you can't write essays, or failing the course?	Probing for the most important inference
SARAH:	Failing the course definitely, I'd feel so ashamed.	

In this example not only are the inferences linked but so are the emotions of anxiety and shame. To get at the irrational belief the counsellor gets the client to assume that his inferences are true for the time being. The technique, known as inference chaining, is also used to identify the critical A – the aspect of A which triggers the B.

The ABCDE model

Two further steps are added to the ABC model to give structure to the counselling process. After assessing the A, B, and C, REB therapists teach clients how to Dispute their irrational beliefs (D) and to replace them with Effective rational beliefs (E). A variety of cognitive, emotive-evocative, imaginal and behavioural techniques are used to implement these two steps.

Cognitive techniques

The main cognitive techniques are the disputing strategies used in the session by the therapist. Clients are taught to use these strategies themselves outside the sessions. In addition a number of other techniques are used to promote belief change. Here are a selection:

Disputing strategies

There are three basic disputing strategies: empirical, logical and pragmatic. The goal of empirical disputing is to help clients understand that there is no evidence to support the absolute demands they are making. As Ellis often says to his clients, 'There are most likely no absolute musts in the universe'. For example, if a client is thinking 'I *must* succeed' the counsellor would ask, 'Where is the evidence that you must succeed?' If it is true that she *must* succeed she would always have to succeed and clearly that is not consistent with reality. Total success is no more realistic than total failure.

Logical disputing challenges the faulty reasoning of the client. In the example above, just because Sarah *wants* to write a good essay it does not follow that she *absolutely must* write a good essay. 'How does it follow that just because you would prefer something to happen that it absolutely *has* to happen?' Logically the demand does not follow from the preference.

Finally, the counsellor can dispute an irrational belief by focusing on the pragmatic consequences for the client. The goal is to demonstrate that as long as the client holds on to the absolutist demands she will remain disturbed. As long as Sarah demands that she always succeeds at college she will remain anxious, thus sabotaging her goal to do well. 'What is believing that you *must not* fail the course going to get you other than anxious and depressed?'

Once the irrational belief has been challenged the client is taught to replace it with a new rational alternative. To illustrate this process we have formulated Sarah's problem using the ABCDE model:

A   I might fail the course
B   I absolutely must not fail the course
     If I fail the course, I would be a failure
     I won't be able to stand it if I fail, it will be awful
C   Emotional consequence: anxiety
     Behavioural consequence: inability to concentrate and complete the essay
     Cognitive consequence: thinking about changing courses
D   How does it follow that just because I'd prefer not to fail I absolutely
     must pass?
     What law of the universe states that I must pass?
     Where is the evidence that I must pass the course? I cannot always
     succeed, sometimes I will fail
     Where does believing that I must pass get me?
     Why does failing mean I would be a failure?
E   I'd prefer to pass this course, but it isn't necessary for me to do so, if I
     don't it will be very bad, but not awful
     I can stand failure, although I will never like it

The three derivatives of irrational beliefs, 'awfulising', 'I-can't-stand-it-itis'
and 'damning' are also the focus of disputing strategies. Clients are helped
to discriminate between 'very bad' and 'awful'. Clients are shown that what
they rate as 100 per cent bad could be worse.

> COUNSELLOR: So you say that to fail this exam would be awful. On
>   a scale of 0 to 100 of badness how bad would that be?
> CLIENT: 100 per cent.
> COUNSELLOR: That bad eh? Well how would you rate failing your
>   exam AND having a car accident as you left the
>   examination hall?

The belief that we can't stand something is a common one. It is usually quite
easy to demonstrate to a client that although very uncomfortable they *can*
stand the situation. Clients are shown that what they really mean is that
'I am finding it very difficult to have these feelings, or go through this experience at the moment, but I have stood it in the past and I can do so again'.

When people damn themselves, 'I am bad, I am worthless', this suggests
that they believe that human beings can legitimately be given a single
global rating, contrary to REBT theory. Human beings are much more
complex than this. What we think and do are part of us but they are never
equal to *all* of us. If Sarah fails her course, it means simply that on one

occasion she did not succeed but it does not mean that she is a *total* failure in all that she does.

Tape-recorded disputing

Clients can record themselves playing both the role of their irrational and their rational selves. The aim is to get the rational self to persuade the irrational self that rational beliefs are more logical, more consistent with reality, and are more pragmatic than irrational beliefs.

Teaching REBT to others

Clients are encouraged to teach the principles of REBT to their friends and relatives. This gives them the opportunity to discover how well they understand the theory and to develop their abilities as a philosopher as they defend their rational beliefs and demonstrate to others the flaws in their own logic.

Semantic precision

People tend to exaggerate when describing their experiences, using words such as 'awful', 'totally', 'impossible' when usually what they actually mean is 'bad', 'a lot', and 'difficult'. This careless use of language can perpetuate irrational beliefs. Clients are encouraged to examine their own use of language and identify statements they use either in self-talk or in talk with others that are 'over the top' and change them to more precise, accurate words and phrases. A typical example of this would be to change 'I can't do that' to 'I am not doing that at the moment'.

Rational coping self-statements

Learning a new way of doing something, whether it is new strokes in tennis or new ways of thinking, requires practice. New effective rational beliefs also need to be practised to make them part of clients' repertoires. Clients are encouraged to have a range of statements that they can repeat to themselves during the day. For example, a client who normally has the irrational belief, 'I must be a perfect father, I'm a worthless person when I fail' would be encouraged to practise the rational alternative, 'I'd like to be a good father, but I don't have to be, nobody can be perfect and it just shows I am a fallible human being when I don't succeed'.

Emotive-evocative techniques

Clients often say that they *know* that their beliefs are not helpful and they *know* what would be a useful rational alternative but they don't *feel* it. 'I know it in my head but I don't feel it in my gut'. Emotive-evocative techniques are used to help clients engage their emotions in the change process. They give clients the opportunity to acknowledge and work with their feelings enabling them also to understand the difference between healthy and unhealthy emotions. Human beings can have great difficulty giving up self-defeating emotional reactions. REBT holds that by encouraging clients to strongly engage their emotions they are helped to see more forcefully that they can change.

Therapist self-disclosure

The egalitarian therapeutic relationship allows counsellors to be open in that they will sometimes disclose personal information *if* it is therapeutically useful to the client and providing they can be sure that the client will not use the information against them. The use of self-disclosure can have a strong effect. By making reference to their own past emotional problems and how they overcame them, therapists serve as credible role models, demonstrating to their clients that they too are fallible. They don't have to damn themselves for having such difficulties and that REBT can be used effectively to resolve them.

Humorous techniques

Ellis believes that one factor in emotional disturbance is the serious way clients view themselves, their problems, other people and the world. He therefore suggests that counsellors make good use of humour in the sessions. This does not mean that the counsellor laughs *at* the client but rather *with* the client at their self-defeating thoughts and behaviours. Again the principle of flexibility comes in here, not all clients will benefit from such humour even though it is not directed at them.

In group therapy Ellis sometimes gives his clients a sheet of humorous songs he has written which they are encouraged to sing. An example, set to the tune of 'God save the Queen', follows:

> God save my precious spleen
> Send me a life serene
> God save my spleen
> Protect me from things odious
> Give me a life melodious
> And if things get too onerous
> I'll whine, bawl and scream

Shame-attacking exercises

Clients are encouraged to carry out behaviours they consider shameful and embarrassing in public. At the same time they work on their beliefs about what they are doing and they practice self-acceptance. The idea is that the more forcefully clients confront their feelings the less likely they are to disturb themselves. Examples are wearing bizarre clothes in public, asking for small sized condoms in chemist shops, and talking loudly in libraries. Clients that carry out such tasks report that although initially they experience discomfort they find that they can tolerate it and can accept themselves even when they receive disapproval from those around. The aim is to demonstrate that it is not the behaviour that is causing the feelings of shame and embarrassment, but the irrational beliefs the client holds about the behaviour.

Behavioural techniques

A wide range of behavioural techniques are used, including stimulus control, skills training (such as assertiveness and communication skills), response cost and penalty. The reader will find these described in chapter 5. The use of behavioural techniques facilitate philosophic change by encouraging clients to put into practice what they have learned. They also enable clients to dispute their irrational beliefs behaviourally as well as cognitively by demonstrating to themselves that they can stand it, nothing is so awful that it can't be tolerated.

In vivo desensitisation – facing the fear in reality

Clients experiencing fear in certain situations are encouraged to face those fears directly by going into the feared situation. For example, someone with a spider phobia would be encouraged to be in the presence of spiders several times a day. The idea is that by exposing themselves to situations they believe they 'can't stand' clients demonstrate to themselves that in fact they can survive and live through high levels of discomfort. While carrying out the activity they are encouraged to rehearse rational self-statements forcefully such as, 'I'd prefer not to be with these spiders, but I can stand these uncomfortable feelings'. REBT favours full implosive exposure rather than gradual exposure to feared situations as being more effective in overcoming low frustration tolerance.

'Stay in there' activities

This is similar to in vivo desensitisation. These activities require clients to stay in situations in which they feel uncomfortable while disputing the irrational beliefs they hold about the experiences. For example, a young man who feels angry in the company of his neighbour because of his racist attitudes might take on the assignment of purposely visiting him and staying there while disputing his irrational beliefs.

Anti-procrastination exercises

Procrastination is often the result of individuals saying to themselves that they cannot stand short-term discomfort in order to achieve their long-term goals. While writing this book, this was very familiar to one of the authors! 'I absolutely shouldn't have to put up with this discomfort' was the belief and many ways were found to avoid sitting down to the task. One way of helping clients overcome this is to encourage them to push themselves to start earlier than they had planned and/or setting aside a specific time each day for the task. At the same time clients are encouraged to dispute their unhelpful beliefs and practise their helpful beliefs. 'This feels uncomfortable but I can stand it.' By doing this, they show themselves that they can tolerate the discomfort and eventually will be rewarded by completing the task.

Risk-taking exercises

When Ellis sat in the Bronx Botanical Gardens and forced himself to approach and speak to the women there, he was carrying out a 'risk-taking exercise'. It was risky for him because he feared rejection and there was a very strong possibility that he would be rejected – and as we know he was! But he learned that is was not awful even when he was unsuccessful and eventually discovered that not only did he overcome his fear but in the long term discovered he actually enjoyed the company of women. In REBT clients are encouraged to take risks in the areas they find difficult and wish to change. The example of Ellis and the hundred women also illustrates the importance of repetition to reinforce the lessons learned.

Imagery techniques

REB counsellors prefer to help clients identify and dispute their irrational beliefs through action in real life rather than in their imagination. In the actual session however, imagination is sometimes used to promote change.

Rational-emotive imagery

This technique involves encouraging clients to imagine as vividly as possible the worst activating event that could happen to them, for example, being rejected by someone whose love they believe they *must* have. They are then encouraged to experience the upsetting emotions associated with the event. The next step is to ask the client to change the unhealthy emotion to the healthy alternative (for example, anger to annoyance) at the same time as maintaining the vivid image of the activating event. When clients are successful at carrying out this task the psychotherapist asks them how they managed to change their feelings. Ideally the clients notice that in order to change their feelings they have in fact changed their irrational beliefs to rational ones. Again repetitive practice is recommended so that the process of having healthy instead of unhealthy emotions becomes automatic.

This use of imagery can also be used to help clients identify the beliefs that underpin their emotional disturbances. It is often easier to access thoughts when experiencing the emotions that go along with them.

Imagery rehearsal

Sometimes imagery can be used to help clients build a bridge between knowing what they had better do in the real world and actually doing it. Before carrying out one of the behavioural assignments, for example, clients may be encouraged to practise the task in their imagination first.

Time projection

Often clients imagine that future events will be terrible. For example, 'If Barry dumps me it will be awful'. This belief can be challenged by going along with this evaluation while asking the client to imagine how she will feel about this at increasing intervals in the future. Indirectly, as the client realises that in fact such feelings rarely last beyond a given length of time, the therapist is encouraging the client to change the irrational belief about this 'terrible' event.

Homework

Self-help skills are an important feature of REBT. The use of homework assignments promotes the efficiency of the approach by encouraging the client to regard their whole week as therapy time and not just the usual hour they are with their therapist. Homework also encourages clients to become their own counsellor rather than becoming dependent on their therapist. The assignments are negotiated with clients in the therapy session. At the next session the therapist checks what the client did and what he/ she learned from it. If clients fail to carry out their homework the reasons for this are explored using the ABC model to identify what clients were telling themselves. Various homework assignments are used, limited only by the imagination of the counsellor and client. Many of the tasks used have already been described above, for example, in vivo desensitisation, teaching others about REBT, and shame attacking exercises. Here are some other common examples.

Biblio- and audiotherapy

Clients are encouraged to use some of the REBT educational materials available. Albert Ellis and Windy Dryden have written many self-help books. Ellis has also made several audio and video cassettes which clients usually find helpful. These materials help clients gain a better understanding of the rational philosophy thus aiding their progress in therapy. A list of some of these is at the end of this chapter.

Self-help forms

A variety of forms have been designed to help clients identify and dispute their irrational beliefs. These usually have columns for recording the activating event (A), the consequences (C), and the irrational beliefs which lead to those consequences (B). In the next column clients record how they dispute those beliefs (D) and in the next column they record the effective alternative rational beliefs (E). The final column is used to record any feelings, behaviours or thoughts they experience after the process of disputing the irrational beliefs and practising the rational alternatives – the new consequences.

Another self-help form known by its acronym DIBS (Disputing Irrational Beliefs) consists of six questions that clients can apply to their unhelpful philosophies. These questions are:

1   What irrational belief do I want to dispute and surrender?
2   Can I rationally support this belief?
3   What evidence exists of the falseness of this belief?
4   Does any evidence exist of the truth of this belief?
5   What worst things could actually happen to me if I don't get what I think I must (or do get what I think I mustn't)?
6   What good things could I make happen if I don't get what I think I must (or do get what I think I mustn't)?

CLOSING COMMENTS

A large number of books have now been written applying REBT to a wide range of client problems such as anxiety, substance abuse, alcoholism, depression and obsessive-compulsive disorder. It is used with individuals, couples and families. Rational emotive behaviour therapy has become a popular approach in the United States and is practised by thousands of mental health professionals there. It is also taught and used in many other countries of the world such as France, Italy, Germany, India and Australia.

In Britain, training opportunities are still limited and the approach has not gained the popularity it deserves. In 1995 Windy Dryden established an MSc in Rational Emotive Behaviour Therapy at Goldsmiths College, University of London. This is the first Master's course in REBT in Europe. A programme of certificate courses is run at the Centre for Rational Emotive Behaviour Therapy in Blackheath, London. The number of REBT therapists in Britain is therefore increasing.

This chapter gives the reader merely a brief glimpse into one of the most important cognitive behavioural approaches to counselling and psychotherapy. Albert Ellis has developed a powerful model out of his own success in overcoming considerable personal difficulties. Today's two main protagonists, Albert Ellis in the United States and Windy Dryden in Britain, continue to develop this approach by publishing numerous books and papers, and running training courses. Recognising the capacity that human beings have to help themselves they have also made their ideas available to the lay person in the form of numerous self-help books. At the end of this chapter in the reference list you will find both text and self-help books.

REFERENCES

Beck, A. (1967) *Depression*. New York: Harper.

Dryden, W. (1989) 'Albert Ellis: an efficient and passionate life'. *Journal of Counseling and Development*, 67, 539–46.

Dryden, W. (1990) *The Essential Albert Ellis: Seminal Writings on Psychotherapy*. New York: Springer.

Dryden, W. (1991) *A Dialogue with Albert Ellis. Against dogma*. Buckingham: Open University Press.

Dryden, W. (1996) 'Rational emotive behaviour therapy', in W. Dryden (ed.) *Handbook of Individual Therapy*. London: Sage.

Ellis, A. (1945) The sexual psychology of human hermaphrodites. *Psychosomatic Medicine*, 7, 108–25.

Ellis, A. (1951) *The Folklore of Sex*. New York: Doubleday.

Ellis, A. (1955a) 'New approaches to psychotherapy techniques'. *Journal of Clinical Psychology*, 11, 1–53.

Ellis, A. (1955b) 'Psychotherapy techniques for use with psychotics'. *American Journal of Psychotherapy*, 9, 452–76.

Ellis, A. (1957a) 'Rational psychotherapy and individual psychotherapy'. *Journal of Individual Psychotherapy*, 13, 38–44.

Ellis, A. (1957b) *How to Live with a Neurotic*. New York: Crown.

Ellis, A. (1958) *Sex without Guilt*. Secaucus, NJ: Lyle Stuart (rev. edn, 1965).

Ellis, A. (1960) *The Art and Science of Love*. Secaucus, NJ: Lyle Stuart.

Ellis, A. (1963a) *Sex and the Single Man*. Secaucus, NJ: Lyle Stuart.

Ellis, A. (1963b) *The Intelligent Woman's Guide to Manhunting*. Secaucus, NJ: Lyle Stuart.

Ellis, A. (1968) *Biographical Information Form*. New York: Institute for Rational-Emotive Therapy.

Ellis, A. (1973) 'My philosophy of psychotherapy'. *Journal of Contemporary Psychotherapy*, 6(1), 13–18.

Ellis, A. (1976) 'The biological basis of human irrationality'. *Journal of Individual Psychology*, 32, 145–68.

Ellis, A. (1977) 'The basic clinical theory of rational-emotive therapy', in A. Ellis and R. Grieger (eds) *Handbook of Rational-Emotive Therapy*. New York: Springer.

Ellis, A. (1980) 'The value of efficiency in psychotherapy'. *Psychotherapy: Theory, Research and Practice*, 17(4), 414–19.

Ellis, A. (1987) 'On the origin and development of rational-emotive therapy', in W. Dryden (ed.) *Key Cases in Psychotherapy*. London: Croom Helm.

Ellis, A. (1989) 'Rational-emotive therapy', in R. J. Corsini and D. Wedding (eds) *Current Psychotherapies*. Itasca, IL: Peacock.

Ellis, A. (1991) 'My life in clinical psychology', in C. E. Walker (ed.) *The History of Clinical Psychology in Autobiography*, Vol. 1. Pacific Grove, CA: Brooks/Cole.

Ellis, A. (1993) 'Changing rational-emotive therapy (RET) to rational emotive behavior therapy (REBT)'. *Behavior Therapist*, 16, 257–8.

Ellis, A. (1994) *Reason and Emotion in Psychotherapy. A Comprehensive Method of Treating Human Disturbances*. (Revised and updated) New York: Birch Lane Press.

Meichenbaum, D. (1977) *Cognitive-Behavior Modification*. New York: Plenum.

Palmer, S., Dryden, W., Ellis, A. and Yapp, R. (1995) *Rational Interviews*. London: Centre for Rational Emotive Behaviour Therapy.

FURTHER READING

Dryden, W. (1999) *Rational Emotive Behavioural Counselling in Action*. London: Sage.

Ellis, A. (1994) *Reason and Emotion in Psychotherapy*. (Revised and updated.) New York: Birch Lane Press.

5 The multimodal approach

INTRODUCTION

> Actions may not bring happiness, but there is no happiness without action.
> Benjamin Disraeli

The story behind the development of multimodal therapy is an interesting one. Unlike most other approaches to counselling and psychotherapy it did not develop out of a theory but as a result of one man's quest to help his clients to find happiness more effectively. This man is Arnold Lazarus. He recognised that individuals were unique and had many dimensions or parts to their personality – we can think, behave, sense, imagine, feel, relate to others, and at base we have our biological make-up. He therefore called his approach to counselling and psychotherapy multimodal – many ways or dimensions. By considering the interaction of all these different modes, Lazarus believes we can explain almost any psychological problem.

When a carpenter goes into a toolshop to buy some tools, she doesn't necessarily choose the tools she is familiar with, but will select the best ones for the job. A good carpenter will have a wide range of tools in the toolbox and will always add to them when necessary. So it is with multimodal therapy: individuals are usually troubled by a wide variety of specific problems, so a wide variety of specific therapeutic techniques are needed to treat them. Problems and difficulties rarely occur in isolation and often we need more than one approach to a solution. Multimodal therapy takes a pragmatic approach to helping clients. If a technique has been shown through research to be helpful for a particular problem then it is added to a counsellor's or psychotherapist's toolbox and used.

As with so many innovators before him, Lazarus's ideas were not new. Hippocrates, who lived about 2300 years before Lazarus, was already aware that the human personality has many layers. Hippocrates, like Lazarus, also stressed the need for taking a comprehensive life history of his patients.

ARNOLD LAZARUS

Family background and early life

Arnold Lazarus was born in Johannesburg, South Africa in January 1932, the last of four children. He grew up in a large extended family group which included many aunts, uncles and cousins. Arnold was very much the youngest in this family and often felt ignored, as if his opinion did not matter. Even in his twenties he felt they still bullied him and put him down. Not only was he the youngest but he was also very small and skinny and he became shy, hyper-sensitive and felt inadequate.

When Arnold was five years old, his sister gave him piano lessons and by the age of seven he was performing in public, playing 'like a talented twelve year old'. His talent did not progress beyond this level so when he reached the age of twelve he decided to quit; an early demonstration of his pragmatic view of life which was later reflected in his approach to counselling and psychotherapy.

As a result of being bullied he became very interested in body-building, weight lifting, wrestling and boxing. He had to learn to fight in order to avoid being completely trampled on; but now he regards these activities as an overcompensation. At seventeen he dropped out of school, intending to open up a health and training centre. In order to earn money he worked in department stores, in a pharmacy and even tried his hand at selling houses. Like many well-known therapists, Lazarus showed an early interest and apti-tude for writing and had some of his stories published in the local newspapers during his teenage years. Linking his two interests, he became the Associate Editor of a South African body-building magazine.

His family had a small retail business and Lazarus has said that the stock-taking mentality necessary to run such a business successfully influenced the approach to therapy that he later developed. He believes therapists should constantly be taking stock of what is happening in therapy and only use methods which have been shown to be effective.

By the age of nineteen Lazarus had been persuaded to return to high school to complete his education so that he could go to university. In 1955 he enrolled at the University of the Witwatersrand in Johannesburg majoring in English. He intended to become a journalist. This was also the year he married his wife Daphne. He has two children, Linda who was born in 1957 and Clifford born in 1961.

University life

Lazarus says that he has always had in interest in the working of the human mind. During his teenage years, his friends often turned to him for help and support. They said that he was easy to talk to, a good listener and was usually able to help them. Lazarus had not considered a career in psychotherapy since he was under the impression that in order to do so he would first have to become a medical doctor. Spending long hours pouring over anatomy, physiology and biochemistry text books did not appeal to him at all. When he discovered that he did not need a medical degree after all, he decided to change the focus of his study to psychology.

In 1957 Lazarus spent three months in England as an intern at the Marlborough Day Hospital in London where he was influenced by a psychiatrist called Joshua Bierer, an Adlerian (see p. 25). Lazarus graduated from the University of the Witwatersrand with an honours degree in Psychology and later a Masters degree in experimental psychology. In 1959 he was registered with the South African Medical and Dental Council as a clinical psychologist which enabled him to start up a private practice. He completed his PhD dissertation in 1960; his thesis title was *New Group Techniques in the Treatment of Phobic Conditions*.

He often cites his experiences of being bullied as a child as a reason for turning to mental activities. He remembers that he began to use psychology against his parents and siblings when they gave him a hard time. By the time he received his doctorate his family were finally showing him some respect.

Early career and professional development

After he had completed his PhD, Lazarus continued to work in private practice as well as working as a part-time lecturer in the department of psychiatry at the Witwatersrand Medical School. He became interested in hypnosis and was elected the president of the South African Society for Clinical and Experimental Hypnosis.

In 1963 he was invited to Stanford University in the United States by Albert Bandura, whose social learning theory was to have a considerable influence on his ideas. Bandura had read a paper written by Lazarus based on his PhD dissertation and was very impressed. After a year as a visiting assistant professor in the psychology department, Lazarus returned to South Africa with his wife and two children. They felt homesick and wanted to return to their family group.

However, because of their increasing unease over the political situation in South Africa, they returned to the United States in 1966. At first Lazarus directed the Behavior Therapy Institute in Sausalito in California. Then in 1967 he became a professor of psychology in the department of behavioural science at Temple University Medical School, Philadelphia, where he worked with his former PhD supervisor Joseph Wolpe, a well-known behaviourist. From 1970 to 1972 he was director of clinical training in Yale University's department of psychology. In 1971 he published his book *Behavior Therapy and Beyond* which is probably the first book written about cognitive-behaviour therapy. In 1972 he moved to Rutgers University in New Jersey where, until his retirement, he held the post of Distinguished

Professor II at the Graduate School of Applied and Professional Psychology. He became a naturalised American citizen in 1976.

Over the years Lazarus has been elected president of several professional associations and has served on the editorial board of a large number of scientific journals. Among the many honours he has received are the Distinguished Service Award from the American Board of Professional Psychology and the Distinguished Career Achievement Award from the American Board of Medical Psychotherapists.

Arnold Lazarus, the person

Lazarus says he has three priorities. His first priority is his family. His second priorities are significant friendships and having fun. Work is his third priority, which includes intellectual stimulation, making enough money to live and making some kind of social contribution. Unlike many other innovators, Lazarus has avoided becoming a 'wise man' in the therapy world and has made no attempt to commercialise his approach.

DEVELOPMENT OF THE MULTIMODAL APPROACH

Initial approach to therapy

At the time when Lazarus began his studies, the psychotherapy practised at the University of the Witwatersrand was mainly psychoanalytic and person-centred. At first he used psychoanalysis with his clients but he found it a very lengthy process and it did not seem to be effective. Lazarus spent much of his time observing experienced therapists treating clients behind one-way mirrors. Joseph Wolpe was also working at the University. Wolpe had invented a form of behavioural treatment called systematic desensitisation[1], which he was using effectively on a number of clients. After watching Wolpe successfully treat a woman with agoraphobia, Lazarus became convinced of the usefulness of this approach. Before seeing Wolpe this client had received drug treatment and psychotherapy from some of the best psychotherapists in Johannesburg and yet had not got better.

Lazarus began to realise that methods based on behaviour and performance were better at bringing about change than those based on verbal approaches alone. So despite the strong feelings against behaviourism in the psychology department at the University of the Witwatersrand, Lazarus was so won over by the dramatic change in this woman's mental health that he began to use behavioural methods himself. In 1958 he was the first to introduce the term 'behaviour therapy' into the research literature with the publication of a paper he wrote called 'New methods in psychotherapy: A case study'. Lazarus became one of the leading figures in its development. During the

1960s his interest in writing was evident in the many articles he published introducing new techniques into the behavioural literature. He used these methods because they worked – and this was to become an important refrain in Lazarus's approach.

Dissatisfaction with behaviour therapy

Nevertheless, by the time he moved to the United States, Lazarus was already questioning what he called the 'narrow band behaviour therapy'. By this he meant therapy focusing narrowly on only one or two aspects of human person-ality. Continuing his inclination to question the effectiveness of what thera-pists were doing with clients, Lazarus had noticed that follow-up inquiries indicated that many so-called 'cured' patients treated with pure behavioural methods had relapsed. In contrast he observed that those clients who had not only changed their behaviour but had also changed their outlook on life, acquiring positive attitudes towards themselves, maintained their improvements. They stayed well.

The key case

In 1966 while at the Behavior Therapy Institute in Sausalito, he met the female client whose experience of therapy was to give birth to a whole new approach to counselling and psychotherapy. This woman, Mrs D, had similar symptoms to those of the women Wolpe had treated and therefore Lazarus expected to obtain similar success. Mrs D had been seeing a psychodynamic therapist for eighteen months and although some improvement had been made, this therapist told Lazarus that the client had 'a passive-dependent per-sonality who . . . had regressed to a pre-oedipal level of fixation' adding that the chance of future improvement was poor (an explanation of these terms will be found in chapter 2). After treating her with various behavioural techniques including systematic exposure and assertion training (see pp. 163 and 168 for a description) for a period of five to six months, Mrs D was much improved and Lazarus was about to discharge her. He had also seen Mrs D with her husband to deal with their marital problems.

Despite improvements in many areas of her life, however, Mrs D was not happy. She said that she remained 'kind of blah', a commonplace person, with nothing much to contribute to society. She wanted more. It was then that Lazarus recognised that the behavioural approach was not enough for this client. Metaphorically going to the toolshop, he searched for other tools to address Mrs D's self-downing thoughts. He used cognitive techniques, such as those described in the chapter on rational emotive behaviour therapy, to challenge her unhelpful beliefs about herself. As a result Mrs D came to the conclusion that 'If you want to feel useful you have to *be* useful'. She then went on to found a charitable organisation which fed and clothed poor people all over the United States and emerged feeling happy and fulfilled.

At this time behaviourists like Wolpe believed that bringing thinking into the therapeutic process was a dangerous, heretical activity and would only lead psychology back to wallow in psychoanalysis. It was not easy for Lazarus to swim against the tide, and his decision to use cognitive techniques with Mrs D and other clients, created turmoil in his own mind. It also resulted in his being branded a heretic by Wolpe and the pure behavioural circle of psychologists.

Transition

His experience with Mrs D led Lazarus to realise that behaviour therapy may not be 'both necessary and sufficient' and that to achieve sustained improvement, more was needed.

Lazarus realised he had to take stock of his position and asked himself what had to be added or taken out of his toolbox, to make therapy more effective for his clients. Aspirin may be a very useful drug in many conditions, but if it was the only drug available doctors would be somewhat limited in how they could help their patients. Doctors are therefore constantly on the search for new and better medicines to treat the very wide range of medical conditions. In the same way Lazarus argued that if only one technique is available to counsellors they too will be somewhat limited in what they can offer clients. Thus Lazarus gradually changed from his original unimodal approach (pure behaviourism) to a bimodal approach (cognitive-behavioural).

Final developments

After his success with adding the cognitive dimension to therapy, Lazarus still was not satisfied. He noticed that, despite behavioural and cognitive change, some clients retained disturbing negative images and were therefore still having difficulties. So he added another dimension or mode to the list of targets requiring change, namely that of imagery. But even then some clients were still complaining, for example, about tension headaches, or that their marriage was still shaky. Finally, Lazarus identified seven different dimensions or modalities as he calls them, which he believed embraced all the different aspects of a human personality. These seven modes are: behaviour; affect (feelings); sensation; imagery; cognition (thought); interpersonal relationships; and biology. Noticing that the first letters of these words created the list of letters BASICIB, Lazarus changed the last one to Drugs/Biology so that the meaningful and memorable acronym BASIC ID could be created.

What Lazarus wanted to do was provide therapists with a whole toolbox of techniques that would satisfy any and all of their clients' needs. In this way a treatment programme can be devised that really fitted the client, like a bespoke tailor makes a suit to fit the customer as perfectly as possible. This is quite unlike all other therapies which tend to expect the client to fit the theory. Clients are normally assessed and treated according to the therapist's particular theoretical approach, be it psychodynamic, cognitive or humanistic. During his developmental journey Lazarus learned that by providing this more comprehensive approach that did not exclude any modality from the therapeutic scene, therapy was more likely to be effective and its effects long lasting. The first official appearance of multimodal therapy was in 1973 when Lazarus published an article outlining his ideas. Since then many counsellors and psychotherapists have used the BASIC ID framework to assess and help their clients. Lazarus himself continues to practise in the United States where there are now several multimodal therapy institutes.

THE THEORY

Overview

Multimodal counselling is a very practical approach to treating psychological problems. Lazarus was not so concerned with theory, preferring to leave the theorising to others. He was much more interested in 'what works for whom and under which particular circumstances' than in theories that might or might not be helpful. He has noted that theories tend to come and go: one minute all the rage and the next something to be laughed at. Nevertheless the multimodal approach is not without an underlying theory. His approach is also based on a broad social and cognitive learning theory, and also on systems and communications theory partly because these theories have been scrutinised through research.

Four people have influenced Lazarus in the development of the multimodal approach. Wolpe we have already seen influenced his initial emphasis on behaviour therapy. Arnold Lazarus selected the quote by Disraeli for the beginning of this chapter because he believes it reflects the fact that the multimodal approach is underpinned by behaviour theory. The ideas of Albert Ellis (see chapter 4) influenced Lazarus to include the cognitive dimension to his therapeutic approach. In 1963, while a visiting lecturer at Stanford University, Lazarus met Perry London who was already looking at what he described as the inherent limitations of both the psychodynamic and behavioural approaches to counselling and psychotherapy. London wrote 'that people are considerably simpler than the Insight schools [psychodynamic] give them credit for, but that they are also more complicated than the Action therapists [behavioural] would like to believe' (London, 1964: 39). He also said that it was 'techniques not theories that were actually used on people'. Like Lazarus, London was a clinical pragmatist and believed that the important questions to ask were: do the techniques work, and on whom? The theory about how they work and why are for later consideration. Lazarus states that it was London who opened his eyes to the value of a technically eclectic approach. The fourth person to have an influence on Lazarus was Joseph Bierer, the Adlerian psychiatrist he met in London. Lazarus was deeply impressed by the genuine kindness which Bierer showed in the hospital he ran. Lazarus also believes that the multimodal emphasis on 'social awareness, holistic education, active interventions, egalitarianism and respect for people, are decidedly 'Adlerian'. So is the emphasis placed on the impact of the family constellation, . . . and the view that clients are basically the victims of faulty learning rather than [being] sick people' (Nystul and Shaughnessy, 1994: 373).

Multimodal therapy is an eclectic approach: selecting what has been shown to be effective from many different methods and ideas. There are many psychotherapists and counsellors today who describe themselves as eclectic. Lazarus, however, was keen to stress that his eclecticism related only to the techniques and not to the theories behind them. In other words a counsellor could use behavioural techniques without necessarily accepting the learning theory that produced them. He called the multimodal approach systematic technical eclecticism – systematic because it is characterised by careful method and planning, technical because it is more concerned with techniques than theory.

Personality theory

The principle of parity

Lazarus believes that we are all equal to one another – no one is superior, not the queen, nor the prime minister, nor religious leaders, not even Mother Theresa. He calls this the principle of parity. The fact that some people have superior skills in certain areas does not make them superior human beings. He believes we should respect people's abilities without making them gods. He agrees with Ellis that we are all fallible yet acceptable people – we all have limitations as well as assets.

The seven modalities

As we have already seen, Lazarus believes that the human personality can be completely described through the seven modalities of the BASIC ID. Although these modalities are described as if they are totally separate they actually interact with each other. Lazarus assumes that everything we experience from sadness to joy, from boredom to great excitement, from greed to generosity can be explained by looking at each component of the BASIC ID and at the interactions between each modality. If change occurs in any one of the modalities, it is likely to affect the functioning of other modalities. The interactions can be very complex and unravelling them is part of the assessment process.

Other factors such as our culture, social group, political climate also have an impact on our personality. Cultural differences, for example, are often stereotyped like the stiff upper lip of the British, and the 'go for it' attitude of the Americans – these can also affect our personality.

Behaviour refers to all that we do or say. It includes habits, reactions to people and events, the responses we make, whether we laugh or cry and so on. Our behaviour is often a response to one of the other modalities.

Affect includes all the emotions we experience such as anxiety, regret, disappointment, anger or guilt. Unlike all the other modalities, emotion cannot be dealt with directly. We cannot change our emotions except through another modality. For example we can generate anger by thumping a cushion (behaviour), we can lessen anxiety through relaxation (sensation) or we can reduce fear by changing the way we think about an event (cognition). All these alterations in mood are brought about by producing change in other modalities.

Sensation refers to the experience of the five main senses: taste, smell, touch, seeing and hearing. These sensations can be pleasant such as the taste of ice cream, the smell of roses, the sight of the Atlantic Ocean, or the sound of Mozart's *The Magic Flute*. They can also be unpleasant such as pain, dizziness, headaches or palpitations. This modality triggers emotional reactions or accompanies them. Sensation can be stimulated by the other modalities such as an image of a sunset encouraging a sense of relaxation. They can also affect other modalities; for example, sensing a lump in the throat can lead to thoughts of death and the emotion of anxiety.

Imagery involves thinking in pictures including dreams, and auditory images (tunes or sounds that we hear in our minds). We are often not very aware of our use of imagery. For example, when you are in conversation do you have pictures in your mind of whatever the other person is talking to you about? When you read a book do you develop images of each of the characters? Do you hear their voices? Sometimes the images take over and may become sinister or disturbing. As with the other modalities, images can lead us to behave in certain ways, or experience certain emotions or sensations.

Cognitions are the thoughts, ideas, values, opinions, and attitudes that we have. Sometimes these are helpful and enable us to lead useful happy lives. Others are less helpful such as 'I am worthless' or 'this situation is awful, I can't stand it'. Thoughts have a powerful influence on our actions and emotions.

Interpersonal relationships refer to our social interactions with others: family, friends and any individuals we meet during the day, employers, shop assistants and so on. It also includes our perception of the way others treat us, and what we desire from them.

Drugs/biology addresses all aspects of physical well being. It includes diet, exercise, sleep, fitness as well as any physical problems we might experience such as low back pain. The basis of all human existence is biological. All modalities are influenced by our biology and in turn it is influenced by them. If you are under pressure at work and home, eventually you will experience the physiological symptoms of stress such as tense muscles, fatigue, palpitations and so on.

How does our personality develop?

Lazarus sees human personality as the result of an interaction between our genetic make-up, the physical environment in which we were brought up and live, and our social learning history. Thus what we inherit, the D part of the seven modalities, underlies the other six which are largely learned through experience; they are all products of various social and psychological processes. Before we look at each factor in our development we need first to explain a little about learning theory, for this is where Lazarus began.

Learning theory

Most people agree that association plays an important role in the learning process. For example, when a baby first sees a bottle he does not know that it contains milk and therefore is unlikely to react to it. However you have possibly seen babies getting excited and salivating at the sight of a bottle. This is because after a few feeds the baby has learned to associate the bottle with milk. This type of learning was called classical conditioning and was first studied by the Russian animal physiologist called Ivan Pavlov. He noticed that the dogs he was working with would often start to salivate when they saw the assistant who normally brought them their food, regardless of whether they were carrying food or not (Pavlov, 1927). Unfortunately sometimes we learn associations that are unhelpful. We can, for example, learn to fear quite harmless things. If you were to have a painful experience at the dentist and experienced fear, while at the same time the scent of roses wafted through the open window, then at a later date just the smell of roses is likely to lead you to experience that fear again. You will have learned to associate the scent of roses with fear. This is how many phobias are thought to develop.

Another type of learning involves the use of rewards and punishment. An American psychologist called Thorndike had noticed that cats finding a way to escape a puzzle box in order to reach food, initially used trial and error. Then after a few trials they seemed to learn how to escape and after a while were able to escape almost at once. Another American psychologist named Skinner extended this work and called this type of learning operant conditioning, because the responses the animals were making are learned as a result of the animal operating on its environment.

Skinner explored the effects of both reward and punishment. Rewards he called positive or negative reinforcements. Positive reinforcements are those given whenever an animal makes the correct response. For humans comfort, praise, money, are examples of positive reinforcers. Negative reinforcement involves the removal of unpleasant experiences once the correct response is made and therefore in a sense are also rewards. For example, depressed people may learn that by doing exercise the level of depression lifts. They are rewarded by the removal of depressed feelings. Or someone who goes to confess to the priest will be rewarded by the removal of feelings of guilt. Following a severe car accident, a person may avoid driving again and is rewarded by the absence of fear. Interestingly Skinner found that punishment was not as effective in encouraging learning as positive or negative reinforcement.

All these associations that we learn through experience, can be unlearned through a process known as extinction. Babies will stop getting excited at the sight of a bottle if they are no longer given milk in it. It is extinction, or this process of unlearning, that is used by behaviour therapists to obtain change. We shall be looking at some of these methods later in this chapter.

Genetic make up

Returning to the development of our personality, each individual differs in their ability to tolerate pain, frustration and stress. Lazarus uses the term threshold to describe this ability and regards it as largely inherited. This is our genetic endowment and is at the physiological level. Some people can tolerate more pain than others, some more stress or frustration.

Social learning theory

Social learning theory does not regard the laws of conditioning sufficient to explain all learning. Bandura (1977) observed that we learn from the experiences of others through imitation and observation. We can see this clearly when we observe a young child follow its mother around the house imitating her activities such as dusting, or painting a room. This is not simply learning through association as the learning theorists would suggest. Also young children observing the results of their big sister's 'bad' behaviour may strive to be 'good' in order to avoid the same consequences. Or alternatively when they see a fellow pupil rewarded by the teacher for good work they will try to imitate this in order to receive the same reward.

This ability to imitate and observe the consequence of behaviour in others, speeds up the learning process because we do not actually always have to go through the experience ourselves and learn through trial and error. This theory suggests that children are influenced by the behaviour of others and especially those who are most important to them like their parents.

This is an efficient way to learn especially for many of the complex skills like language.

The descriptions of conditioning given above suggest that many of our responses are automatic. Bandura disagreed with this view and said that people do not always respond automatically to what is happening around them. How we think about those events will determine whether we even notice them. Also we do not always react to the real environment but to the environment as we see it. In addition we can think ahead and anticipate the consequences of our actions. This acknowledges that we are more than animals who simply react, we are animals who are also capable of conscious thought.

But there are other events in our heads apart from thoughts. We also have images that can have an affect on learning, we have feelings and sensations. For example, people who are depressed have a different awareness of their environment – they will tend to notice negative events. A man who has strong images in his head of his children coming to harm will be unable to learn that leaving them at school in the hands of capable teachers means that the children will be safe. In fact any of the seven modalities can have an effect on what we learn.

Nonconscious processes

An assumption made by the multimodal approach is that learning is not always conscious or deliberate. Lazarus spoke of nonconscious processes meaning that we have different levels of awareness and many stimuli can affect our thoughts, feelings and behaviour without our being aware of them. For example the person in the dentist's chair may not be consciously aware of the smell of roses because of the distraction of the pain experienced. Nevertheless for the association between fear and the smell of roses to be learned, at a nonconscious level that person was aware of the smell. Lazarus's choice of the term 'nonconscious' rather than unconscious was mainly because of the Freudian use of this word, which implied some kind of entity or structure.

Systems theory

Systems theory states that we need other people in order to give meaning and purpose to our lives. It recognises that our problems are usually linked to interpersonal difficulties with family members, friends and acquaintances. These links and interactions between the system's members mean that often in order to improve the situation, the whole social network of the person needs to be taken into consideration. Multimodal therapy therefore will often include family or group therapy.

Communications theory

Communications theory simply states that all behaviour has some sort of message (Watzlawick, Weakland and Fisch, 1974). It is impossible not to communicate. Communication is more than what is said. It includes also messages conveyed through non verbal means such as posture, eye contact, mood or even silence. The theory also states that these messages do not only give information but they also says something about the relationship between the people communicating. For example, a father might say to his child 'I would like you to tidy up your room now' or he might say 'I am tired of the mess in your room, tidy it up this instant'. Both messages make the same request but the relationship between father and child is clearly different. Sometimes relationships get into difficulties because the messages are unclear, insufficient or perhaps conveyed through a third person. This theory also addresses the reaction of the listener who might respond in three ways. First the listener might accept the message accurately and respond in an appropriate way. Second, they might reject the message perhaps by not listening to it properly or by ignoring it. Finally they can reply but not in a relevant way. Politicians for example, when asked questions often answer in this manner.

How our problems develop and how we maintain them

Lazarus has described a number of ways in which he considers people make themselves disturbed (Dryden, 1991). During the development process of learning, outlined above, Lazarus believes that various factors can combine and interact. This can lead to the development of problems and can also prevent us from overcoming them. Underlying these factors is the biological dimension. Lazarus recognises that a chemical imbalance especially in disorders such as severe depression may be involved and such cases often call for a psychiatrist to prescribe medication. Nevertheless, he recognises that even if a person's problems do have a biological base any or all of the factors discussed in this section may also be present. Multimodal therapy is therefore directed at these.

Misinformation

During the social learning process people acquire beliefs and assumptions about life. If these are counterproductive or unhelpful they will lead to emotional problems. Lazarus refers to such beliefs as misinformation. For example, the belief prevalent in our society that fame and fortune leads to happiness is an incorrect assumption – as we have seen in Britain following wins on the National Lottery. It can lead to the development of perfectionist ideals and people then place great demands on themselves to succeed. These demands can lead to stress and anxiety and, when the person fails to achieve fame and fortune, to depression.

Another unhelpful belief is that we are victims of circumstance: 'It's not my fault I failed my examination, the teacher was hopeless' or 'It makes me so angry when my father speaks to me like that'. Other individuals spend much of their time trying to please others in the mistaken belief that they will then be liked and approved of. The belief that by avoiding problems and unpleasant situations these will then disappear is another example of misinformation. Difficulties do not vanish just because we ignore or avoid them.

In the chapter on rational emotive behaviour therapy we have described irrational or unhelpful beliefs such as making demands on ourselves and others. Other ways of processing information identified in the same chapter such as overgeneralization (drawing general conclusions from one isolated incident) are examples of misinformation. Not only do these unhelpful beliefs and assumptions lead to emotional problems but as long as they remain in place, they also maintain them.

Missing information

During the social learning process, if we are denied the opportunity to learn through our own experience or by observing and imitating others then we can fail to acquire the skills we need in life. Some people have very obvious areas where they display ignorance or naiveté: they don't know how to behave in social situations, in job interviews, how to ask for what they need, how to solve problems. Children brought up by overprotective parents, for example, when they become adults and have to move out into the adult world, may not have the assertiveness skills needed to deal with difficult, aggressive people they meet. Unless these skills are acquired, it is likely that they will continue to have emotional difficulties.

Defensive reactions

In order to lessen our awareness of situations that cause pain and discomfort, we acquire defensive reactions, or avoidance responses, again through our social learning experiences. There are some similarities here to the theory of defence mechanisms described by Freud. Lazarus is careful to stress that multimodal therapy is not a blend of psychoanalysis, behaviour theory, and other theories. Defensive reactions help us to avoid negative emotions such as hurt, anger, guilt which may otherwise seem unbearable. They include denial, losing touch with ourselves, deceiving ourselves. For example people often deny the seriousness of a loved one's illness because they think they cannot stand the associated pain and anxiety. These defensive reactions are largely nonconscious. Lazarus regards them as distractions – for example sublimation is simply the redirection of effort and energy from one direction to another. A woman unable to have a child may redirect her mothering needs into the care of animals. Multimodal counsellors do not make fixed interpretations. For example if a client arrives late for an appointment, it will not be assumed that this is a defence but rather all possible explanations will be considered.

Unhelpful habits

We have already seen how easy it can be to acquire associations between events, often at what Lazarus calls a nonconscious level. People acquire these habits without thinking about them and they are often maintained through positive and negative reinforcement. An unhelpful habit such as avoiding or backing away from events we fear will be maintained by the negative reinforcement of avoidance of fear. The body learns to respond automatically in times of stress. Sometimes this stress can be prolonged or severe enough for a strong association to form. For example, Graham experienced a bad car crash and formed a strong association between the smell of the burnt rubber of the tyres and panic. Every time after the crash that he smelt rubber he experienced panic. This is a habitual response and is likely to remain in place until 'habit retraining' is carried out.

Unless individuals become aware of these learned habits they will be unable to change them so they will be maintained by the nonconscious processes. In order to lessen our awareness of situations that cause pain and discomfort, we acquire what Lazarus has called defensive reactions, or avoidance responses, again through our social learning experiences. Defensive reactions can be useful coping strategies but they can also help maintain unhelpful habits.

This is often evident after a person has gone through a traumatic experience. Prakash was involved in the King's Cross Underground station fire. He had always believed that he must be in control at all times and not express his emotions. During the fire he experienced intense fear and panic. He was afraid for his life. Afterwards he described his feelings as 'kind of numb'. Using defence reactions he defended himself against the feelings of helplessness and terror he had felt during the fire by shutting off his emotional life, by avoiding talking or thinking about the fire, and by avoiding anything that might remind him of it. This led to emotional problems as the memories and thoughts intruded in the form of nightmares, flashbacks, panic attacks, and anger.

Traumatic experiences

Lazarus recognises that events over which we have no control, such as the King's Cross fire, are so terrifying and threatening that inevitably some people will 'break down'. Lazarus does not believe that this response to such events is due to the person's perception of the environment or to the person's thoughts about what has happened. He uses the concept of thresholds to explain why some people are more susceptible than others: some people are biologically stronger than others. However the resulting psychological difficulties can be maintained by maladaptive habits and misinformation. In Prakash's case his strong belief that he must at all cost be in control and his habit of avoiding anything that distressed him maintained his difficulties.

Lack of self-acceptance

We have already addressed the difference between self-acceptance and self-esteem in the chapter on rational emotive behaviour therapy. Like Ellis, Lazarus believes that lack of self-acceptance leads to and maintains emotional problems. This is not something Lazarus regards as separate from all the other factors mentioned above, but it interacts with them. For example, George had the mistaken belief that his happiness depended on people seeing him as a successful businessman. Through no fault of his own he was made redundant and became depressed. He had worked on building up his 'self-esteem' which was dependent on his work: accepting himself as fallible was foreign to him. Without his job he was nobody. Until George learns to accept himself with all his shortcomings and personal limitations he is likely to remain depressed.

Interpersonal sabotage

As we have seen, none of us live in isolation but within systems. Sometimes other people in these systems can stop us changing in the way that we want. For example, John realised that he was rather passive in his relationships with other people. Not wanting to be taken for granted any more he underwent assertiveness training. In his workplace, his colleagues noticed his attempts to change and encouraged him enabling him to become a more useful and effective member of the organisation. However at home, his wife enjoyed the control she had in their marriage and did not want him to change. By becoming more assertive he was disrupting the system. His wife was not initially aware that she was preventing him from changing. This is often the case: the sabotage can be unwitting or witting.

THE THERAPY

One of the basic beliefs of the multimodal approach is that people are more likely to remain well after successful counselling or psychotherapy, if they have been helped by the therapist to address all of the seven modalities of personality. Lasting change, Lazarus believes, is more likely to happen if all relevant issues are addressed. This does not mean that change has to occur in all modalities but by focusing on only one or two means that important factors in the other modalities might be missed. If Lazarus had ignored the cognitive dimension when treating Mrs D as other behaviour therapists would have done, she would have been discharged while still distressed. This approach stresses the uniqueness of each person and therefore the programme of therapy is carefully devised for each individual. What is suitable for one person suffering from flying phobia for example, may not be suitable for another.

Distinctive features

One of the distinguishing features of all the publications by Lazarus is the very large number of questions they contain. He is a true scientist, always testing out his ideas against the evidence he finds from observing his clients. This questioning strategy runs right through the multimodal approach and is an integral part of the therapy.

Multimodal therapy is based on the principle of individuality and believes therefore that there is no one correct way to deal with psychological problems. This principle guides and informs all aspects of the practice of multimodal counselling, from initial assessment, to the therapeutic relationship through to the actual techniques chosen. This emphasis on the attention paid to the 'goodness of fit' is unique to this approach.

Lazarus describes six features that distinguish the multimodal approach from any other. They focus on the comprehensive assessment procedure which involves not only each specific modality on its own but also how these modalities interact with each other, with the aim of achieving a thorough understanding of all aspects of the individual and the social environment. Each of the distinctive features listed here will be described later.

1   The specific and comprehensive attention given to the entire BASIC ID
2   The use of second-order BASIC ID assessments
3   The use of modality profiles
4   The use of structural profiles
5   Tracking the modality firing order.
6   Deliberate bridging procedures to enhance the therapeutic relationship.

Lazarus, 1992: 250

Assessment

In order to answer the all important question 'what works for whom and under which particular circumstances' a comprehensive assessment at the beginning of psychotherapy of all the seven modalities is often seen as necessary. Only then can the right tools for the job be chosen. The exception is when a person is in a crisis or has only one or two obvious problems in a single modality. Then a full assessment is superfluous. Assessment is seen as a continuous process throughout therapy.

The initial interview and the thirteen determinations

As with most other counselling approaches, one of the main aims during the first meeting with the client is the establishment of a good therapeutic relationship. Lazarus describes how he often uses small talk to give the client time to adjust to the environment of the counselling room and to enable them to relax and not feel threatened by the process. The formal details of taking down name, address, marital status and so on provide useful opening topics.

During the initial interview good multimodal therapists will seek to find answers to a number of questions. Lazarus has listed twelve questions that the counsellor ought to be able answer by the end of the first session but at least by the end of the second. These questions are (based on the twelve determinations of Lazarus, 1992: 240):

1 Are there any signs of psychosis (for example bizarre behaviour, strange thoughts, delusions)
2 Are there any signs of any organic problems (for example, disorientation, memory lapse, odd mannerisms)
3 Is there any evidence of depression, self-blame, suicidal or homicidal tendencies?
4 What problems has the client brought to counselling and what seems to have triggered them?
5 Why is the client coming for counselling now and not last week, last month, or last year? Is anyone forcing them to come or strongly influencing them? Or has some crisis occurred?
6 What factors seem to have preceded the difficulties? How did it all start?
7 Is there someone or something that is maintaining their problems, preventing the client from solving them?
8 Is it clear what the client hopes to gain from coming for counselling?
9 Are there any indications that one particular therapeutic style is more helpful or more unhelpful than another? Is a directive or non-directive style preferred by the client?
10 Are there any indications that it would be best for the client to be seen individually, or as part of a dyad (eg with partner or spouse) or as part of a family unit, or in a group?
11 Can a relationship develop that is satisfactory to both client and counsellor or should the client be referred elsewhere?
12 What are the client's strengths, what are the positive attributes?

To this list compiled by Lazarus, Palmer and Dryden (1995) have added an important thirteenth question.

13 Has the client had previous experience of counselling and if so, what was the outcome? What did the client find helpful or unhelpful?

Palmer and Dryden, 1995: 19

This is an important question. If the client has already had behaviour therapy and found it unhelpful or describes the directive approach of the therapist as 'too bossy' this provides important clues to the counsellor regarding therapeutic style and also perhaps the avoidance of, at least initially, interventions in the behaviour modality.

At this early stage counsellors or psychotherapists collect information and listen out for underlying themes. While listening to the client they take a note of the preferred modalities used to describe the difficulties.

CLIENT:	I am trying to stop drinking (behaviour) but my wife just doesn't help, she just keeps nagging and thinks it's all will-power (interpersonal). I feel so depressed about it all (affect). I'll never be able to quit (cognition).
COUNSELLOR:	A sense of hopelessness? (underlying theme).
CLIENT:	Yes that's it, I can't do it alone (cognition) and I keep seeing pictures of my wife leaving me (imagery) and I don't think I could stand that (cognition).

Multimodal life history inventory

At the end of the initial interview, the client is usually given the multimodal life history inventory. This is a fifteen page comprehensive questionnaire that has several sections. The first asks for general biographical information and includes questions about the client's relationships with their parents. The next section asks for a description of the presenting problem and about the client's expectations regarding therapy. The next seven sections ask numerous questions across all the modalities. Here we give a couple of examples of the types of questions asked in each modality.

Behaviour

What are some of the special talents or skills that you feel proud of?
What would you like to stop doing?

Feelings (affect)

List your five main fears.
When are you most likely to lost control of your feelings?

Sensations

Check any of the following physical sensations that often apply to you. (List includes abdominal pain, headaches, dizziness, flushes and so on.)

Images

Describe a very pleasant image, mental picture or fantasy.
Describe any persistent or disturbing images that interfere with your daily functioning.

Thoughts (cognitions)

Are you bothered by thoughts that occur over and over again? If yes, what are these thoughts?
What worries do you have that may negatively affect your mood or behaviour?

Interpersonal relationships

What do like most/least about your partner?
Describe your parents' attitude toward sex. Was sex discussed in your home?
Complete the following: One of the ways people hurt me is: . . .

Biological factors (drugs/biology)

Please list any significant medical problems that apply to you or to members of your family.
Do you get regular exercise? If yes, what type and how often?

The advantage of completing this to clients is that it facilitates the therapeutic programme, saves therapeutic time and, if they are paying, also their money. Clients are usually told that they do not have to complete all the questions if they don't want to and that any queries can be dealt with at the next session.

Clients have described it as thought provoking – 'It made me think about things in a different way, I hadn't realised how important that aspect was to me'. Some also describe it as rather tedious and intrusive. The reaction to it can form part of the next session's discussion.

Modality profile

A modality profile is a chart based on the seven modalities and is used to provide a summary of the information obtained during the assessment process. Its function is to enable the therapist and client to identify difficulties in each modality and also to plan out the techniques to be used to overcome

Table 5.1 Modality profile for a client with anxiety

Modality	Problem	Intervention
Behaviour	Avoids disagreeing with people	Assertiveness training
	Sleep disturbance	Self-hypnosis tape or relaxation programme
	Avoidance of public transport	Exposure programme
Affect	Anxiety	Educate about anxiety
		Dispute unhelpful beliefs
		Relaxation techniques
	Panic	Breathing exercises
	Depression	Increase rewarding activities
		Coping imagery
Sensation	Dizziness	Relaxation of neck muscles
	Tension	Biofeedback
		Relaxation exercises
	Heart palpitations	Educate about effects of anxiety
		Dispute catastrophising beliefs
Imagery	Images of train crashes	Imaginal exposure
	Images of lying dead in hospital with heart failure	Positive imagery
Cognition	I am useless	Dispute unhelpful beliefs
	No-one likes me	
	I can't stand these panic attacks	
Interpersonal relationships	Few close friends	Friendship training
		Social skills training
	Marital problems	Communication skills training
		Couples counselling (refer if necessary)
Drugs/biology	Little exercise	Fitness programme
	Takes a lot of aspirin	Relaxation training
	Eats junk food	Nutrition programme

these difficulties. It is seen very much as a working document and can be revised as therapy progresses. Sometimes the client is asked to produce their own modality profile as a homework assignment. This can then be compared in the next session with one drawn up by the counsellor. Table 5.1 illustrates an example of a modality profile for a client with anxiety problems.

Structural profile

Some people are doers, some thinkers, others are primarily people-orientated. The clients are asked to rate themselves using a seven-point scale on each of the dimensions by answering questions such as the following:

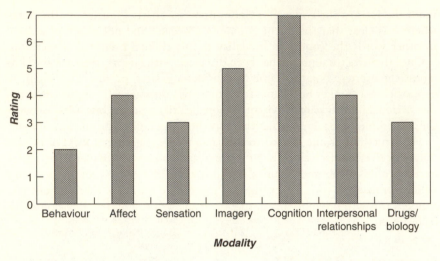

Figure 5.1 Current structural profile

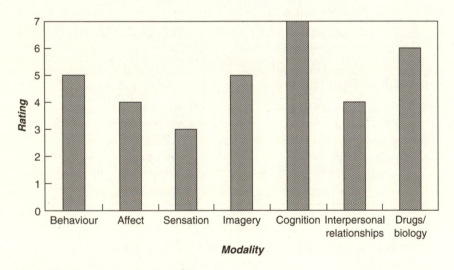

Figure 5.2 Desired structural profile

Behaviour: How much of a doer are you?
Affect: How emotional are you?
Sensation: How aware are you of your bodily sensations?
Imagery: How imaginative are you?
Cognition: How much of a thinker are you?
Interpersonal: How much of a social being are you?
Drugs/biology: To what extent are you health conscious?

From the ratings the counsellor draws up a bar chart. Figure 5.1 illustrates where it is clear that the client is mainly a thinker and not much of a doer. In other words the cognitive modality is this client's preferred dimension.

Once the structural profile has been discussed with clients, they are asked to repeat the exercise but this time to consider a desired profile. This client is happy being a thinker but wants to be more of a doer as well, to put thoughts into action. She also wants to become more health conscious but is happy with the other dimensions. Figure 5.2 illustrates how this desired profile might look.

The structural profile is used to illustrate to the client what kind of person they perceive themselves to be at present and to compare this to their preferred profile. Structural profiles can also assist the counsellor in deciding which approach to use. For example if the profile indicates that a client is a thinker, this will probably mean that he or she will respond well to cognitive techniques.

Second-order BASIC ID

Sometimes, despite careful assessment and use of appropriate techniques, clients do not seem to resolve their problems. When this happens second-order BASIC ID assessments can help. This involves taking just one specific problem and constructing a Modality Profile relating just to that problem.

After trying relaxation and other stress reducing techniques, Mehtap was still experiencing tension headaches. A modality profile was constructed just for this symptom by asking questions relating to each modality. When you have a severe headache what do you do? What do you think? What images do you have? Mehtap's answers were as follows:

Behaviour	lie down in darkened room
Affect	anxious
Sensation	tightness in throat and throbbing head
Imagery	keep seeing cousin who died from meningitis
Cognition	I'm sure I've got a tumour
Interpersonal relationships	can't face anyone at present, keep to myself
Drugs/biology	I take paracetamol but it doesn't help

From this the counsellor can get a few clues on Mehtap's problem. Is she using her headaches to avoid social contact and is this maintained by holding on to her belief that she has a brain tumour even though her doctor has ruled this out?

Tracking

Tracking involves the assessment of the 'firing order' of the different modalities. Lazarus recognises that since we are all unique, we do not respond to problem situations in a set sequence. For example, a man faced with having to speak in public may become aware of a tight chest and palpitations (sensation) as he climbs onto the platform, then think 'this is awful what is wrong with me' (cognition), have a picture of himself collapsing on the floor (imagery), and decide to escape the situation by leaving (behaviour). The modalities have fired in the order SCIB. Another person might experience the modalities in a different order. She might think 'I'm going to make a right mess of this and that will be awful' (cognition), leave the platform (behaviour), imagine the audience are laughing at her behind her back (imagery) and experience palpitations and a racing heart (sensation). This time the order is CBIS.

The selected techniques are geared to the firing sequence. To begin by aiming at the modalities occurring later in the firing order may be unsuccessful. In the case of the man above, techniques are more likely to be effective if used in the same firing order as the problem. So the psychotherapist would start with sensory techniques moving on to cognitive, imagery and behavioural techniques. For example, he might be instructed to use relaxation (sensation) and say to himself 'it is only the increased adrenalin that is causing my heart to beat faster, it feels bad but I can stand it' (cognition).

One principle that Lazarus stresses is that therapists should know their own limitations and other therapists' strengths. They should be prepared to refer their clients elsewhere. They need to be able to ask themselves 'Am I best for this client?' Who might be more effective? For example, an alcoholic might be better served by going to Alcoholics Anonymous or a special clinic, or someone with an eating disorder to a therapist who specialises in this area. In other cases it might be that another counsellor or psychotherapist has skills or personal qualities that will blend better with a particular client.

Goals

Lazarus describes the overall general aim of multimodal therapy as the reduction of psychological difficulties and the promotion of personal growth.

In addition more specific goals can be identified. Problems in each of the modalities can be drawn up for each individual and any excesses and deficits examined. Since the treatment is to be tailored to fit the client, it is important that the goals take into account the person's wishes in each modality. Lazarus has found that goals agreed on by client and psychotherapist that are stated explicitly, result in more effective outcomes than vague obtuse goals. They also need to be achievable in order to inspire hope in the person. Changes in any modality may involve a decrease or an increase or a difference. For example a sales person suffering from stress, who drives her car for many hours a day may wish to find a way to decrease this behaviour by reducing the amount of time spent at the wheel. Alternatively or as well as, she might recognise the advantages to driving in a different way, perhaps slower and more relaxed.

Therapeutic relationship

Therapist style

The multimodal approach encourages therapists to be flexible and adaptable. Sometimes this might mean relating in quite a formal manner or conversely with the person-centred stance of warmth and empathy. Therapists may need to change their approach even within one session. With each client the therapist needs to ask, how supportive need I be with this client and how directive?

> Tony made it quite clear at the beginning of the initial session that he had not liked his previous counsellor because she asked too many questions which felt intrusive. His multimodal counsellor therefore took a very gentle approach using very tentative ways of encouraging Tony to open up. During the third session after hinting at some special secret that no one knew, Tony suddenly said that he had been abused as a child, and then abruptly changed the subject. It was not until the fifth session that the counsellor began to ask questions about his life.
>
> In contrast Tracy, a high-flying business woman, got irritated with the warm empathic responses of her client-centred counsellor and wanted instead to have a directive, get-down-to-business relationship with the multimodal therapist.

Whatever specific approach or style is needed, an overall consideration is for the counsellor to work together with the client. Lazarus has used the metaphor of the 'authentic chameleon' to describe the way that multimodal counsellors change their styles to suit the clients' experiences, personalities, problems and goals. Lazarus tends to work in quite a directive manner combined with giving support. This is because he sees counselling as an educative process correcting the misinformation and missing information from the client's past. Nevertheless when required he will adopt a very gentle non-directive approach.

Bridging

We mentioned earlier that individuals tend to have a preferred modality. Bridging is a technique designed to enhance the therapeutic relationship and involves the counsellor being aware of and tuning in to the client's preferred modality. In the following example, the counsellor becomes aware that the client's preferred modality is cognitive, so rather than pressure the client into expressing his feelings, the counsellor first joins the client in the cognitive preference, moves her to sensation and uses this as a bridge from the cognitive modality to the affect modality.

COUNSELLOR: When your boss fired you, how did you feel?

CLIENT: Oh I felt it was so unfair, I did not deserve to be sacked (expressing her thoughts and opinions rather than feelings).

COUNSELLOR: (going along with the thoughts) You did not think you had done anything to warrant being sacked?

CLIENT: No, not at all.

COUNSELLOR: When you think of that time, standing in her office and the way she treated you, are you aware of any sensations in your body? (Using sensation as a bridge.)

CLIENT: I feel kind of tense, sort of tight across the chest and there's a lump in my throat – I had those feelings that day too.

COUNSELLOR: Concentrate on that tension now, the lump in your throat and that tightness and tell me any feelings or mental pictures that come to mind.

CLIENT: I think I feel angry, yeah I do, angry with her and scared because I might not get another job.

COUNSELLOR: Tell me more about that anger.

If the counsellor had persisted in probing for emotions at the beginning, the client might have felt alienated and concluded that the counsellor just did not understand her.

Techniques

Selection of multimodal techniques

Having assessed the needs of the client and therefore the focus of therapy, the counsellor turns to the tool box to select the techniques that are likely to be most effective. This means that multimodal counsellors need to be familiar with and skilled in the use of a wide variety of techniques. In the selection of these Lazarus stresses the importance of choosing those that have research data to support their effectiveness. He warns against using procedures that the counsellor has heard of but knows nothing of their effectiveness in dealing with a particular problem. Much criticism has been levelled at counsellors for using a particular technique that happens to be in vogue. For example when psychodrama first appeared on the scene – everyone was doing it from occupational therapists to tutors at the local evening classes. The use of untested techniques in this way by untrained people is not only unlikely to be effective but can actually be dangerous and harmful.

Multimodal counsellors start with the well established procedures: those that are known from the research literature to be especially effective for a particular problem. As with all stages in this approach, constant assessment and reassessment means that the effectiveness of the chosen approach needs to be carefully monitored for the particular client and changes made as required.

What follows is a list of the techniques most commonly used in each modality with a brief description of each. It is by no means a complete list. Some of these techniques may be used in other modalities too. For example relaxation which is a sensory technique, can also be used to help changes in behaviour, for example, like helping a person to sleep or feel less anxious in social situations.

Behavioural techniques

Behavioural techniques are based on the assumption that since behaviours are largely learned they can be unlearned and replaced with more helpful or desirable behaviours. The originators of these techniques have given them technical names which sometimes sound a little strange and obtuse. We will use them but explain each one carefully.

Behaviour rehearsal

Clients unable to behave in a desired manner may rehearse a particular behaviour with their counsellor or psychotherapist – just like an actor will rehearse a new role. For example, if a client is unable to return a faulty kettle to a shop, perhaps because he is too afraid to do so, he can rehearse the scene with the counsellor. The conversation can be recorded to enable the client to listen to and assess his performance. When the client feels no anxiety and is familiar with the scene, he is encouraged to go and test his new skills in the real life situation.

Modelling

We have already spoken of how we can learn from modelling our behaviour on that of others. In therapy, counsellors can provide role models for their clients. In our example above, instead of, or perhaps as well as, rehearsing returning the kettle to the shop, the counsellor could model the assertive behaviour for the client to imitate.

Nonreinforcement

Counterproductive associations formed during the learning process can be broken by a process known as extinction (described on p. 145). For example, a client Miss K aged 28 has learned that childish requests for reassurance from her parents are always met with love and attention. This behaviour is maintaining her grief following the death of her boyfriend and is reinforced by her parents' ever available sympathy. To break the association thereby leading to the extinction of this response, the parents would be instructed to ignore their daughter's behaviour rather than reinforce it. At the same time they can encourage more appropriate behaviour, such as talking about her boyfriend to resolve the grief, through the positive reinforcement of praise.

Recording and self monitoring

This involves the client keeping careful notes of their progress in changing behaviour and is aimed at giving the client a greater sense of self control. Also seeing progress in a positive direction can serve as a positive reinforcer.

Response cost or penalty

Here the client agrees to increase or decrease specific behaviours with the understanding that failure to achieve agreed goals will result in an agreed penalty. For example, a client with a back problem who fails to complete her exercise regime either has to perform an activity she does not like doing or has to forego an activity she does enjoy.

Stimulus control

Behaviour may be encouraged by the presence of certain stimuli. For example, those who wish to reduce the amount of alcohol they drink each day will find this harder to achieve if there is alcohol in their house. Stimulus control, in this case, would involve removing the alcohol from the house. Desired behaviour can also be increased in a similar way by arranging the environment with cues to trigger the behaviour. An author writing a book can encourage himself by arranging the desk so that there are no distracting stimuli present and by ensuring that he only sits at his desk to write. The desk then becomes a stimulus that is associated with writing his book.

Systematic exposure

Two of the common symptoms that individuals present with are the avoidance of situations they are afraid of and the refusal to take risks. It has been shown clearly that by staying in the feared situation levels of anxiety initially rise but after a time start to reduce until they reach normal levels. Usually this is carried out by clients gradually exposing themselves step by step to the feared situations. For example, an individual with a fear of transport of any kind would first be asked to travel by the method they are least anxious about until they no longer feel the anxiety, then move up a step to the next most feared mode of travel. In learning theory terms this is the extinction of the association between anxiety and the event or object.

Affect or emotional techniques

Most of the work therapists do is concerned with treating emotional disorders such as depression, anxiety, guilt or grief. Lazarus states that we cannot deal directly with emotion, it can only be reached through the other six modalities. This may seem strange to you but try for a moment to feel guilty without first conjuring up a thought or an image that provokes feelings of guilt in you. In order to change emotions, the counsellor has to use techniques from other modalities. For example, if a person wants to become less anxious the psychotherapist might use anxiety-management training. However what this actually involves is relaxation training (behavioural technique), coping imagery (imagery technique), perhaps also biofeedback (sensory technique) and various cognitive techniques to challenge unhelpful beliefs. Similarly anger management training will consist of similar combinations of techniques from other modalities.

Sensory techniques

Some of these may be for specific problems, for example sexual problems. Others are aimed at more general problems which will have an indirect effect on specific problems, for example reducing general body tension will have a specific effect on raised blood pressure. Included in this group is relaxation and hypnosis.

Biofeedback

There are a number of devices that can be used to monitor certain physiological functions such as heart rate, blood pressure and muscular tension.
This information is fed back to the client via any of the senses – most commonly auditory or visual feedback is used. The purpose of using such devices
is to bring about desired change in the physical sensations we experience.
A very popular device is the so-called galvanic skin response (GSR) monitor.
This measures skin conductivity and indicates the level by producing a tone of
a certain pitch. When our autonomic nervous system is aroused we start to
sweat which increases skin conductivity. You may recall getting sweaty
hands for example as you enter an examination room. If you had a GSR connected to you, it would respond to the change in your skin conductivity by
increasing the pitch of the tone. Using such devices, clients can learn to maintain a low pitch or even to eliminate the tone altogether. This is a very useful
way to illustrate how different thoughts and images can stimulate the stress
response very quickly. After getting the client to relax and maintain a low
tone, asking the client to think of something that frightens him or her will
instantly cause the GSR to rapidly raise the pitch indicating a very rapid
change in the body's physiology.

Sensate focus training

This is a well known and useful method for couples having sexual problems.
This is usually the first step taken in their therapy. It really refers to sensual
rather than sexual pleasure as it involves the stimulation of physical sensations
resulting from touch, massaging, caressing of any part of the body except for
the genital organs and female breasts which are to be avoided. The idea
behind this method is to encourage the couple to enjoy intimacy and pleasur-
ing of the other without the pressures or expectancies of sexual performance.

Imagery techniques

Unlike the techniques described for the other modalities there is at present
little research evidence to show that the imagery techniques described here
are effective. Nevertheless Lazarus has suggested a number of exercises he
has found useful to help individuals improve their powers of imagery. One
way to help people cope with stressful situations is to get them to imagine
themselves coping first. If they have difficulty doing this they will first
need help with their powers of imagery. Through careful assessment the
therapist should already know whether the use of imagery is difficult for
the client. Care needs to be taken by the counsellor in the use of images
because of the chance that certain ones may trigger off unpleasant memories
such as past traumas. The aim of imagery exercises is not to evoke unhelpful
emotions but to increase imagery skills.

Imagery exercises are best carried out with the person sitting comfortably and relaxed in a quiet place. You might like to try one or two of these yourself.

A white board technique

Clients are asked to concentrate on their breathing and relax. Then with their eyes closed they are asked to picture a white board on which one can write. They are asked to imagine themselves writing the number one, then the number two and so on putting as many numbers as possible on the board. Through practice the total numbers should increase as should their clarity.

The common object

Clients chose a common object and closely examine it until they believe they know it in detail They are then requested to close their eyes and imagine they are still studying the same object, trying to see it as clearly as they can and from all angles. After a couple of minutes they open their eyes and re-examine the real object to see if they forgot any detail or changed any aspect of it.

Once the clients use of imagery has improved sufficiently any of the following techniques may be used.

Anti-future shock imagery

Sometimes people are anxious about events that are likely to happen in the future, such as a daughter's marriage, one's retirement, or going on a date. The client may have negative images of for example, being alone, getting old, or being socially inadequate. One way to help clients overcome these images is to get them to visualise themselves coping with these changes. Lazarus called this 'emotional fire-drills'. For example on retirement, clients often imagine that life is over and they may see themselves miserable and alone. The counsellor will encourage them to brainstorm various coping strategies such as joining the local sports club, taking up new interests via adult education and then getting them to visualise themselves carrying out these activities successfully. By seeing, literally, that there are other ways of thinking about the future and of experiencing the future, the individual is enabled to cope with changes in a more constructive manner.

Imaginal exposure

Like systematic exposure, this technique exposes clients to situations they fear but here it is done in imagination. Sometimes it is not possible to expose the client to real life feared situations. People who have been through a trauma certainly do not want to repeat it in reality. By reliving it in imagination, these events eventually tend to lose their ability to trigger anxiety. First of all a hierarchy of fears is constructed and then the situation at the bottom of the list is imagined until the fear subsides. Then the next one is taken and imagined and so on until the worst feared situation is conquered.

Positive imagery

Positive imagery can be used to reduce anxiety and tension and literally means picturing any scene, real or imaginary, that the individual finds pleasant. For example, Mary was feeling so anxious that she could not relax. The counsellor knowing that she had pleasant memories from childhood holidays asked her to imagine one she particularly enjoyed. She pictured herself sitting on the cliffs above Dingle in Ireland watching the evening sun set over the Atlantic. As she recalled this memory she began to feel less tense.

Step-up technique

Another way to help a client with a future event such as a woman making a retirement speech is to use this technique which basically involves imagining the worst event that could possibly happen. Then the client is asked to imagine successfully coping with the most unlikely horrors deliberately called into fantasy. The counsellor may need to help the client identify possible solutions to the nightmare that was dreamed up. For example, the worst scenario might be that as the woman rises to make her speech, her dress catches on a nail underneath the table and gets completely ripped off revealing herself in her underwear. One coping strategy might be to grab the remains of the dress, drape it around herself and say loudly 'Just thought I'd try being a dress designer'.

Time projection imagery

Time projection imagery guides the client backwards or forwards in time. In this way past events can be re-lived thereby placing them into perspective. Clients can also imagine what might happen in the future. This is particularly helpful after experiencing a loss, such as the ending of a long term relationship. By asking the client to visualise themselves some time in the future, enjoying the things they used to enjoy the client's mood can lift. This can sometimes help the client to see the temporary nature of life events perhaps enabling them to see the proverbial 'light at the end of the tunnel'.

Cognitive techniques

In this section we will describe cognitive techniques commonly used in multimodal therapy. Other methods often used have already been described in the chapter on rational emotive behaviour therapy, such as disputing strategies, semantic precision and rational coping self-statements.

Bibliotherapy

There are now many very good self-help books, videos and audio-cassettes on the market which can be used to augment counselling sessions. Very often education about anxiety and how it can affect the bodily functions is very useful in reducing that anxiety as clients come to understand why many of their symptoms arise. Well chosen books also reinforce many aspects of what the client learns within a session. Lazarus has written some very useful self-help books such as *I Can if I Want To'* (Lazarus and Fay, 1992), *Don't Believe it For a Minute!* (Lazarus, Lazarus and Fay, 1994) and *The 60-second Shrink: 101 Strategies for Staying Sane in a Crazy World* (Lazarus and Lazarus, 1997).

Self-instruction

Many people experience failure or anxiety because of the way they think about what will happen. For example, before taking his driving test, Mark was telling himself that he was bound to fail and he would look really stupid to his friends if he did. He became very anxious and his anxiety affected his performance so that he did in fact fail as a result. Just as he had talked himself into failing, so he was helped to talk himself out of failing next time. Before he was due to take the test again the therapist helped him understand how his self-defeating thoughts, his anxiety and his poor driving performance were related. Then Mark was helped to become aware of his self-defeating inner speech. Next the therapist and Mark together identified some coping self-statements such as 'Calm down, you know you can drive well, breathe slowly, it doesn't matter if you feel a little anxiety, you can manage it'. These were practised by getting Mark to repeat them out loud, then *sotto voce* and then silently to himself until he was familiar with them.

Problem solving

Clients faced with problems often feel overwhelmed and unable to even begin to think of solutions. Problem solving is a method of dealing with problems that might require practical solutions and with problems that the client is emotionally disturbed about. There are a number of steps involved. The first is to identify the problem – what is the concern? Sometimes the problem may need breaking down into smaller parts. After identifying what the person wants, what their goals are, the second step is to generate possible alternative solutions to the problem. Brainstorming is a useful way of doing this. Then the advantages and disadvantages of each possible solution can be considered. Additional information may need to be obtained and used to strengthen or weaken the solutions under consideration. The solution most likely to succeed with the least negative consequences is then chosen and implemented. The final consideration being 'Did it work?' If this solution was not successful, the process can start again and either the first chosen solution can be modified, or a different solution can be tried.

Correcting misconceptions

People often have mistaken ideas about themselves, others or the society in which they live. For example they may believe that the HIV virus can be spread by hugging, or that they are going mad because they keep having nightmares. By correcting these misconceptions through education of the facts and not the myths, much distress can be alleviated.

Interpersonal relationship techniques

Interpersonal techniques are directed at difficulties clients have in relating to others. Interpersonal skills are important to anyone not living as a hermit yet so often these skills are missing from a person's repertoire. Some of these skills are easier to learn in a group rather than in individual counselling. For example, assertiveness training groups are often run by local adult education organisations in Britain.

There is considerable overlap between the skills described below. For example, communication skills overlap with assertiveness training since part of being assertive involves being able to clearly express what one wants. Most interpersonal techniques make use of techniques such as behaviour rehearsal, modelling and role playing.

Assertion training

Lack of assertiveness is a common problem and one that is addressed by some excellent books on the subject. Many people need to learn about their personal rights and how to stand up for them without violating other people's rights and without being aggressive or passive. Certain verbal and nonverbal behaviours are associated with being non-assertive such as using the words 'I wonder if you could' or standing with hunched shoulders looking down. Assertiveness skills are taught and practised through modelling and role playing in the counselling session before clients put what they have learned into practice outside.

Communication training

Communication involves the skills of both sending and receiving messages. To improve sending skills the client learns about the importance of eye contact, body posture, tone of voice, and the importance of not attacking the other person or making critical comments and statements about them. The skill of receiving messages can be improved by active listening, checking with the speaker to be sure that they have understood correctly and acknowledging what the speaker has said.

Friendship/intimacy training

This includes all of the above but also involves learning about such things as sharing, self-disclosure, caring, and not being competitive.

Social skills training

Social skills training involves acquiring, practising and integrating the skills needed in people's repertoires so that they feel confident in using them. These skills include assertiveness, communication and friendship skills described above. More frequently they include skills such as maintaining eye contact, smiling, and body posture, such as leaning forward to show interest. We need these skills to relate to people in a variety of settings including work and leisure. Often as a result of what Lazarus calls missing information, perhaps through lack of experience, many people simply do not know how to behave or converse in an appropriate manner in certain situations. For example, someone brought up in a very closed community like a strict religious sect will never have had the experience of meeting strangers in diverse social situations. For the best results, social skills training needs to take place in groups in order to give the person an opportunity to learn and practice new skills in a social setting.

Drugs/biological techniques

An educational approach is usually necessary when working in this modality. Sometimes counsellors and psychotherapists will need to have information about drugs clients are taking so that they can educate them about likely side effects that are often similar to symptoms of stress. It is also important that the counsellor refers clients back to their doctors if there is any suspicion that their problems have a medical origin. For example, someone complaining of persistent severe headaches may not be suffering from stress but from some more serious medical complaint.

Drugs/biological techniques are mainly concerned with lifestyle changes encouraging good health habits and with referral to other agencies. Sometimes general advice is all that is needed, but for clients a programme of change may be needed addressing the areas discussed below.

Exercise

Exercise has been shown to improve both physical and mental health. In fact research has suggested that running can be more effective than psychotherapy in the treatment of depression since exercise stimulates the production of a substance in our body called endorphin which naturally acts to raise our mood. For other clients exercise is indicated as part of a stress management programme. Most towns have physical fitness centres where qualified instructors give advice about fitness programmes. A good multimodal counsellor should have information available about local facilities. Clients are encouraged to spend at least two periods a week of a minimum of fifteen minutes each in some kind of aerobic exercise (swimming, brisk walking, running, cycling).

Diet

Despite advertising campaigns many people still eat unhealthy foods such as convenience foods, or foods that contain saturated fats. General advice on avoidance of such foods and on eating plenty of fibre, fresh fruits and vegetables can be given. Individuals who smoke, drink alcohol in excess or have a high intake of caffeine are encouraged to cut down.

Rest, relaxation and leisure

Many people ignore this aspect of life. It is important to both physical and mental health since it allows the body to recover from the effects of a stressful life. Good sleep is also essential. Some clients benefit from engaging in relaxation techniques such as meditation or yoga.

CLOSING COMMENTS

Lazarus continues in his search for more effective assessment and treatment methods so that he can more easily fulfil his 'greatest joy and major feelings of achievement' which 'come from turning around someone's life so that he or she manages to find happiness and calm in place of misery and fear' (Nystul and Shaughnessy, 1994: 383). This joy he feels is quite private; Lazarus is not a man who seeks guru status. He does state, however, that he wants to share his ideas more widely not only with other professionals but also with the general public through books and radio. Lazarus and his son Clifford have a weekly radio show called 'Mental Health Matters'.

In America multimodal therapy has been rated as one of the most important approaches and Lazarus is considered among the top five most influential therapists there – the other four being Freud, Rogers, Ellis and Wolpe. British and European students are much less familiar with this approach. In Britain the main leading figure is Stephen Palmer who has taken multimodal counselling and developed it further so that it can be applied to stress problems and in industrial settings (Palmer and Dryden,1995).

Multimodal therapists believe that in order to cope with life we need to learn as many skills and coping responses as possible. Lazarus uses an educational model 'Let's see how many coping responses we can possibly learn, and the more we learn the better off we will be, and we will find life easier to take' (Nystul and Shaughnessy, 1994: 383). Lazarus believes that the practice of multimodal therapy is quite demanding. Not only does the counsellor or psychotherapist have to have a well stocked tool box, they also have to be proficient at using each and every tool. In addition they have to be flexible in order to respond to the client's uniqueness and individuality. Almost a Sherlock Holmes strategy is required to fathom out the puzzle that each person brings. What seems to be causing this client's problems? Who or what seems to be maintaining them? What seems to help them, what doesn't? If change is not happening, then why not? Who or what else might help?

NOTE

1 This technique involves first teaching the person to relax. Then the person is asked to imagine the objects or situations they are afraid of, gradually increasing the intensity of the exposure. For example a person with arachnophobia (fear of spiders) would first be asked to imagine a very small spider perhaps twenty feet away, then a larger spider gradually getting nearer.

REFERENCES

Bandura, A. (1977) *Social Learning Theory*. Englewood Cliffs, NJ: Prentice-Hall.

Dryden, W. (1991) *A Dialogue with Arnold Lazarus. 'It Depends'*. Milton Keynes: Open University Press.

Lazarus, A. A. (1958) 'New methods in psychotherapy: A case study'. *South African Medical Journal*, 33, 660–4.

Lazarus, A. A. (1971) *Behavior Therapy and Beyond*. New York: McGraw-Hill.

Lazarus, A. A. (1992) 'Multimodal therapy: Technical eclecticism with minimal integration', in J. C. Norcross and M. R. Goldfried (eds) *Handbook of Psychotherapy Integration*. New York: Basic Books.

Lazarus, A. A. and Fay, A. (1992) *I Can if I Want To*. New York: Morrow.

Lazarus, A. A. and Lazarus, C. N. (1997) *The 60-second Shrink: 101 Strategies for Staying Sane in a Crazy World*. San Luis Obispo, CA: Impact.

Lazarus, A. A., Lazarus, C. N. and Fay, A. (1994) *Don't Believe it For a Minute! Forty Toxic Ideas that are Driving You Crazy*. San Luis Obispo, CA: Impact.

London, P. (1964) *The Modes and Morals of Psychotherapy*. New York: Holt, Rinehart and Winston.

Nystul, M. S. and Shaughnessy, M. (1994) 'An interview with Arnold A. Lazarus'. *Individual Psychology*, 50, 372–85.

Palmer, S. and Dryden, W. (1995) *Counselling for Stress Problems*. London: Sage.

Pavlov, I. (1927) *Conditioned Reflexes* (ed. and trans. by G. V. Anrep). New York: Dover (reprinted 1960).

Watzlawick, P., Weakland, J. A. and Fisch, R. (1974) *Change: Principles of Problem Formation and Problem Resolution* New York: Norton.

FURTHER READING

Lazarus, A. A. (1989) *The Practice of Multimodal Therapy*. Baltimore, MD: Johns Hopkins University Press.

Lazarus, A. A. (1997) *Brief but Comprehensive Psychotherapy: The Multimodal Way*. New York: Springer.

Palmer, S. and Dryden, W. (1995) *Counselling for Stress Problems*. London: Sage.

6 The four approaches compared

> Comparisons are odious.
>   Fifteenth-century proverb

In this final chapter we have attempted to make the business of comparisons among the four approaches less odious and more interesting by presenting you with a case vignette and interviews from four well-known therapists. Mary is a real client of one of the authors (JM), who has kindly given permission for us to use her story (names and identifying details have been changed to protect the anonymity of the client). The interviews were semi-structured in that each therapist was asked identical questions. We complete the chapter by comparing their responses to these questions and using them to illustrate a number of points made in the previous chapters.

MARY'S STORY

Mary was referred by her family doctor because she was feeling depressed. She has had bouts of depression since she was 15 years old – she is now 51. The current bout began about six months ago. As well as being on anti-depressants she is also on hormone replacement therapy.

Mary was first married at 17 and has three sons from this marriage. She divorced this husband when the children were in their mid teens. He now lives in Canada, where the three children also now live with their families. Mary remarried a few years after her divorce, to Robert who has an adult daughter from his first marriage. She says that she feels guilty towards her own children for depriving them of their father and also towards her step-daughter for splitting up her family – although in fact this had already happened by the time she met Robert.

Mary's father died ten years ago; she still grieves for him. Towards the end of his life they had to put him in a nursing home because he was terminally ill – she feels guilty about this and thinks she should have looked after him. After his death there was a major family argument which has to some extent been healed, although Mary still feels hurt and the relationship with her sister is still very difficult. Her mother died seven years ago. She described her childhood relationship with her mother as good but her father she described as domineering and at times quite harsh.

Both her husbands she also described as domineering. She finds it very difficult to speak about her problems to Robert – she experiences him as critical and says he puts her down. He was made redundant two years ago and they had to move into a small house, which she says does not feel like hers. She normally works full time for an estate agent but currently, due to her depression, she is on sick leave. Outside work she does very little and she has few friends.

During the first session she reported feeling very down, continually tired and having problems with sleeping. She wanted help to change things so that she could stop feeling guilty and miserable all the time. She was very concerned about her relationship with her husband and seemed afraid that this was failing too. She presented as a very quiet, gentle woman, almost apologetic when talking about her problems and needs. She seemed to expect the counsellor to do the work, through questioning and the giving of advice. She was open to talking about these expectations however, and came to realise that magic wands were not on offer from the counsellor, although it was unclear whether this realisation was genuine or out of compliance and a desire to please.

THE INTERVIEWS

The psychodynamic approach – Judy Cooper

Judy Cooper is a member of the British Association of Psychotherapists and is in private practice. She is the author of *Speak to Me as I Am: The Life and Work of Masud Khan* (London, Karnac Books, 1993) and co-editor of two books *Narcissistic Wounds: Clinical Perspectives in Psychotherapy* (London, Karnac Books, 1995) and *Assessment in Psychotherapy* (London, Karnac Books, 1998).

How would you deal with this client's problems? Would you take a problem-focused approach, exploratory, or some other approach and why?

I would take an exploratory approach but I would definitely have some psychoanalytic guidelines in mind, so I would want to know more about her childhood and her inner world. I would also try to note patterns and repetitions that appear; for example, the fact that she seems to have had difficulty at both adolescence and menopause. It is a complicated story, there are threads of repetition but one would need to flesh the story out about her childhood, her marriages, her parents' relationship, and her relationship with her children.

What hypotheses would you have about Mary that would inform your assessment of her difficulties and why?

She has had so many losses in her life and is still grieving the death of her father ten years ago. Her mother also died three years after that. In some of these losses, however, including her divorce and the difficult relationship with her siblings, she may have played a contributory role. This would seem to be confirmed by the fact that her three children and their families are all in Canada where their father lives. Mary, in fact, acknowledges her guilt at having deprived her children of a father when they were younger and in her second marriage blames herself for causing her stepdaughter unhappiness even though her new husband's marriage had already broken down.

When Robert lost his job she lost her nice house, and with her depression she is experiencing a temporary loss of her job. Menopause is also linked to loss. Now she must be very frightened about her current marriage breaking up because she does not appear to have many resources and has few friends. She doesn't sound as if she is able to share or give very much and actually sounds quite solitary, as if she feels that she hasn't got much to give so it isn't altogether surprising that her children chose to live near their father.

It is possible that, from my assessment of her, I would get a slightly fuller picture of Mary than the one you have given. In my opinion, she seems to show traits of both aggressiveness and passivity, which are quite likely to alienate people. She doesn't appear to own her aggression which seems to come out in depression or guilt. She seems to relate as a victim. She becomes a victim and that has probably got its roots in her childhood experiences. Obviously there is much more information I would need to know about her relationships while growing up. She seems to have difficulty in sharing. I wonder how, after her divorce, she shared the parenting of the children with her ex-husband, and what happened in that period leading to them all choosing to live abroad near him.

I would want to know why she has come for counselling now and I might link it for her with the physical and emotional changes around the menopause and see how she responds.

One hopeful thing is her relationship with her mother. I would be most interested in what sort of a mother she was, and whether Mary was able to use that relationship to be a mother herself. I would also be interested in how Mary's mother related to her father. Was her mother a victim and has Mary therefore identified with the victim role and consequently became a victim in her own marriages? She is full of guilt and very ready to see herself as the victim. Even when it has got nothing to do with her, as is the case of splitting up her second husband's family, she still takes it on board.

What theoretical constructs would inform the process of assessment?

What I look for is the importance of childhood experience, then unconscious factors and, in a wide sense, infantile sexuality, in the sense that different phases are attached to different sexual development. Being aware of her capacity to form a transference relationship would also be around if I was assessing her and noting how she saw me, whether as benign or threatening.

What kind of therapeutic relationship would you seek to develop with Mary? Which therapeutic style would you aim to use and why?

I would hope to form a relationship where she felt safe enough and free enough to reveal as much of her inner and external worlds as possible. She obviously has such difficulties with relationships – all her relationships seem to go bad, so I would hope that we would be able to use this fact creatively in the therapeutic relationship which would be likely to repeat this disappointment for her.

I would use a psychodynamic style, which on the whole is non-directive so that the client can choose her own solutions. Giving advice doesn't usually stick, people don't listen anyway, people have to find their own choices and solutions. For real change to take place it has to be that they are in control of their choices. Being directive would be feeding into the problem of her passivity.

How important would the therapeutic relationship versus specific techniques be with Mary?

The therapeutic relationship would be very important and I don't know what you mean by specific techniques. I would use interpretation, and also as far as possible explore her dreams with her and whatever comes to her mind, free association in the sense of not censoring whatever comes up even if it seems trivial or embarrassing or irrelevant. I think lying down on a couch makes it easier for someone to focus on their own issues and their internal world without being distracted by cues from me.

What would be your broad therapeutic aims and objectives?

The aim in psychodynamic work is to explore the person's inner world and to make the unconscious conscious so that they can have more control over the choices they make. There are more options if one is conscious of where things come from, what one's moves and reactions are about. In Mary's case the aim would be to make destructive thoughts and actions ultimately transformed into more constructive and creative ones. I would aim to develop her sense of self because of her lack of confidence and resources.

What is your stance on goal setting; would you help her set goals or not and if so would you do that now or later on?

I wouldn't set goals, no not in that sense. Patients have their own goals, their own ideas. I would ask, if I was doing an assessment session, what would be her expectations of therapy, what would she hope for.

If you would not encourage her to set goals, why not?

I think that the aim of therapy is not goals as such, though change is certainly an aim. I don't think you can tell in which way change will occur and I think things actually alter as a person develops in therapy. Energy is dynamic and moves, and things change all the time, so it's not relevant to set goals as such. I think goals can restrict one.

What problems would you envisage emerging from the therapeutic process and how would you address them?

I think the problems that would emerge with this woman are her passivity and her anger. I think that beneath her depression she is actually very angry and hostile but she is not in touch with this. There is a dissociation somewhere. I would imagine all this coming out in her relationship with me as a therapist. I should imagine it might be either quite difficult to get into these feelings because she may not be able to see it this way or if she did there may be quite a negative transference to get through so that might be quite difficult. The other anxiety, I suppose, is would she stay with the therapy if it got really deep and into these aggressive feelings? For fifty years she has avoided them.

What do you imagine will be the therapeutic outcome?

I don't know if she'd stay the course but if she did I should imagine she'd be a rewarding patient to work with. It's obviously at these transition points, adolescence and menopause, that things have got very difficult for her and she's got to a crossroads maybe in part through hormonal changes which alter her whole way of dealing with situations and her lifestyle. She has never really dealt with any of these things and much of her life she has been living with these dysfunctional relationships and rifts. Whether she can deal with ending the therapeutic relationship in a mutual and considered way at the end of therapy is a question mark but if she could, she would get a lot from therapy. If she couldn't she may find it too painful and take flight.

The person-centred approach – Brian Thorne

Brain Thorne is professorial fellow and director of the Centre for Counselling Studies at the University of East Anglia, Norwich. He is also a professor of education in the College of Teachers and co-founder of the Norwich Centre for Personal and Professional Development. Brian is author or editor of a number of books, including *Person-centred Counselling in Action* (London, Sage, 1988) with Dave Mearns and *Person-centred Counselling and Christian Spirituality* (London, Whurr, 1998).

How would you deal with this client's problems; would you take a problem-focused approach, exploratory, or some other approach and why?

I would take a person-centred approach. This means I would try to offer Mary the deepest possible respect of which I am capable through establishing, I hope, my acceptance of her and offering, I think in this particular instance anyway, a very detailed empathy, trying to convey that I really do want to know the intricacies of her inner world. So it would be very much focused on Mary as a person and trying to offer her the kind of relationship in which she can feel respected, valued and truly understood. This would be very different from the relationships she has had with the significant men in her life.

What hypotheses would you have about Mary that would inform your assessment of her difficulties and why?

The hypothesis I would be working on would be that Mary does have the capacity to be a self-accepting person. She is also capable of, and here's a funny word, uplifting other people. By uplifting I mean giving to them a sense of value and worthwhile-ness. I would hypothesise that if Mary can actually become the person she has it within her to be, she will be a rather glorious person.

I would work on those hypotheses because that's what I actually believe about all human beings. It seems particularly important to have those hypotheses well to the fore when I'm responding to someone who clearly at this point in her life, feels very far from a self-accepting person and I suspect very far from appreciating herself as somebody who can offer a life-giving force to others.

What theoretical constructs would inform the process of assessment?

I think I can interpret that word assessment so that I'm comfortable with it. I would interpret it in terms of what will enable me more fully to understand the inner world of this person. So taking that as the starting point, what theoretical construct from my own person-centred position would enable me more fully to understand the inner world of Mary?

I would say, something like this, that I would hypothesize that Mary, at this particular time in her life, and probably for a very long time previously too, has been almost totally divorced from what in my jargon I call the actualising tendency. But she's been beset probably from very early times indeed, by massive conditions of worth — another theoretical construct that would have meaning for me. And that therefore her self-concept, again a fundamental notion in person-centred therapy, is deeply self-denigrating.

I would also be assuming that because of all that in her life, she's very far away from any internalized locus of evaluation, that she would find it really quite difficult to make decisions for herself, to have any sense that she has within her a capacity to make her own judgements. So in a nutshell: actualising tendency, conditions of worth, self-concept, and the locus of evaluation. And all those I think would be of assistance to me in understanding more of the nature of Mary's inner world.

What kind of therapeutic relationship would you seek to develop with Mary? Which therapeutic style would you aim to use and why?

In a way I've answered this partially by what I said at the outset. It would seem to me that even more than usual I would want to be very deeply respectful of Mary and I would want to try and enable her to feel that I genuinely want to understand her inner world in detail. And I do put quite a bit of emphasis on the detail, because I think it's by sensitively offering a person the opportunity to explore in detail and in depth, that respect is really conveyed. It's not just a kind of passing interest but a deep interest.

What follows from that is that I would be trying to establish a relationship with her where gradually she feels less afraid. We're talking really about trust; we're talking about the establishment of intimacy where she can feel that it's going to be safe to self-explore, it's going to be safe to acknowledge and admit her vulnerabilities and that's going to be quite something for her given her experiences, particularly of men. So I would see this as being not easily achieved and probably not rapidly achieved either. I would sense that this relationship of trust, the relationship of intimacy, will be quite a difficult thing to move towards.

I think the fact that I am a man is going to make her initially and perhaps for quite some time, deeply uneasy, probably deeply suspicious. I think that the experience of real acceptance and empathy can at one and the same time be both desirable and quite frightening.

The response to 'and why' is that Mary has had experiences with men which for her have been damaging, which have made it almost impossible for her to have a sense of the worthwhile-ness and validity of her own being. If that repeated experience can therefore be changed then this will be enormously important in her life experience and in the way that she's going to conceptualize herself and think and feel about herself in the future. It will be worth hanging in there for.

All human beings have a particular way of presenting themselves in the world. They have in that sense a style and, as a person-centred therapist, I'm going to be concerned that the way I am, the way I try to give expression to my being with this person isn't so divergent from their style, is not so incompatible that they find it enormously difficult to relate to me. I would be at pains to make sure that I wasn't somehow presenting myself to them in a way which was incompatible with their own way of being, so that they felt almost that they were speaking to a person from a different planet.

I certainly wouldn't be in the business of imitating Mary's submissive style, but on the other hand I would be very careful that I was not giving expression to my own way of being in such a fashion that she felt almost immediately intimidated. There is something here about, I suppose, tailoring one's way of being so that it is acceptable to the other.

How important would the therapeutic relationship versus specific techniques be with Mary?

This question is, I think, a non-starter for the person-centred approach. Specific techniques are not part of the armamentarium of the approach. The therapeutic relationship is of paramount importance and specific techniques not at all.

Specific techniques furthermore are likely to be detrimental to the building up of the relationship which I would desire. They might breed the notion of some kind of manipulation, some kind of power-trip. Behind so much of the work that I do as a person-centred counsellor is the issue of enabling people to feel parity of esteem, to feel that they actually do have their own power and their own resources and that they're not going to be diddled out of that by their therapist. The notion of parity of esteem or equality of relationship is I think quite central to the whole endeavour.

What would be your broad therapeutic aims and objectives?

I'm going to try and express that in a slightly different way. My therapeutic aim would be to understand Mary's inner world so that I can become an acceptable companion there and can gradually assist her to become more self validating and as a consequence therefore more likely to be in touch at least from time to time with her actualising tendency.

What is your stance on goal setting; would you help her set goals or not and if so would you do that now or later on?

I think that depends on what the *client's* stance is towards goal setting. If the client is very keen on setting goals, well then that's fine, because that's what the client wishes to do. Mary is quite clear, she says she wishes to stop feeling guilty and miserable all the time. So she has a goal for herself. And that particular goal is very much in self-concept terms isn't it? She wants to feel differently about herself and that fits extraordinarily well into the person-centred framework. And I think goal setting in person-centered therapy is nearly always to do with self-concept and usually also to do with relationships – perhaps relationship with others, perhaps relationship with self. So I wouldn't be averse to setting goals if that's what the client wants.

In Mary's case I can imagine that it is possible that I might find myself working with her on precisely what she has said she wants to do. How are we going to set about enabling her to feel less guilty and less miserable? What at the moment is causing her to feel this way? I can imagine that through teasing out the goals she's already setting herself, we might very quickly move into some of the conditions of worth, some of the things that have happened to her in the past which have conditioned the way in which she currently feels about herself. On the other hand (so I hedge my bets here) there could be real dangers about explicitly establishing goals because she might then fall into the trap of wanting to please me. She might see me as the person who's going to evaluate her ability to achieve these goals and she might pretend to achieve them or, worst of all, therapy might turn out to be another failure. She would go away feeling even more guilty and inadequate and miserable because she couldn't even make a go of therapy.

I think there is a kind of myth around, that person-centred practitioners are against goals and objectives. As in so many other things in person-centred therapy it depends on what the client wants.

If you would help her set goals, what kind of goals would you imagine would be helpful to Mary and why?

What I'm actually saying is that I'm not at all sure if I would or if I wouldn't. A lot would depend on what really emerged as we began to look at some of the things she says she wants. If I were to find myself helping her to set goals, the goals would be clearly in the area of self-validation. The goal of feeling all right about herself, of not feeling guilty. I think very often person-centred therapists are working on what one might term implicit rather than explicit goals but that those goals are none the less shared by client and counsellor even though they might not ever be fully articulated.

To answer the 'and why', it is because if we can actually set goals which are to do with shifts in self-concept and are to do inevitably therefore with the forming of different kinds of relationship, we shall be doing a great deal to undo those conditions of worth and to remove the impediments to her development. So the setting of those kinds of goals, if it proved to be appropriate, could be enormously significant. But as I say those goals may well be there implicitly rather than explicitly.

If you would not encourage her to set goals, why not?

As I have said I might not encourage her to set goals because she might try to please me.

What problems would you envisage emerging from the therapeutic process and how would you address them?

Whether this is a problem or not I'm not sure, but what I would envisage is that if we are successful in creating an environment where gradually she does begin to feel safe, where she does begin to trust, where the fear has been diminished, then it's quite likely that there will be a deep attachment to me. I think it's quite likely to happen although previously that's never been possible. It's never been safe enough for her to allow dependency with a man, so therefore there must be a willingness in me to permit that, as a really vitally important stage in the process towards interdependency. Or another way of putting that is a willingness on my part to accept her love of me. Because to reject that would be to reinforce the feeling that she hasn't got anything worth offering other people, that she hasn't got it within her to uplift others. I've got to be prepared to accept the dependency, to accept the positive feelings she may have towards me and not in fact to be frightened. I think some person-centred therapists get very frightened. It's a potential problem but I think one I've experienced so often, it's not actually problematical for me. Although that isn't to say that it doesn't have to be handled with enormous sensitivity.

What do you imagine will be the therapeutic outcome?

My hope is that the therapeutic outcome will be a movement forward in her sense of self-worth and if that occurs within the therapeutic relationship, there will come increasingly a need in her to develop more validating relationships and that may well mean that at some point or other if she desires it, her present husband will begin to feature in this current therapy. He might actually start coming to sessions as well. And I can see that one possible outcome is an enrichment of her marriage as a result of this, or the reverse, a recognition that the marriage is in fact destructive to her, that it simply reinforces her old feelings of worthlessness and she may sadly have to separate from this man too.

The rational emotive behavioural approach – Windy Dryden

How would you deal with this client's problems; would you take a problem-focused approach, exploratory, or some other approach and why?

I would take a problem-focused approach in the sense that I would encourage her to come up with a list of problems that she would like to deal with in therapy. I would then give her an opportunity to talk about each of these problems. Thus, I would be exploratory within the context of a problem-focused approach. While I am flexible on this point I believe that therapy is best approached in a problem-oriented manner. With Mary I think exploration would give her the opportunity to hear the sound of her own voice which is important since she appears to be somewhat diffident and frightened, and may well see the therapist as controlling and domineering. Thus, I think that it is important for her quite early on to have the sense that she has a definite influence over the direction of her therapy.

What hypotheses would you have about Mary that would inform your assessment of her difficulties and why?

I would hypothesise that Mary has a dire need for approval, that she is an individual who hasn't really considered her own desires to be of much importance and hasn't really pursued personally meaningful projects in life. She may have been brought up in an environment where putting others first was seen as a virtue and to put oneself first was seen as a sin and thus forbidden. I would hypothesise that Mary has problems with self-assertion so other people think that she goes along with them and therefore they continue to be in control. Whether she chose a domineering husband or whether she ended up with a domineering husband as a result of lack of assertion is something I would need to explore with her. Certainly, Mary does seem to be the kind of person who has a poor opinion of herself in the sense that she does not see herself as important or efficacious in life. As a result I would hypothesise that she does not experience herself as being in charge of her life and believes that if she were to take control bad things would happen for which she would be responsible. The idea that Mary is responsible for the break-up of her husband's previous family before she had even met him is testament to the fact that she has an unhealthy attitude towards responsibility. I would again test out this hypothesis with her.

I would also be curious to discover why Mary is still grieving for her father whom she describes as domineering and quite harsh and is not still grieving for her mother whom she describes as good. I would need to explore the nature of her grief with her – is it a healthy grief where she cries for her father often but then gets on with her life, or is she weighed down by her grief? I would want to discover what role her grieving plays in her life.

I also wonder and would seek to discover whether Mary comes from a family where there is a strong inherited tendency toward depression. I would explore with her the history of her depression. Are we talking about a lifelong unremitting depression, does it fluctuate according to her situation, or does it come out of the blue? I also wonder whether she is taking the correct antidepressant medication. If her GP has been prescribing the medication I might want to suggest to her that she has it checked out by an expert, because GPs quite often aren't that expert at prescribing anti-depressant medication.

Although REBT recommends zeroing in on people's beliefs it does allow for the fact that people hold these beliefs in a much broader context, so I would want to view Mary's beliefs in a wider context. I would look at her present relationship with her husband which seems to be failing and would want to find out more about this relationship and why it is failing. Also I would seek to discover what her attitude is towards feeling and expressing anger since people with Mary's story and background often have great difficulty with anger.

What theoretical constructs would inform the process of assessment?

First of all the construct of irrational beliefs would obviously be to the fore. With Mary I would anticipate that she would hold irrational beliefs about responsibility, approval, assertion, and anger. It is also important to consider the behaviour which stems from Mary's irrational beliefs and which helps to shape her interpersonal world. For example, Mary seems to believe that she must have the approval of her husband. If this is so, a typical interaction might go something like this. When her husband starts to control Mary, she may not say anything. Her lack of action then may encourage him to see that she will go along with him. So her passive unassertive behaviour might help to explain why her husband is so domineering. Therefore the link between irrational beliefs, the behaviour that stems from these beliefs and the impact that her behaviour has on other people needs assessment. If her behaviour encourages other people to act in domineering ways, Mary unwittingly will have helped to create the very problems that she is grappling with.

I would also be informed by Lazarus's BASIC ID framework. However, I would highlight, perhaps more than Lazarus would, the role of cognition and irrational beliefs in particular as the core of her difficulties, not the only factor to be considered but the core factor.

*What kind of therapeutic relationship would you seek to develop
with Mary? Which therapeutic style would you aim to use
and why?*

One has to be mindful that with Mary we are probably dealing with a woman
who is likely to be compliant, meek and mild. Therefore I would be quite
gentle in my work with her, encouraging her to get used to talking to me
and to having a major say in the direction of her therapy. As a male I
would wonder whether Mary would be better off talking to a female therapist.
I might suggest this to her if it became clear at the outset that she was questioning her role as a woman, and this was a central issue for her.

I would be mindful of my own power and the degree to which I would
adopt an active directive style with Mary. It would be very easy to become
overly active and overly directive with her. Consequently I would emphasise
the Socratic rather than the didactic aspects of REBT and attempt to get her
involved in the process as much as I could. Assuming that she could use this
Socratic approach, I imagine she would say 'I don't know' a lot to encourage
me to take the lead. This might be problematic because I would not want to
do the work for her. Because of her need to be compliant and respectful she
may look towards me as the fountain of advice and wisdom and it would
be a grave error if I assumed that role. Thus, I may suggest that she reads
other people's self-help books rather than my own, because I would not
want to overemphasise my expertise. I would predict that Mary wants to
be told what to do, which would not of course be good for her in the long
run. Consequently I would seek feedback from her throughout therapy and
tailor therapy according to her desires, as long as it is in her long term healthy
interests for me to do so.

I think I would spice my approach to Mary with a little humour. Reading
her case vignette, I picture her as a grey, dowdy, overly serious individual.
Does she have a sense of humour? I might make a few trial humorous comments to see how she resonates to humour. Also as I have said it would be
wrong to adopt an expert style with her. I would thus encourage her to use
my first name to equalise the relationship in terms of power. I would adopt
a formal–friendly style with Mary and de-emphasise my expertise.

*How important would the therapeutic relationship versus specific
techniques be with Mary?*

I think that if I were to get the therapeutic relationship wrong with Mary
then the specific techniques would lose their potency. If I get the relationship
right in the sense that I am successful in encouraging her to be powerful
and efficacious then this is the soil in which the specific REBT techniques
would take root. If, on the other hand, I emphasise my own efficaciousness
and power, then Mary would look at me admiringly as a fountain of all knowledge and the techniques would lose their potency.

What would be your broad therapeutic aims and objectives?

My therapeutic aims and objectives for myself would be to establish the kind of relationship that I spoke about before, and to teach her the tasks and techniques of REBT but in a way that emphasises her personal power and agency.

What is your stance on goal setting; would you help her set goals or not and if so would you do that now or later on?

I would definitely help Mary to set goals that are within her control. I would help her to see that remorse is a healthy alternative to guilt if you violate your moral code, and to see that sadness is a healthy alternative to depression. Her behavioural goals would follow from these emotional goals and would lead to a discussion of such issues as:

i   to what extent is putting oneself first selfish?
ii   can one avoid hurting others' feelings and if one does is this a sin?

I would do this before encouraging her to be assertive.

In the main, I would encourage Mary to set goals right from the start of therapy but would be mindful of the fact that these goals may well change later.

If you would help her set goals, what kind of goals would you imagine would be helpful to Mary and why?

The goals I believe would be helpful to Mary are first of all to see herself as more of an assertive individual. Becoming more assertive would mean her standing her ground more with people and going for what she wants. I would like to see her being concerned rather than overconcerned about pleasing others but to see pleasing them as secondary to pleasing herself. Another goal might be developing a healthy sense of responsibility. Thus I would want her to stop taking responsibility for what she is not responsible for and to stop blaming herself. A third goal would be integrating the death of her father better. Finally perhaps to look at her relationship with Ron perhaps in a couples' therapy context. I don't think I would be best placed to do this myself but I think that it might be a useful thing for her to do with her husband.

While all these would be my objectives, the important thing is helping Mary to meet her objectives. I would be mindful of the fact that she may set goals that she thinks I want her, to have rather than goals that she herself wants to set. Thus, I might say to her, 'Now if I didn't want you to set that goal would that change things for you?'

What problems would you envisage emerging from the therapeutic process and how would you address them?

The main problem would be if Mary came to see me as another domineering man in her life. I would be very careful to avoid this happening. As a therapist I recognise that I do have personal power and thus need to be especially vigilant of this particular aspect of the therapeutic process. I wonder to what extent Mary would be open about expressing her dissatisfaction with therapy or her difficulties with the counselling process. This is something I would be very mindful of. She may be dissatisfied but would say that things were fine. I also think that Mary might either do her homework too religiously or not do it and make excuses. She would not be forthcoming and say things like 'that was not a good homework assignment' or 'you pushed me into it'. What I would do is to put my hypothesis to her and say something like 'Mary I wonder if it would be hard for you to tell me about aspects of counselling that you find uncomfortable, difficult or aspects about my behaviour that you have problems with?' I would put this issue on the table and deal with it there and then but I would not do so too soon because that might be frightening for Mary. At the outset I would ask her what she thinks counselling is about, what her understanding of it is and what her hopes and fears for counselling are. I would want to show that I am a person who will take her seriously and not somebody who will try to push her into something against her will.

What do you imagine will be the therapeutic outcome?

It depends. If Mary is only prepared to take a passive role in therapy and if her relationship with her husband runs into overt difficulty, these elements could be problematic. But if Mary is prepared to work and if the relationship with her husband can be contained I think she would be a good client. I think she would work diligently in therapy and if so there could be a good outcome. If her husband is amenable to therapeutic intervention there could be a very good outcome.

The multimodal approach – Stephen Palmer

Dr Stephen Palmer is director of the Centre for Multimodal Therapy and the Centre for Stress Management in London. He is honorary visiting senior research and clinical fellow at City University, a chartered psychologist and UKCP registered psychotherapist. He is one of Britain's leading exponents of multimodal therapy and has authored and edited a number of books including *Counselling for Stress Problems* (London, Sage, 1995), *Counselling: The BAC Counselling Reader* (with S. Dainow and P. Milner, London, Sage, 1996) and *The Future of Counselling and Psychotherapy* (with V. Varma, London, Sage, 1997).

How would you deal with this client's problems; would you take a problem-focused approach, exploratory, or some other approach and why?

Both. I would take a problem-focused approach because multimodal therapy is generally problem-focused; we'd look at Mary's problem areas to help her eliminate, manage or overcome them. I would also use an exploratory approach because certain issues, such as grief or child abuse may require more exploration by the client. In this case we have what sounds like complicated grief. It would probably be useful to explore her feelings and attitudes towards her father, partly because she may not realise that her relationship with her father has had a repeating theme in her relationships with her two husbands.

In the first session I normally spend about twenty minutes listening to the client's story using an exploratory approach. Then I would suggest that, to make it easy for both of us to understand the client's problems, we could note them down in seven key areas (i.e. BASIC ID modalities) on the white boards I have in my room. This would be a problem-focused approach. In Mary's case the initial exploration may take longer than twenty minutes because there are many problematic areas in her life.

What hypotheses would you have about Mary that would inform your assessment of her difficulties and why?

Several hypotheses came to mind when I read this case vignette. First of all there is a lack of external positive reinforcements in many areas of her life underlying her depression. Certain of these areas we can do something about in concrete terms. For example, if we focused on the interpersonal modality we could look at her lack of friends and discuss ways to help her meet people and make more friends. Second, there is a lack of internal reinforcement evidenced by her lack of interests and hobbies.

My next hypothesis is that she is very anxious about being assertive and standing up for her own rights probably because of her relationship with her father, repeated with her husbands and possibly also with others in her life, for example, her work colleagues. The key point is that she has constructed the belief in her head from her relationship with her father that if she stands up for herself the significant other person – usually a man – would be 'cruel' to her or treat her badly and this idea prevents her from being assertive in her life.

Finally because of her medical condition there is possibly an organic problem helping to make her depressed. People usually take hormone replacement therapy because of difficult symptoms and some of these may remain despite the treatment. For most women the menopause is an important life-stage change. Mary may have become more aware of her own mortality – a fact of life she already knows about through her father's death.

What theoretical constructs would inform the process of assessment?

Learning theory, social learning theory and systems and communications theory inform the multimodal assessment process and the formulation of a counselling programme. The constructs relating to these theories that I would have in mind when assessing Mary would include: misinformation; missing information; unhelpful habits; lack of self acceptance and inter-personal sabotage. The assessment process would focus on the seven key modalities (BASIC ID):

- her self-defeating behaviour, what precipitated and maintains this behaviour;
- her key emotional disturbances; any unpleasant sensations she was regularly experiencing, paying attention to her tolerance threshold;
- possible negative images to do with her father which may exacerbate the emotional disturbance;
- a number of self-defeating beliefs, clarifying whether there is any mis-information or missing information;
- her problems with her dominant husband and her lack of friends;
- issues associated with her general physical condition.

The assessment would be undertaken probably within the first or second session with Mary although it is also an on-going process. With new information, the assessment is revised and regularly updated.

What kind of therapeutic relationship would you seek to develop with Mary? Which therapeutic style would you aim to use and why?

I would need to establish a very open, straightforward relationship which involved talking in concrete, specific terms with appropriate self-disclosure where necessary. No hidden therapeutic or technical tricks, sensitively giving her feedback on her interpersonal skills. I would encourage her to 'rebel' against me and speak her own mind in a forthright manner without fear of criticism. She would need to have an understanding of the concept of the ego-less self – in other words, homo sapiens are too complex to be rated. Therefore teaching her self-acceptance through realising that 'you are not your behaviours'. For example, even if you have a failed relationship it does not logically follow that you are a failure as a person.

Multimodal therapists believe it is important to be an 'authentic chameleon' – that is to adapt interpersonal style to what is most beneficial to working with their clients at any one time over the counselling process. With Mary, to help her stay in therapy and also to match her expectations, I would initially take the approach of a 'coach'. Later in therapy it would become important to take a more passive approach so that she can start taking the lead. This will be a slow process of adaptation. As she comes out of herself in the counselling process and becomes more confident she can start to take the lead and, for example, suggest her own assignments, without any assistance.

How important would the therapeutic relationship versus specific techniques be with Mary?

An experienced multimodal therapist would consider five important areas which I list here in no particular order:

   Client qualities
   Therapist qualities
   Therapeutic skills
   Therapeutic alliance
   Technique specificity – that is which techniques are appropriate for each
      problem

All five go hand in hand and a good multimodal counsellor would consider all of them as important and in need of close attention. For example if a client needs exposure therapy in vivo (in a real life situation) and the therapeutic alliance is poor, it is likely that the client will not undertake the exercise and possibly drop out of therapy. In this case the therapist may choose to negotiate initially a less anxiety provoking intervention like imaginal exposure or coping imagery. These are more likely to be undertaken and less likely to lead to her terminating her counselling prematurely.

   In Mary's case, assertion training is indicated but she is unlikely to attempt to use assertive skills with her husband straight away. However, she may with encouragement from her therapist apply assertive skills with less significant others, for example, colleagues at work. This would serve as a trial run to show her that she has learned the skills and she can then choose to use them later in her life with her husband. Of course, she would probably need a fair amount of practice in the counselling sessions using role play and coping imagery prior to in-vivo exercises. A judicious referral to an assertion training class as an adjunct to therapy may also be indicated.

What would be your therapeutic aims and objectives?

My therapeutic aims and objectives! I would negotiate everything with her, since it is *her* counselling programme and not mine. At the end of the day it is her therapy. If I have a therapeutic aim it is to help clients achieve their goals and objectives by using a range of different techniques, interventions and strategies taken from any particular therapeutic or training approach. Multimodal therapy is an idiographic approach which considers each person as unique and each will need their own carefully tailored counselling and training programme to help them achieve their goals, in this case to help her not to feel depressed and guilty. A BASIC ID modality profile would be developed to help this process (see Table 6.1). If the person does not have clearly defined goals, my job is to help them with this particular problem. This often occurs with clinically depressed clients.

What is your stance on goal setting; would you help her set goals or not and if so would you do that now or later on?

For many clients, goal setting is crucial. Within the first session I'd be developing a BASIC ID modality profile with Mary, focusing on her problems and skills deficits and how to manage or deal with them. This profile is not set in stone as it is updated and modified throughout the client's counselling programme.

If you would help her set goals, what kind of goals would you imagine would be helpful to Mary and why?

I have not met Mary so the modality profile given here is constructed purely from the case description and is therefore hypothetical. The goals for Mary would reflect the problems arising in each modality. For example, I would suggest rekindling her interests in life and increasing her social intercourse, to deal with her depression and guilt, to become assertive, to increase self-acceptance and reduce approval seeking behaviour, to deal with her bereavement and other issues of loss.

A comprehensive programme would not overlook the key areas including the drugs/biological modality. Notice that I have not provided a completed modality profile as I would negotiate the possible techniques, interventions and strategies with Mary. However they would probably include goal-direction (B), relaxation techniques (S), imaginal exposure, coping and step-up imagery (I), cognitive restructuring, self-acceptance, general thinking skills training (C), assertion, communication and friendship skills training (I), exercise and liaising with her medical practitioner (D).

What problems would you envisage emerging from the therapeutic process and how would you address them?

Her being too passive and compliant would be a major concern. Her anxiety about taking any action in the behaviour and interpersonal modalities could prevent her from undertaking assignments discussed during her counselling session. If she didn't undertake an assignment, due to her feeling guilty or ashamed she could terminate counselling prematurely. Therefore a good therapeutic relationship where she didn't feel the counsellor was critical of

Table 6.1 Hypothetical modality profile for Mary

Modality	Problem	Proposed counselling programme
Behaviour	Does little outside work Moved house which she dislikes Apparent lack of goals or interests in life	Goal direction Discuss possible new interests
Affect	Depression Grief Hurt Guilt	Elicit disturbance triggering beliefs and images and restructure accordingly
Sensation	Possible unpleasant physical symptoms of the menopause	Relaxation techniques or Self hypnosis (possibly using tapes)
Imagery	Possible negative images about childhood associated with 'cruel' father Possible negative images about ill/dying father	Time projection imagery 'New ending' imagery Focus on negative imagery until habituation occurs
Cognition	Mind reading Approval-seeking beliefs Low self-esteem/self-worth Self-defeating beliefs about putting father in a home Self-defeating beliefs about own children and stepdaughter	Thinking skills training Challenge unhelpful beliefs Self acceptance training Ellis's ABCDE paradigm Ellis's ABCDE paradigm and listing pros and cons of consequences of beliefs
Interpersonal relationships	Submissive, quiet Non-assertive Marital difficulties Compliant Few friends Approval seeking	Assertion skills training Communication skills training Social and friendship skills training Self acceptance training and disputation of approval seeking beliefs
Drugs/biology	Sleep disturbances Fatigue On anti-depressants Hormone replacement therapy	Relaxation and Thought stopping Check for side effects of drugs For all these problems refer to medical practitioner if necessary

her would be very beneficial and would enable her to return to the next session without fearing critical judgement for failing to undertake her assignment.

Due to her appraisal of her childhood *vis-à-vis* her relationship with her father, the relationship with a male therapist like myself, might be more problematic than with a female therapist. Although a judicious referral to a female multimodal therapist might be a possibility, if the relationship with a male therapist was handled carefully there could be longer term benefits.

What do you imagine will be the therapeutic outcome?

I am concerned that as she started to implement new behaviours and inter-personal skills at home she may encounter difficulties in her relationship with her husband. There may come a point when she would have to weigh up the pros and cons of standing up for herself at home and in other situations. Her submissive behaviour temporarily ameliorates her anxiety and avoids conflict. By being assertive she is more likely to trigger aggressive behaviour in others which she will have difficulty in dealing with. I suspect that, assuming she undertakes the negotiated counselling programme, depending on her husband's responses, she may leave her husband which may temporarily increase her anxiety levels unless she has gained new social support which would be a useful part of her counselling programme. On past experience of similar cases I'm quietly optimistic that the outcome will be favourable for Mary with or without a critical husband.

COMPARISONS

In this section we are going to look at each question posed to the therapists and compare their responses. To assist the reader in this process of comparing and contrasting the four approaches, we have summarised the most important points from each interview in Table 6.2. A quick glance at the whole table gives some indication of which aspect each therapist would focus on. The two predominantly directive approaches, rational emotive behaviour therapy and multimodal therapy, have large sections on hypotheses informing assessment and goals likely to be helpful to Mary. This reflects the problem solving approach taken by these two models.

How would you deal with this client's problems; would you take a problem-focused approach, exploratory, or some other approach and why?

The answers the four therapists gave to this first question reflect clearly their orientations. All four seemed mindful of the fact that Mary needs to explore her problems further. Both the psychodynamic and the person-centred

Table 6.2 The four interviews compared

	Psychodynamic	Person-centred	Rational emotive behavioural	Multimodal
Approach to Mary's problems	An exploratory approach with psychodynamic guidelines in mind	A person-centred (exploratory) approach respect offering and empathy	A problem-focused approach but exploratory within that	A problem-focused approach but exploratory also, especially initially
Hypotheses informing assessment	Mary • has had many losses • is passive-aggressive • relates as victim which has roots in childhood experience • has difficulty sharing	Mary • lacks self-acceptance but has capacity to develop it • lacks self-appreciation but has ability to give life-giving force to others	Mary • has a dire need for approval • has problems with self assertion • has a poor opinion of herself • does not experience herself as in charge of her life • has an unhealthy attitude towards responsibility • may have problems feeling and expressing anger • may have an inherited tendency towards depression • grief for her father may play a role in her life	Mary • lacks external positive reinforcement • lacks internal reinforcement • is very anxious about being assertive possibly because of relationship with men in her life • may have an organic problem
Theoretical constructs informing assessment	• Childhood experience • Unconscious factors • Infantile sexuality • Transference	• Actualising tendency • Conditions of worth • Self-concept • Internalised locus of evaluation	• Irrational beliefs • Behaviour stemming from irrational beliefs • Impact of her behaviour on others	Based on learning theory, social learning theory, systems and communication theory: • Misinformation • Missing information

				• Unhelpful habits • Lack of self-acceptance • Interpersonal sabotage • BASIC ID
Therapeutic relationship and style	Relationship in which • Mary can feel safe and free where her difficulties with relationships can be used Style: • non-directive	Relationship where • Mary can feel safe • conditions of respect, acceptance and empathy present Style: • non-directive Equality in the relationship is central	Relationship where • Mary can have a major say in the direction of her therapy Style: • active directive • formal–friendly • de-emphasising expertise • humorous Equality in relationship	Relationship • that is open, straightforward with appropriate self disclosure • that encourages her to speak her own mind Style: • flexible • initially as a coach, later a more passive style
Importance of the therapeutic relationship versus techniques	Therapeutic relationship very important Uncomfortable with term specific techniques – would use: • interpretation • dream exploration • free association	Therapeutic relationship of paramount importance and specific techniques not at all	Balance between the two important. Specific techniques lose their potency if therapeutic relationship wrong	Five important areas: • client qualities • therapist qualities • therapeutic skills • therapeutic alliance • appropriate techniques All interdependent

Table 6.2 (continued)

	Psychodynamic	Person-centred	Rational emotive behavioural	Multimodal
Therapeutic aims and objectives	• To explore Mary's inner world • To make the unconscious conscious • To develop her sense of self (i.e. strengthening of ego)	• To try and understand Mary's inner world • To help her become more self validating and more in touch with her actualising tendency	• To establish the kind of therapeutic relationship described • To teach her the tasks and techniques of REBT	Focus on her aims and objectives which would: • be negotiated with Mary • be to help her define and achieve her goals
Stance on goal setting? If no goals why not?	Aim of therapy is not goals though change is an aim – goals are restrictive	Depends on what client's stance is on goal setting	Definitely help Mary set goals that are within her control right from start	For many goal setting is crucial In first session help Mary develop BASIC ID modality profile
What goals would be helpful to Mary?	Not applicable	If she wants to set goals, goals would be in area of self validation – feeling all right about herself and not feeling guilty Goals often implicit rather than explicit	Helpful goals might be: • to see remorse as a healthy alternative to guilt and sadness a healthy alternative to depression • to explore notion that to put oneself first is selfish • to explore validity of idea that we can avoid hurting others and doing so is a sin	The goals would reflect the problems arising in each modality and would probably include: • rekindling her interests in life • increasing her social intercourse • dealing with her depression and guilt

	• becoming assertive • increasing self acceptance and reducing approval seeking behaviour • dealing with her bereavement and other issues of loss But the goals would be negotiated with Mary	• become more assertive • develop a healthy sense of responsibility • concerned but not over concerned about pleasing others • integrate the death of her father better • address her relationship with Robert Focus would be on helping Mary to achieve her goals		
	• Her passivity and compliance would be major concern • Problems with undertaking assignments • Termination of therapy • A relationship with a male therapist	• Mary might see me as another domineering man • Mary might not voice her dissatisfaction with therapy • Homework might cause problems – she might do it too religiously or make excuses for non-compliance		
Possible problems in process	Her passivity, anger and hostility could come out in relationship • Negative transference • Doubt over whether she would stay in therapy	Mary might form deep attachment to and a dependency on her counsellor. This is a potential problem and will require great sensitivity on the part of the counsellor and a willingness to accept Mary's dependency feelings.		
Opinions about therapeutic outcome	If she stays the course she would be a rewarding patient	Hope that outcome will be a movement forward in her sense of self-worth. A change in current relationship likely, may be an enrichment but could also mean she separates from Robert	If Mary is passive and marriage runs into difficulty this could cause problems If she works hard and relationship with Robert can be contained, outcome could be good	Mary might encounter difficulties with Robert as she changes and she may leave him Outcome could be favourable from her perspective

approaches emphasise the importance of the therapeutic relationship in helping clients understand their difficulties. Neither Judy Cooper nor Brian
Thorne suggest taking a problem solving approach with Mary, they both
described a purely exploratory approach. We can contrast these two with
the rational emotive behaviour therapy (REBT) and multimodal therapy by
noting that both Windy Dryden and Stephen Palmer would primarily take
a problem solving approach while encouraging Mary to explore within that
more directive style. Both these therapists believe therapy is best approached
in this way.

The psychodynamic and person-centred approaches aim to help the client
develop understanding and both work through the medium of conversation
which is exploratory in nature. In rational emotive behaviour therapy and
multimodal therapy understanding is important but acting on that understanding is even more so. They are practical models aimed at solving the
clients' problems in the most efficient way.

What hypotheses would you have about Mary that would inform your assessment of her difficulties and why?

In the four chapters we made it clear that the psychodynamic approaches,
rational emotive behaviour therapy and multimodal therapy all regard assessment as an important component of counselling, whereas the person-centred
counselling regards formal assessment as unnecessary. Our four therapists
illustrate this in their answers. Judy Cooper (psychodynamic) formulates a
number of hypotheses that would inform her assessment of Mary's difficulties,
which are specific to Mary's story, as do Windy Dryden (REBT) and Stephen
Palmer (multimodal) whereas Brian Thorne (person-centred) uses more
general hypotheses which could be applied to any client. This illustrates
the person-centred approach's belief that all clients are out of touch with
their actualising tendency and therefore no specific hypotheses are necessary.
The client is at the centre of the therapeutic process and the counsellor's job is
to 'take no action'. All except for Brian Thorne mention Mary's difficulty with
being assertive – a theme which recurred throughout the interviews.

What theoretical constructs would inform the process of assessment?

The process of assessment is usually informed by the theories on how
problems are developed and maintained. We can see in the interviews how
the theoretical constructs, mentioned by each of the therapists, relate to
their chosen approach to counselling and psychotherapy. There is little in
the way of commonality here.

Judy Cooper would focus on the client's past (childhood experiences and
infantile sexuality) and present (unconscious factors and transference in the

relationship) to inform her assessment of Mary. This is in line with the psychodynamic beliefs that disturbances in adult life have their roots in disruptions to the developmental process in childhood which are then maintained by largely unconscious processes.

Brian Thorne also has some focus on the past in that he acknowledges that Mary has been divorced from her actualising tendency from very early in life and that she has from early times been affected by conditions of worth. Both these factors are put forward by the person-centred approach as the main mechanisms whereby our development is blocked and distorted. They are still with Mary as are an internalised locus of evaluation and self-denigration. It is the effect of all these constructs in the present that would inform his assessment of her.

Both REBT and multimodal therapy recognise that past experiences can have a role to play in the development and maintenance of an individual's problems but, like the person-centred approach, they do not dwell on these but rather focus on what is in the 'here-and-now'. For example, Windy Dryden mentions the important construct of irrational beliefs. While recognising that the tendency to have irrational beliefs is biological he would focus on assessing what irrational beliefs Mary has now and not on how they originated. He would also focus on her behaviour which stems from these irrational beliefs and the impact that this has on other people. This may be the mechanism whereby her problems are being maintained. The two constructs, irrational beliefs and behaviour, would inform the assessment process which in turn would inform the programme of therapy he would negotiate with Mary.

Similarly Stephen Palmer acknowledged the role of learning in the development of problem behaviours but, like Windy Dryden, would focus on assessing Mary as she is now and not on how the problems arose in the past. Like REBT, multimodal therapy recognises the biological dimension to personality and that many factors interact which lead to the development of problems. Stephen Palmer lists a number of these in his interview and also refers to the belief that our personality can be described through the seven modalities of the BASIC ID. These constructs which would inform his assessment of Mary, would also inform the programme of therapy he would negotiate with her. The assessment process in REBT and multimodal therapy is regarded as crucial to this development of a counselling programme.

What kind of therapeutic relationship would you seek to develop with Mary? Which therapeutic style would you aim to use and why?

In the chapters on the four approaches we described the therapeutic relationship in some detail. The four therapists we interviewed have stressed certain aspects of the relationship, which they consider to be of particular relevance to Mary.

Both Judy Cooper (psychodynamic) and Brian Thorne (person-centred) have identified the need for Mary to feel safe enough to be able to explore her inner world and both highlight the non-directive style adopted by these two approaches. Where they differ is in the amount of involvement with the client. In chapter 2 we described the rules of abstinence, anonymity and neutrality used by psychodynamic counsellors to help their clients in the process of free association without unduly influencing them and to assist the development of the transference within the relationship. Judy Cooper alludes to this in her suggestion that she might suggest Mary lies down in therapy to cut out distracting cues from herself. In direct contrast to these three rules, Brian Thorne emphasised the importance of the three core conditions which enable therapist and client to become more involved in the relationship. Person-centred therapists seek to enter into their clients' worlds and they stress the importance of being genuine and open in the relationship; the ideas of neutrality and anonymity would be anathema to them.

The person-centred stress on authenticity and openness is also found in the multimodal approach (the authentic chameleon). Stephen Palmer stressed the importance of an open and straightforward relationship with appropriate self-disclosure; also in direct contrast to the psychodynamic ideas of neutrality and anonymity. Like Judy Cooper and Brian Thorne, both Windy Dryden and Stephen Palmer would seek to develop a relationship where Mary can 'speak her mind'. However, they both would take an active directive style which would include a certain amount of teaching or coaching.

Both the multimodal and REBT approaches emphasise the equality in the relationship, something they share with Brian Thorne (person-centred) who stressed the centrality of this in the therapeutic relationship. The core conditions used by person-centred counsellors are recognised as being necessary by the multimodal and REBT approach but they do not regard them as sufficient.

How important would the therapeutic relationship versus specific techniques be with Mary?

All four approaches stress the importance of the therapeutic relationship and this is illustrated well in the four interviews. Both Judy Cooper and Brian Thorne had difficulties with the concept of 'techniques'; these two approaches are more relationship than technique driven. The person-centred approach believes that the core conditions in the therapeutic relationship are not only necessary but sufficient for change to occur; techniques are not only superfluous but their use would be against its philosophy of the client being at the centre of the process. Psychodynamic approaches do use techniques such as interpretation and free association but the relationship between therapist and client is of paramount importance.

The two directive approaches on the other hand do use a variety of techniques in several modalities to bring about change. Nevertheless, both Windy

Dryden and Stephen Palmer make it clear that a good therapeutic relationship is essential for these techniques to be effective. Both stress the importance of a balance and interdependency between the two.

What would be your broad therapeutic aims and objectives?

This question has been interpreted in different ways by the four therapists and it is therefore difficult to make comparisons. Both Judy Cooper and Brian Thorne would seek to understand Mary's inner world. Brian Thorne focused on the aim of becoming her companion as she got in touch again with her actualising tendency. Judy Cooper would seek to explore her inner world and make the unconscious conscious. Windy Dryden would have the aim of establishing a helpful therapeutic relationship with Mary and teaching her the tasks and techniques of REBT. Stephen Palmer stressed the need to negotiate everything with Mary and that his role was to help her develop her goals and achieve them.

What is your stance on goal setting; would you help her set goals or not and if so would you do that now or later on?

Both Judy Cooper and Brian Thorne are reticent about the idea of setting goals. Neither the psychodynamic nor the person-centred approach believe that setting goals in therapy is relevant. Each has general goals for counselling, such as making the unconscious conscious in the psychodynamic approach and removing the blockages to the actualising tendency in the person-centred approach. However, these general goals are not goals that are set with clients. Brian Thorne would normally not set goals with his clients – but, in true person-centred style, if Mary wanted to set goals he would help her do so.

In complete contrast, both Windy Dryden and Stephen Palmer regard goal setting as crucial and both would expect to set these right from the start of counselling. This reflects the problem solving process that both the rational emotive behaviour and the multimodal approaches emphasise.

If you would help her set goals, what kind of goals would you imagine would be helpful to Mary and why?

Only the two problem solving approaches actually came up with a list of goals they imagined would be helpful to Mary. Windy Dryden and Stephen Palmer represent approaches that are very goal focused. Once the goals are set up through negotiation, the solution to the problems can then be discussed with Mary and activities worked out. The goals suggested by Stephen Palmer are based on the BASIC ID and some of them are echoed by Windy Dryden, for example, becoming more assertive, dealing with bereavement issues, and changing the feelings of guilt and depression.

202 *The four approaches compared*

Brian Thorne, as we have seen, would set goals with Mary if that is what she wanted and he listed two possible goals which were in fact the two she mentioned herself in the first session; she wanted to stop feeling guilty and miserable. Judy Cooper did not address this question at all since the aim of therapy is not setting goals which the psychodynamic approach sees as restrictive.

What problems would you envisage emerging from the therapeutic process and how would you address them?

All four therapists acknowledged that problems could emerge from the therapeutic process. Three of the therapists focused on problems that originate in Mary and in particular shared a concern about her passivity and the effect that it might have on the outcome. Brian Thorne, on the other hand, did not raise any of Mary's issues as potential problems. He spoke rather of the therapeutic relationship itself possibly being a problem, but a problem for the therapist and not for Mary. During the process of therapy he thought it likely that Mary would form an attachment to the therapist which can be difficult for an inexperienced counsellor to deal with without damaging the counselling process.

Judy Cooper and Stephen Palmer were both concerned that Mary might not stay in therapy although for different reasons. Judy Cooper highlighted one of several reasons why clients sometimes terminate their therapy; that is, it simply becomes too much for them. Stephen Palmer on the other hand focused on how Mary would feel if she failed to complete an assignment they had agreed on; feelings of shame and guilt might prevent her from returning unless she could trust the therapist not to be judgemental.

Both Windy Dryden and Stephen Palmer focused on the potential problems Mary might have completing any homework assignments. This aspect does not apply to the person-centred and psychodynamic approaches as neither negotiate homework assignments. The three male therapists all thought that a relationship with a male therapist might be problematic (Thorne had highlighted this potential problem earlier in the interview). All three believe that if this problem is handled carefully then there would be longer term benefits to Mary, since up to that time all her relationships with significant men had been unsatisfactory.

What do you imagine will be the therapeutic outcome?

All four therapists have the opinion that the outcome could be favourable for Mary but that would be conditional on a number of different factors. Each therapist focused on important aspects of their particular approach. Judy Cooper's main concern focuses on whether Mary would stay in therapy and, if she did, whether the end of therapy could be concluded satisfactorily. Her concerns highlight two important aspects in psychodynamic theory.

First of all the defence mechanism of 'flight into health' which can occur when the client has reached a point in therapy where more difficult material is coming to the surface and they believe they cannot deal with it and so terminate therapy saying 'I'm much better now'. Secondly the termination phase of therapy is regarded an important stage in the therapeutic process.

Brian Thorne focused on the expected movement forward in Mary's sense of self-worth – a central construct in person-centred counselling. He raised the possibility that as Mary develops this sense of self-worth, so the relationship with her husband would be affected and that this could be for the good of the marriage or could lead to her separating from a relationship which reinforced her sense of worthlessness. He did not entertain the idea that Mary might not stay in counselling.

Windy Dryden also focused on Mary's relationship with her husband but his concern was more around whether overt difficulties with Robert would get in the way of the therapeutic process. The rational emotive behavioural approach emphasises that clients have to work hard for change to take place and Windy Dryden stresses that this would be an important condition for a good outcome. Stephen Palmer's response is very similar. He also is concerned about the effect difficulties with her husband might have on Mary's progress and, like Brian Thorne, considered the possibility that separation from him might be the result.

CLOSING COMMENTS

The four approaches to counselling and psychotherapy described in this book can be roughly divided into two groups: the exploratory approaches versus the problem solving. The psychodynamic and person-centred approaches are both exploratory and their main focus is on using the relationship as the main therapeutic tool in which clients feel safe enough to explore their inner lives. Rational emotive behaviour therapy and multimodal therapy are problem solving approaches. Their focus is much more goal and technique orientated.

Despite being able to place the four approaches in this book into two broad groups, we hope we have also made it clear that there are differences within these groups as well as between them. So that, for example, within the exploratory group the psychodynamic approach focuses on past experience and on uncovering the unconscious whereas the person-centred approach focuses on the here-and-now. Within the problem solving group, REBT is more philosophically driven than the multimodal approach and has a more cognitive emphasis. The multimodal approach takes a more pragmatic stance and works in all seven modalities.

Similarities between the two broad groups include the fact that both the problem solving approaches recognise that without a sound therapeutic relationship, techniques are less effective and that some exploration is nearly always necessary. The focus on the 'here-and-now' in the person-centred approach is found also in the two problem solving approaches and the psychodynamic approach shares their focus on assessment.

We have now come to the end of the book. We hope that you have found it valuable and instructive. We invite you to give us feedback (c/o Routledge . . .) which could help us to improve the book in any future editions.

Index

SUNY BROCKPORT

3 2815 00823 9678

THE COLLEGE AT BROCKPORT · DRAKE MEMORIAL LIBRARY · WITHDRAWN

RC 480 .D79 1999

Dryden, Windy.

Four approaches to
  counselling and